IMAGES
of America

EUREKA AND HUMBOLDT COUNTY

CALIFORNIA

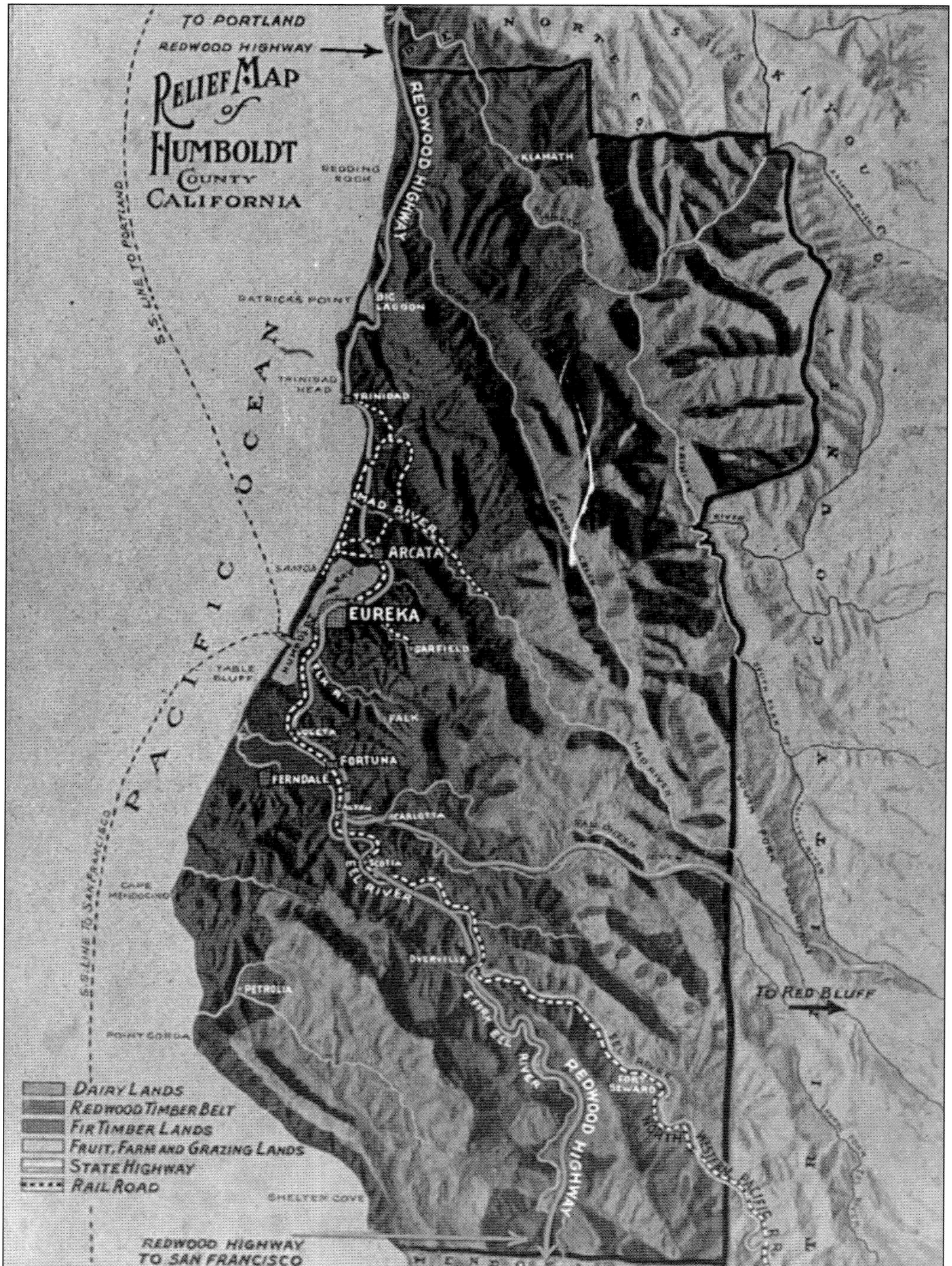

This cover appeared on a promotional booklet put out by the Eureka Chamber of Commerce around 1920. The map was based on a large (12-foot by 8-foot) papier-mache relief map made by Eureka engineer J.N. Lentell for the Humboldt exhibit at the 1915 Panama Pacific Exposition in San Francisco. The original map is now on exhibit at the Clarke Historical Museum.

IMAGES
of America

EUREKA AND HUMBOLDT COUNTY CALIFORNIA

Clarke Historical Museum
Pamela F. Service and Raymond W. Hillman, Principal Writers

ARCADIA
PUBLISHING

ISBN 978-0-7385-1872-5

Published by Arcadia Publishing
Charleston, South Carolina

Printed in the United States of America

Library of Congress Catalog Card Number: 2001090197

For all general information contact Arcadia Publishing at:
Telephone 843-853-2070
Fax 843-853-0044
E-Mail sales@arcadiapublishing.com
For customer service and orders:
Toll-Free 1-888-313-2665

Visit us on the Internet at www.arcadiapublishing.com

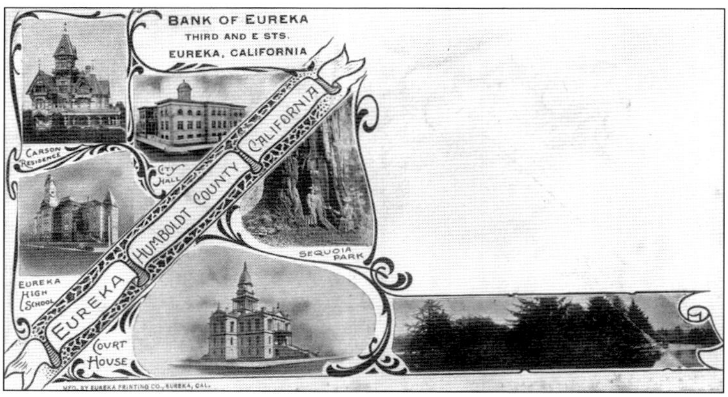

These Eureka-boosting envelopes were made for the Bank of Eureka around 1910. The former bank building, at Third and E Streets, now houses the Clarke Historical Museum.

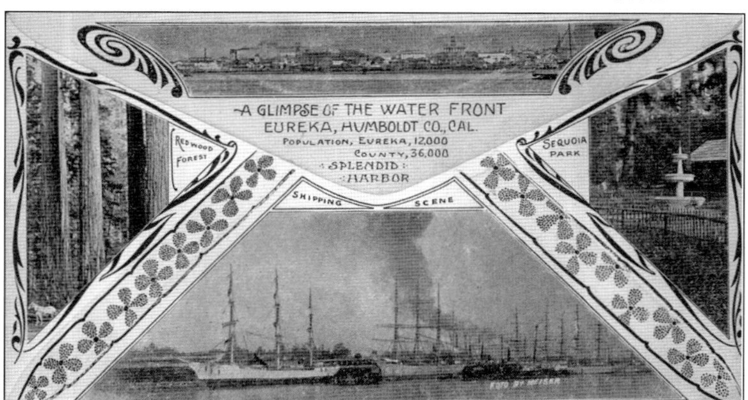

Contents

ACKNOWLEDGMENTS

Pamela Service and Raymond Hillman, principal writers of this book, would like to thank the board of the Clarke Historical Museum for their enthusiastic support, with particular thanks going to Bradley Marshall for his assistance with the Native American chapter. We also appreciate the assistance of Edie Carhart at the Fort Humboldt Museum. Finally, the entire museum staff and board thank the people of Humboldt County for their support of the Clarke Historical Museum in the past, present, and future.

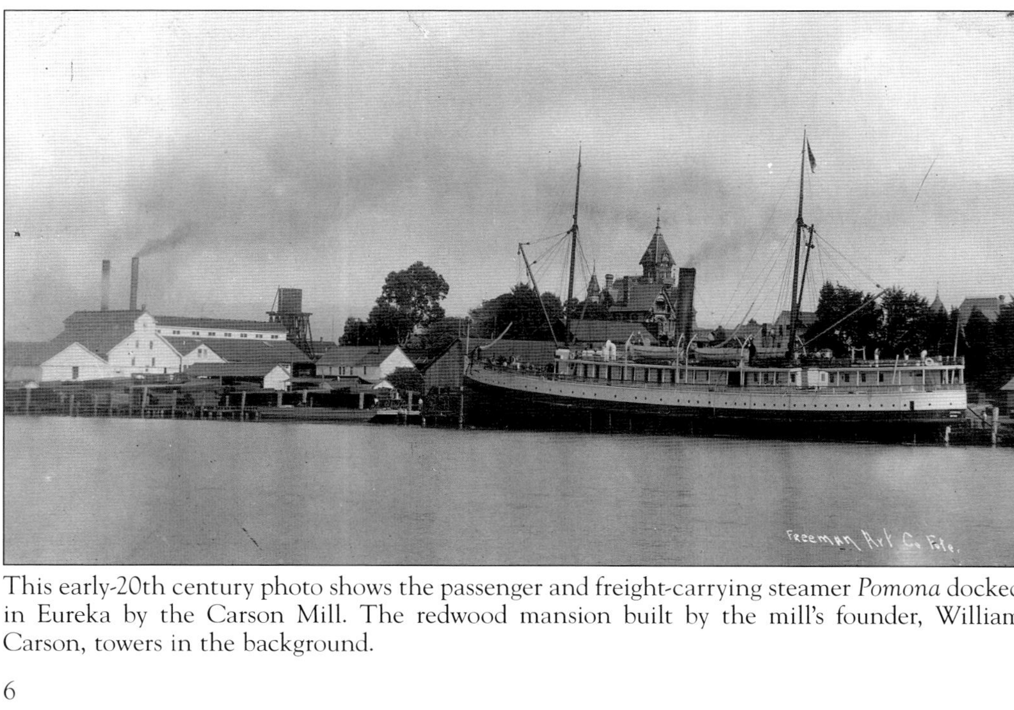

This early-20th century photo shows the passenger and freight-carrying steamer *Pomona* docked in Eureka by the Carson Mill. The redwood mansion built by the mill's founder, William Carson, towers in the background.

INTRODUCTION

"Eureka" is the classical Greek for "I found it!" In 1850, settlers and gold seekers found what they were looking for in what was to become Humboldt County, California. They named their village and future county seat Eureka.

For many centuries before, however, the area had been the ideal home for others. The boundaries of future Humboldt County contained portions of the home territory of several tribes, most prominently the Wiyot, Yurok, Hupa, and Karuk. Though speaking languages from three different language families, these groups shared similar beliefs, social structures, and material culture.

All were hunter-gatherers, but the area's mild climate and abundant resources allowed the people to live in permanent villages and to nurture wild plants. Subsisting on acorns, game, coastal shellfish, and the rivers' abundant salmon and trout, they developed elaborate ceremonials and the art of fine basket making. There was little warfare because disputes within and between groups were usually settled by paying compensation. The people lived in close harmony with their environment and each other.

That harmony was shattered by Shasta County rancher Pierson Reading's discovery of gold in the Trinity Mountains in 1848. Although Spanish explorers and Russian fur hunters had earlier touched Humboldt's coastline, it took a month-long westward expedition led by Josiah Gregg to establish a route from the Trinity gold fields to the coast. In April of 1850, the *Laura Virginia* was the first American ship to enter the bay, naming it Humboldt after the famous German geographer and scientist, Alexander von Humboldt.

Soon fortune seekers flocked to the area by ship and over the mountains. Humboldt County was not a major source of gold, though Orleans and Willow Creek had mining-based economies, and beach sand under Gold Bluffs was worked with limited success. However, the coastal towns of Eureka, Arcata (originally called Union), and Trinidad grew into prosperous and notoriously rowdy ports and supply centers for the mines. Pack trains moved gold seekers and supplies into the mountains, and one of California's first railroads was built in Arcata to transport goods from the docks to the town plaza.

The miners and early settlers, however, usurped or destroyed the resources on which the native populations depended. Conflict led to massacres, the establishment of government forts, and forced resettlement. These policies, plus introduced diseases, destroyed some tribes entirely. Others, however, have retained their identity and many aspects of their culture.

Timber, Humboldt's "red gold," was soon discovered to be a resource as valuable as the area's minerals. Massive redwood trees, some 2,000 years old and growing to heights of over 300 feet, thrive in the narrow fog belt along California's northwest coast. Felling and milling activities began almost immediately as lumbermen, used to smaller eastern trees, developed new techniques and tools to deal with the huge redwoods. Timber companies multiplied, expanding their operations inland, building rail links as they went, and scattering the area with small lumber-based towns and temporary camps.

The need to ship out timber plus the availability of raw materials stimulated a local ship building industry. Fishing for crab, oysters, and various ocean fish, especially salmon, grew into a major industry, and Humboldt, Shelter Cove, and Trinidad bays supported active fishing fleets. Whaling was occasionally carried out as well. The rugged coastline sprouted lighthouses in an attempt to protect shipping, but the area remained the site of numerous spectacular wrecks.

The land itself and the moderate climate proved to be other valuable resources for Humboldt County. Farmers from many countries were attracted to the rich soils around Humboldt Bay and several river bottoms, while the hills provided good grazing. Sheep raised here produced exceptional fleece, and the dairy industry prospered. Fruit growing was also successful, and the area became particularly known for its apples.

Humboldt towns grew, and the more prosperous citizens built elegant homes using local wood. The difficulties of road travel over the mountains, and the dangers and discomfort of sea travel, kept the area fairly isolated. As a result, residents developed an attitude of rugged independence. The "redwood curtain" began to part, however, in the early 20th century with the building of a rail connection, completion of the Redwood Highway, and the rise of automobile travel. Tourism quickly joined timber and fishing as a major industry. A movement to preserve the redwoods led to the creation of local, state, and national parks. Though this cut into timber profits, it bolstered tourism and preserved endangered species. The natural and architectural beauty of the area, combined with relative accessibility to Hollywood, also made Humboldt County the setting of many films from the silent era to the present.

Although vastly changed in the last century and a half, Humboldt County in one respect remains true to its roots. It is an area where people and their natural environment are strongly interdependent—a place where many who long for an ideal home can still cry out "Eureka!"

The following photographs give a varied, though necessarily incomplete, picture of Humboldt County's past. They all come from the extensive collection of the Clarke Historical Museum in Eureka. The collection was begun by Eureka High School teacher Cecile Clarke, who founded the public museum in 1960. In addition to its thorough local history collection, the Clarke is nationally recognized for its excellent collection of Native American basketry and ceremonial regalia from northwest California. The museum is located at 240 E Street in Eureka. Admission is free. Further information is available at (707) 443-1947.

One

NATIVE PEOPLES

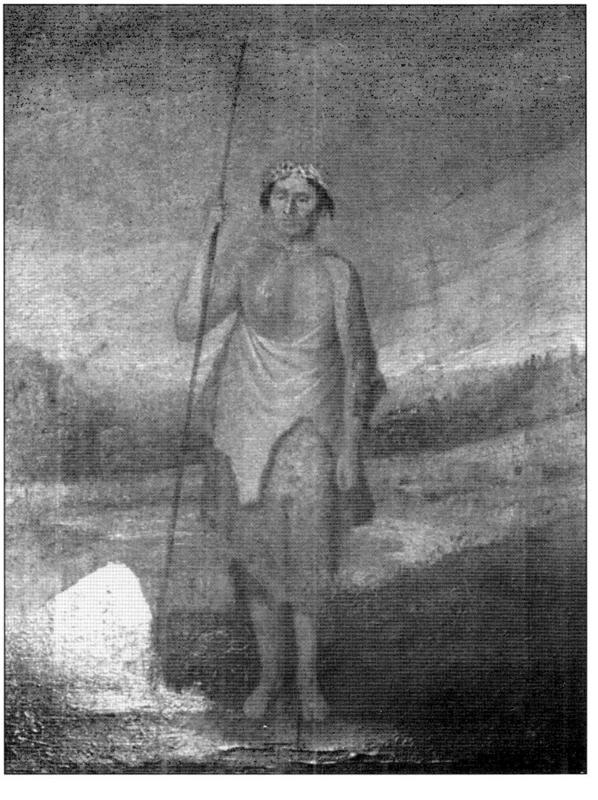

Ki-we-lah-tah, a leader of the Wiyot, painted by Stephen Shaw, welcomed the Gregg Party to *Wigi*-Humboldt Bay in 1849. Within a year, Americans were settling the area and tensions grew. In 1860, one of California's worst massacres took place on Indian Island where most victims were Wiyot women and children. Arcata journalist Bret Harte's newspaper report brought the atrocity to national attention. It also led to his being run out of town and the beginning of his renowned literary career. Today, Wiyot people still live in small numbers around the Bay.

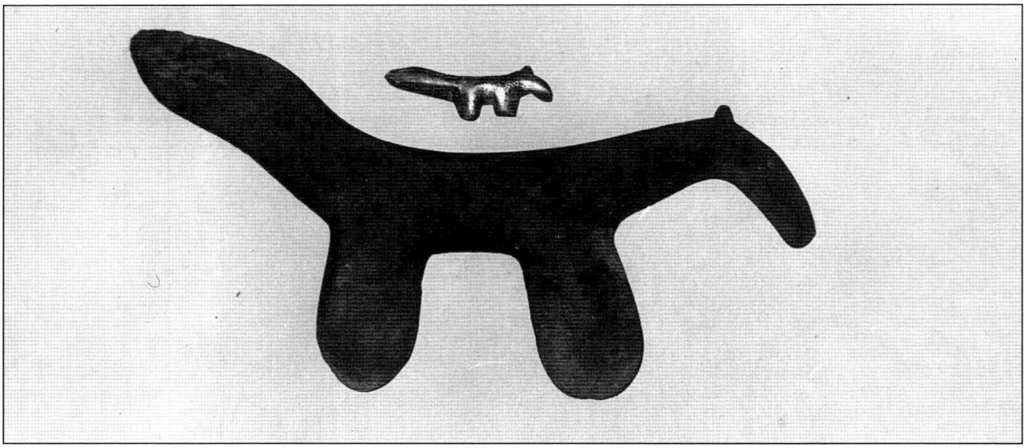

Zoomorphs, stones in the shape of long-tailed animals, have been found in prehistoric Wiyot sites and in some coastal Yurok and Tolowa locations. Similar items are known along the North American Pacific coast as far as Alaska where they are called "slave killers" and were used in ritual destruction of wealth. This practice was not part of Humboldt area cultures, and their use here is uncertain, though possibly they were signs of wealth and authority. The Clarke Museum's collection of zoomorphs is among the world's largest.

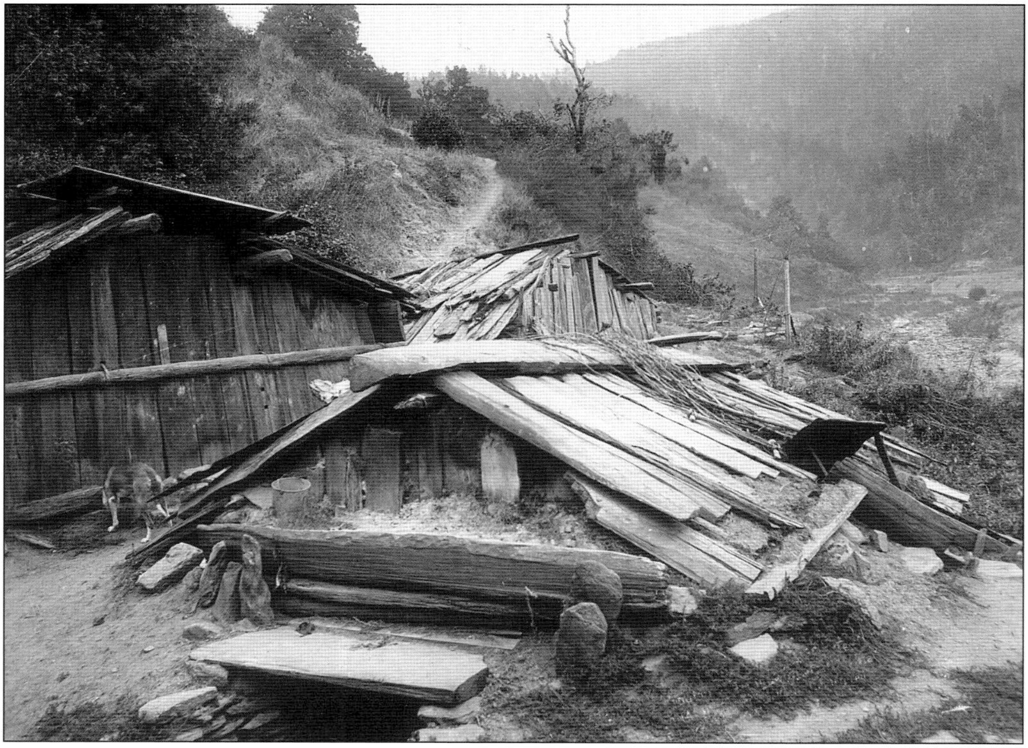

In the 1890s, Pecwan was one of many Yurok villages along the Klamath River. The partly underground sweathouse in the front is where men and adolescent boys slept while women and children slept in redwood plank houses such as that in back. Pecwan is still a location for religious ceremonies of the Yurok people.

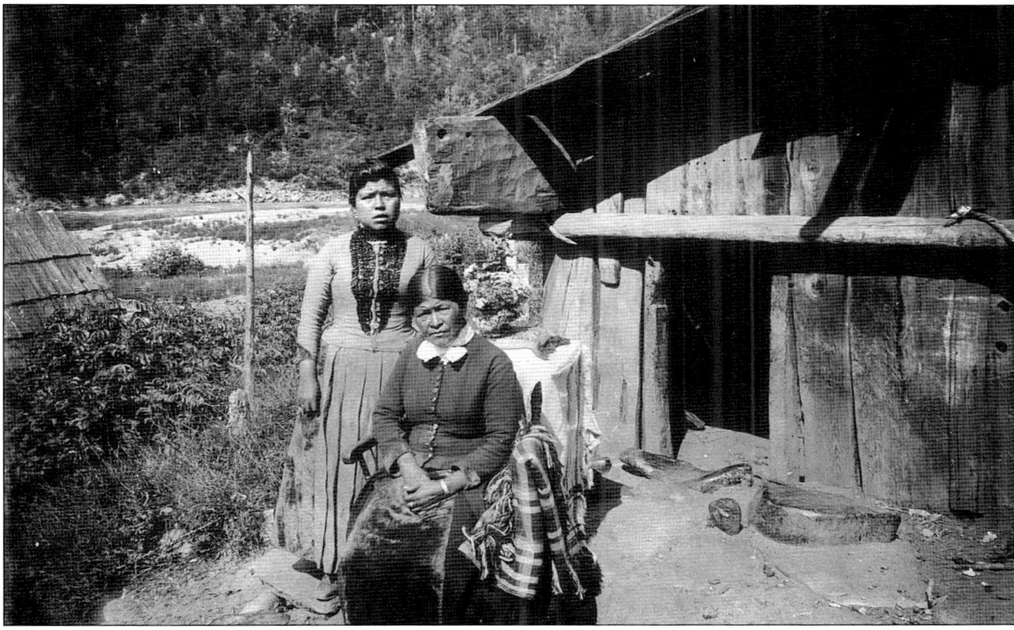

Traditional clothing of the native peoples changed with the encroachment of settlers. Here two Karuk women in western clothes pose in front of their plank house. Villages along the coast made houses of redwood planks, while inland villages used cedar.

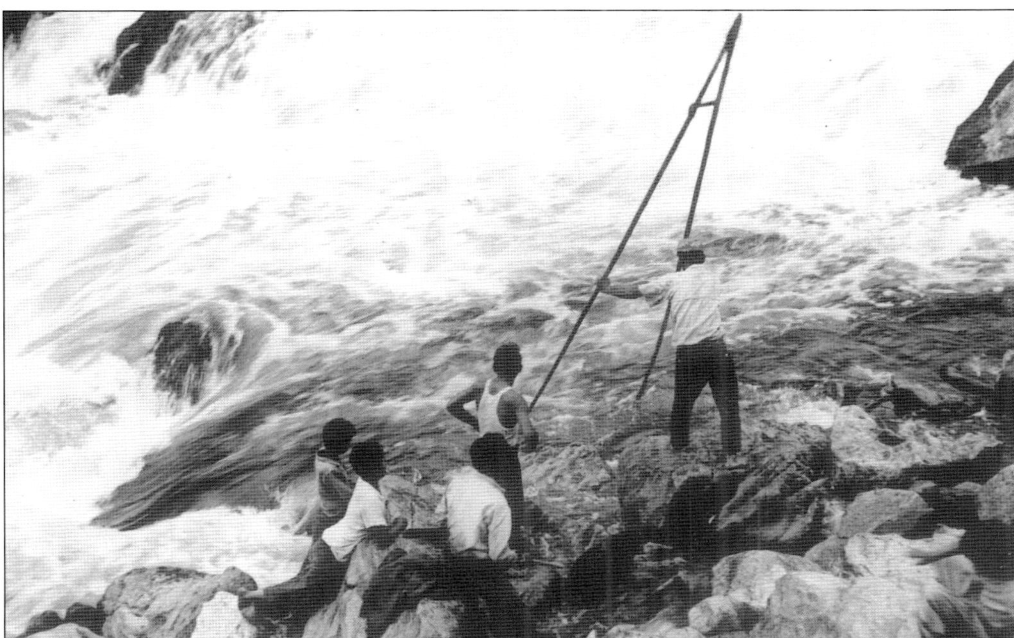

Using a traditional dip net made of wild iris fibers, Elder McGlaughlin of the Karuk fishes for salmon at Ishi Pishi Falls on the Klamath River. Salmon supplemented by trout and eel were diet staples for local native peoples. Spears, weighted nets, and traps were also used for fishing. Fish were roasted or preserved by smoking with alder wood.

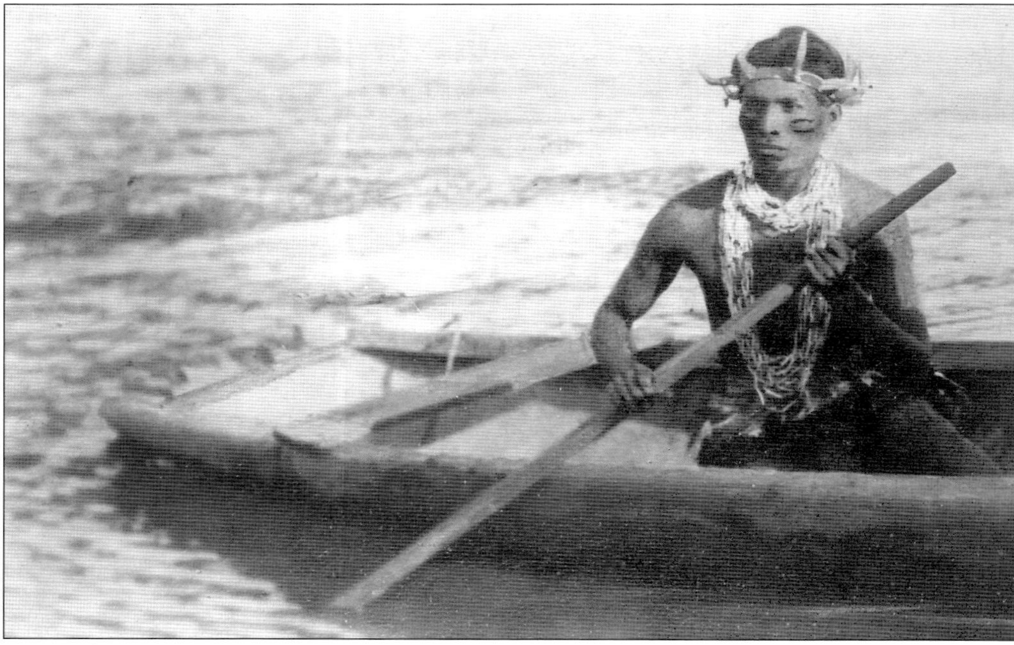

Most redwood canoes were made by Yuroks who traded them upriver to the Karuk and Hupa. Traditionally, half a log was burned then hollowed out with antler and stone tools. Though this design of canoe was not used on the ocean, they were valued for river fishing and transport, as well as for the "Boat Dance" portion of the "White Deer Dance." Here boatman George Reed is shown in dance regalia.

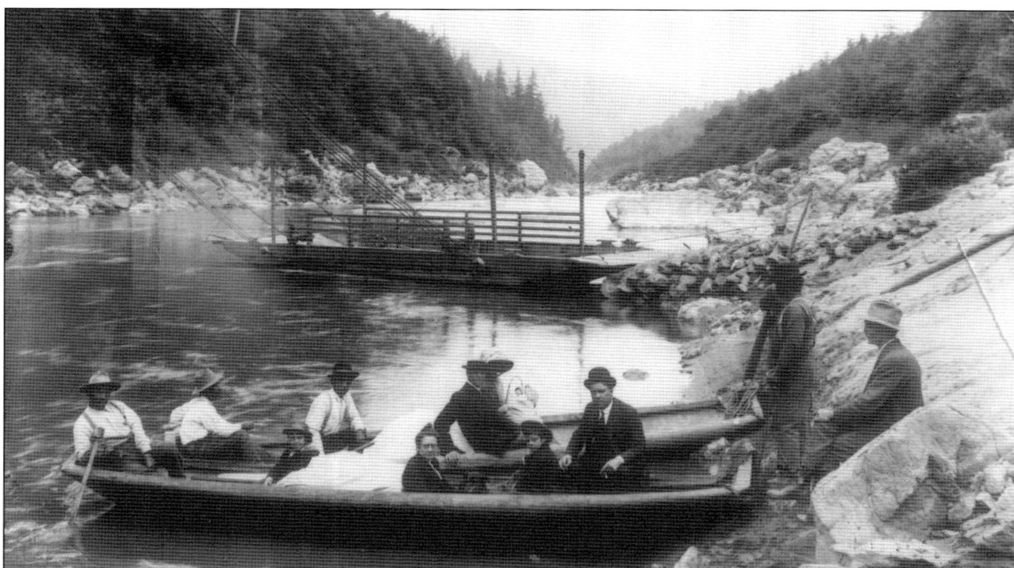

Traditionally, redwood dugouts were used to cross rivers. In 1908 at Martin's Ferry on the Klamath, a cable ferry was operating, but Yurok and Hupa canoes still provided excursions such as this for Jesse Mortsolf and party. Mortsolf was superintendent of the Hoopa Valley Indian Reservation and School.

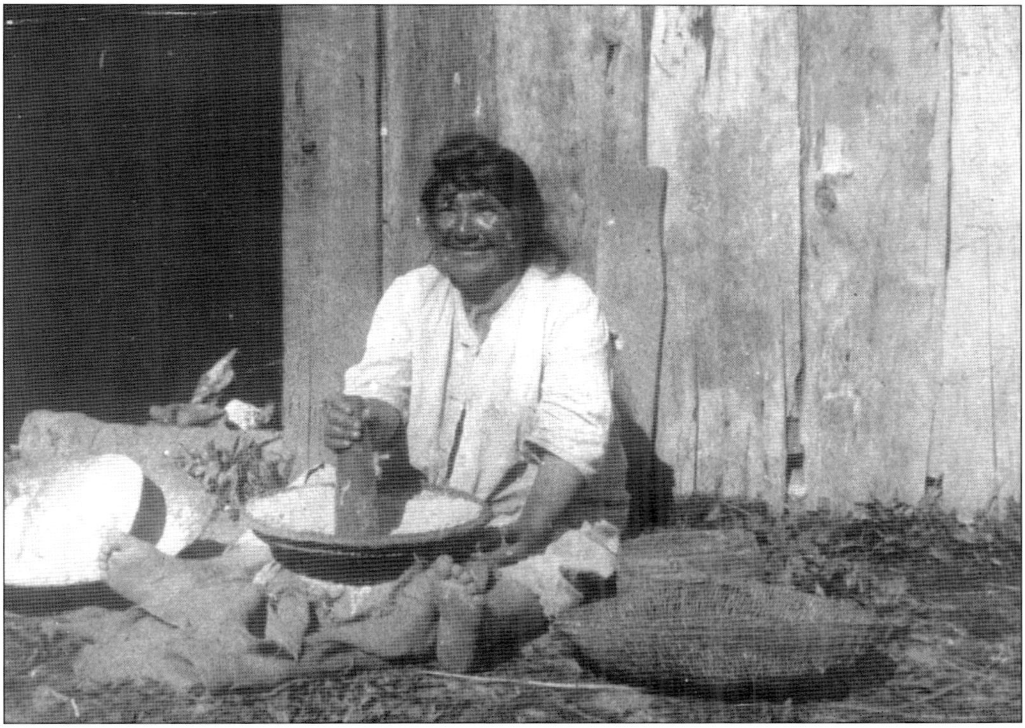

Acorns were the staple of the area's traditional diet. They were gathered in the fall, stored in large baskets, ground into flour, and then washed to leach out the bitter tannic acid. Here Mrs. John Marshall of Hoopa grinds acorn flour using a stone mortar and pestle and a basketry hopper.

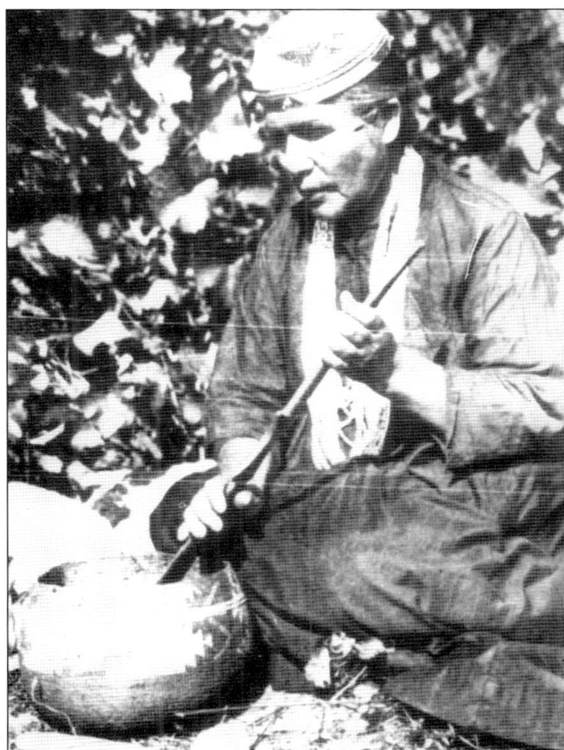

This photograph taken in the 1890s shows a woman making acorn soup. Cooking baskets were woven tightly enough to hold water, which was brought to a boil by adding rocks heated in a fire. The soup was stirred constantly with wooden paddles to keep the stones from burning the basket. This technique is still used today in preparing traditional meals.

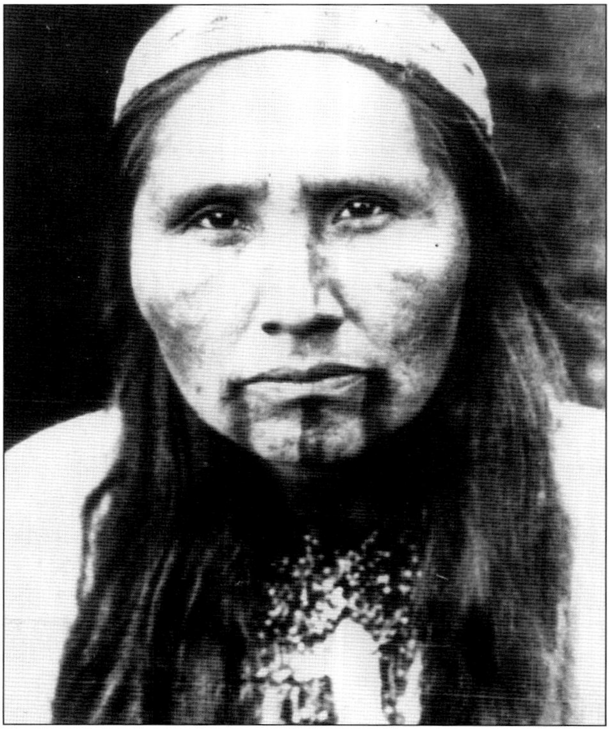

Prior to the early 20th century, many women in area tribes, such as this Tolowa woman, received a chin tattoo as part of their coming-of-age ceremony. The "111" mark was applied by cutting the chin with an obsidian blade and rubbing in soot and bear grease. It was seen as a mark of beauty and family status.

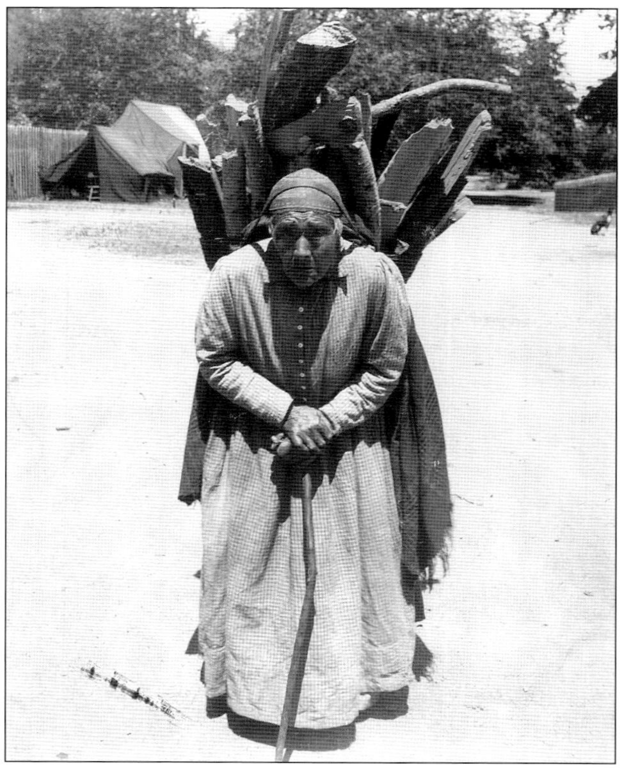

Traditionally it was women who gathered acorns and other wild foods as well as basket making materials and firewood. In this 1890s photograph taken in Hoopa, Mary Major carries firewood in a conical collecting basket supported by a strap over her forehead.

This Tolowa woman, Delia Albert of Smith River, was also called "Traincar" because she was a very swift runner. In this photograph taken at Lake Earl she is preparing for the Nee-dash ceremony. The number of clamshell rolls on her traditional woman's ceremonial skirt shows that she is from a wealthy family. The basketry hat she is wearing is unique to the tribes of this area.

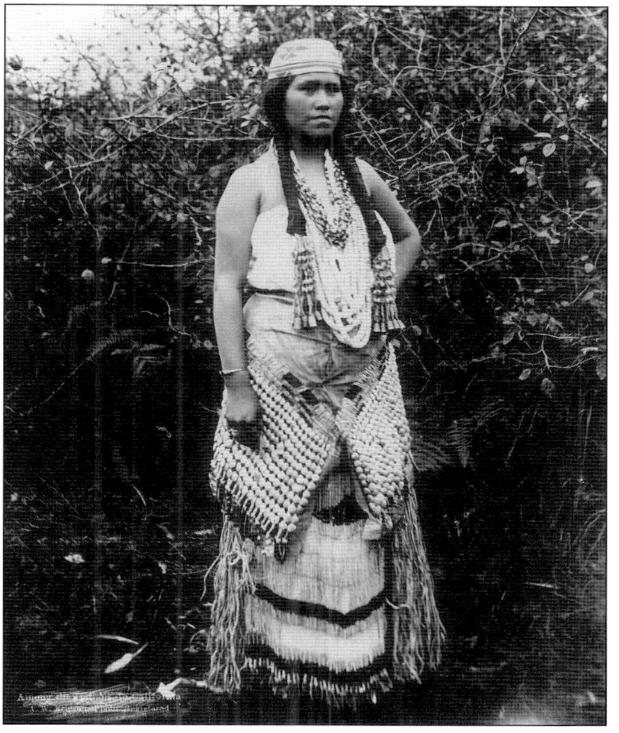

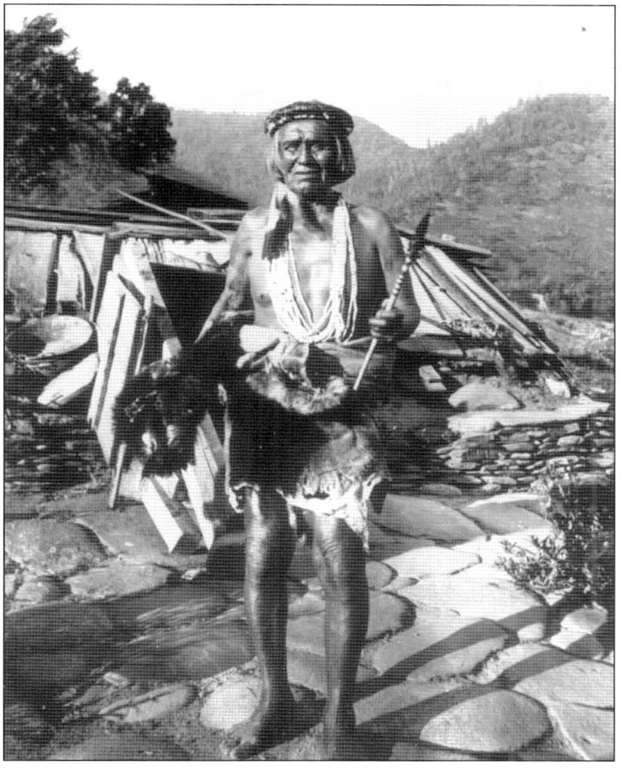

Captain John stands in front of his "Xo'ji-xontah" cedar plank house in the village of Med'dilding on the Trinity River. He was a political, civic, and religious leader of the Hoopa. Here he is wearing men's regalia for the Brush Dance, a three day ceremony for healing sick children. A mountain overlooking Hoopa is named after him.

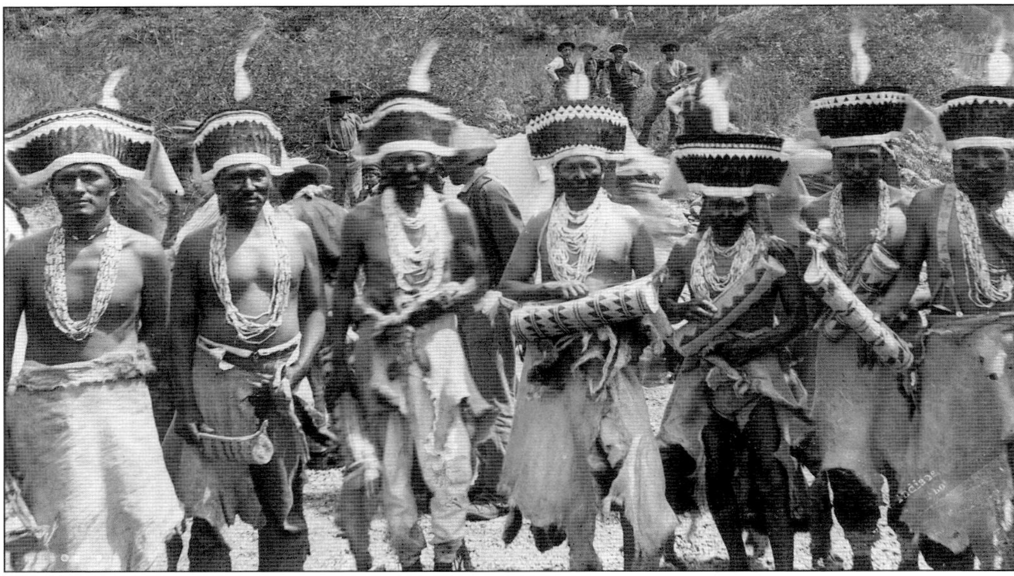

This photograph of men dressed for the Jump Dance was taken in 1901 at the Yurok village of Pecwan downriver from the junction of the Trinity and Klamath Rivers. The ceremony is performed in order to bring balance back into the world and is common to the Hupa, Karuk, Yurok, and Wiyot peoples.

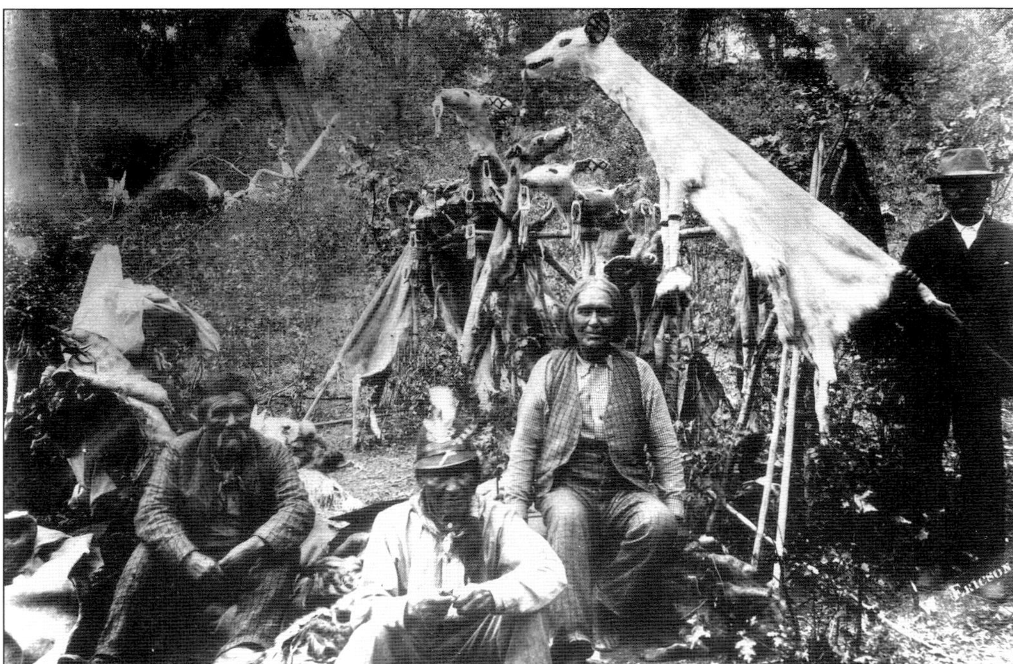

Taken around 1900, this photograph shows the men's camp at a Hupa White Deer dance. This area is where men prepare themselves and their regalia for the ten-day world renewal ceremony. Central to the ceremony are the decorated hides of white deer carried on poles. The seated man in the vest is the dance leader. These dances continue to this day on ancient ceremonial grounds.

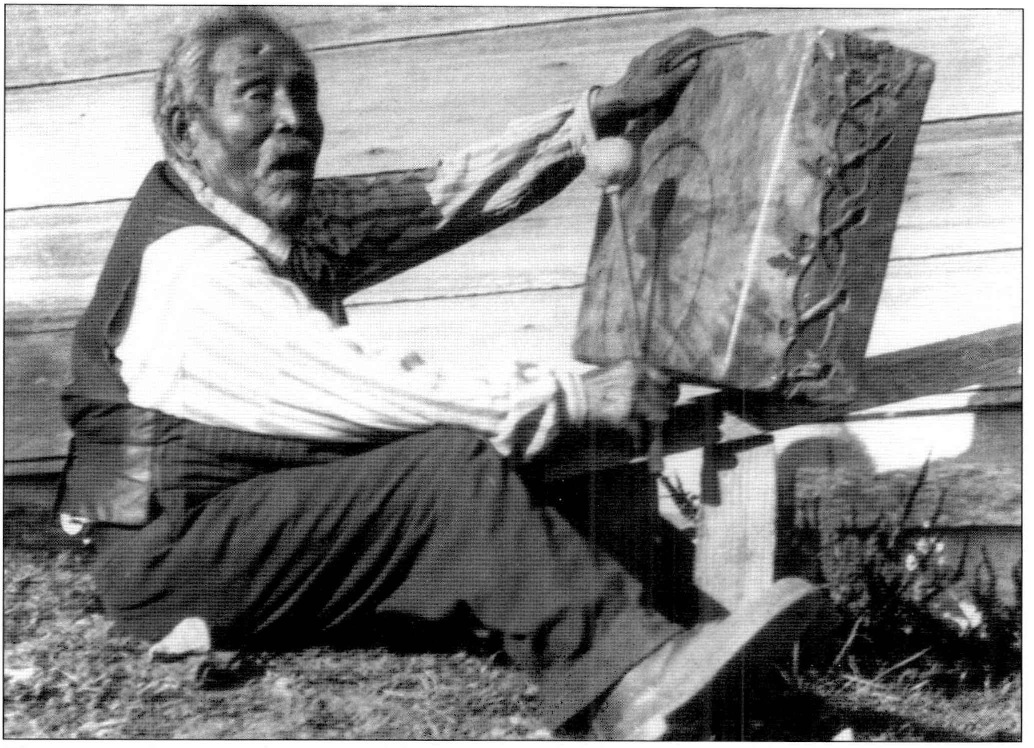

The square drum in this turn-of-the-century photograph is a style unique to northwest California. The man is playing it to accompany a men's gambling game where players try to guess which of the dealer's hands holds a specially marked stick.

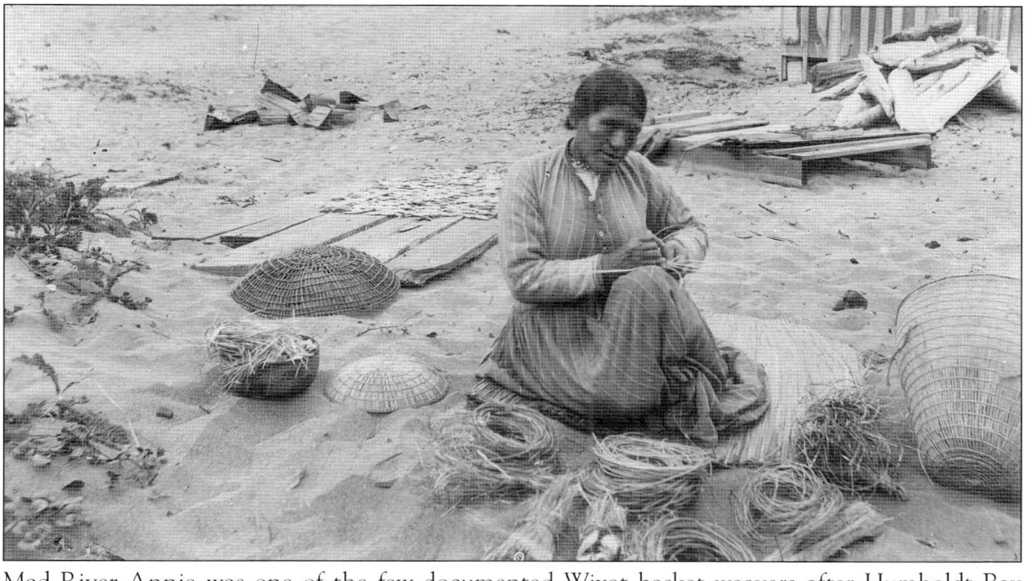

Mad River Annie was one of the few documented Wiyot basket weavers after Humboldt Bay settlers killed many of the Wiyot and pushed those that remained into more marginal dune country. Today the tradition of basket weaving is alive and growing among Wiyot tribal people.

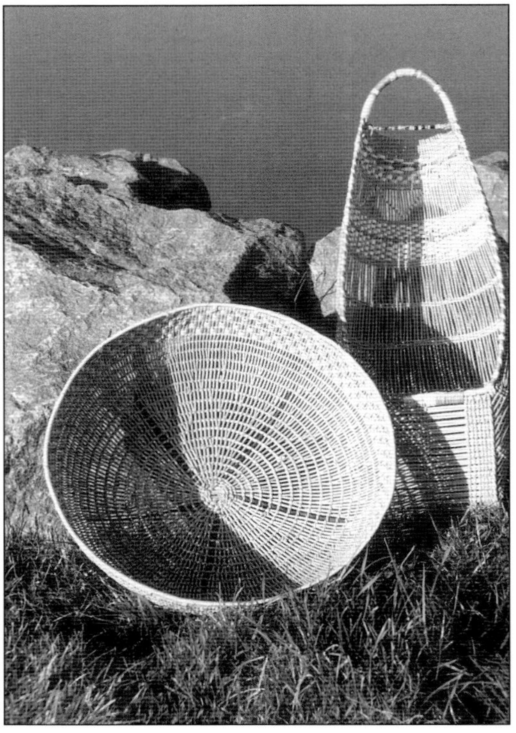

This acorn flour sifting basket and baby carrier were made by Mad River Annie in the early 1900s. They are now part of the Clarke Historical Museum's collection and are frequently on exhibit.

Mrs. Childs was photographed at age 100 weaving a collecting basket at Tsurai, a Yurok village overlooking Trinidad Bay. Most villages along the coast depended heavily on shellfish, and their sites can be identified by the centuries worth of discarded shells. Tsurai was inhabited until 1914, and, although their way of life was disrupted by the settlers, Mrs. Childs kept weaving because basket making was a fundamental part of her life.

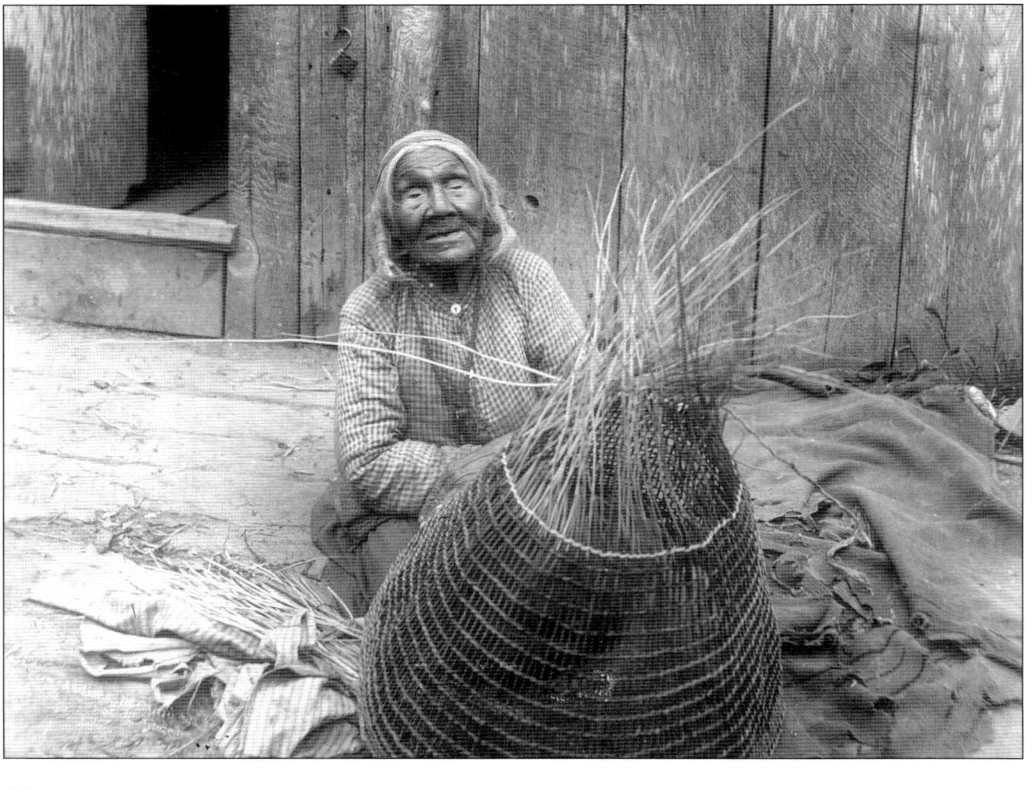

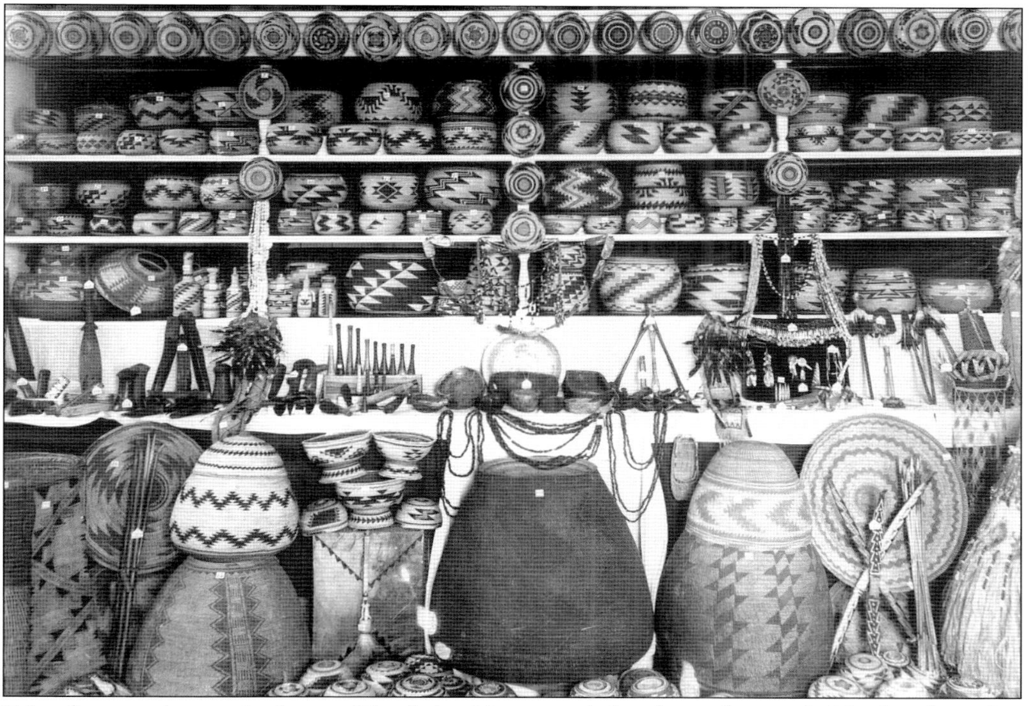

Brizard's general stores in Arcata, Blue Lake, Hoopa, and elsewhere often traded food and supplies for baskets and other native-made items. This photo shows part of the Brizard collection, much of which was then sold to museums and private collectors outside the area, though many pieces are now in Eureka's Clarke Museum. The basketry of northwestern California is particularly valued for its fine twining technique and overlay designs. Some pieces were specifically made for trade to tourists, collectors, and art dealers.

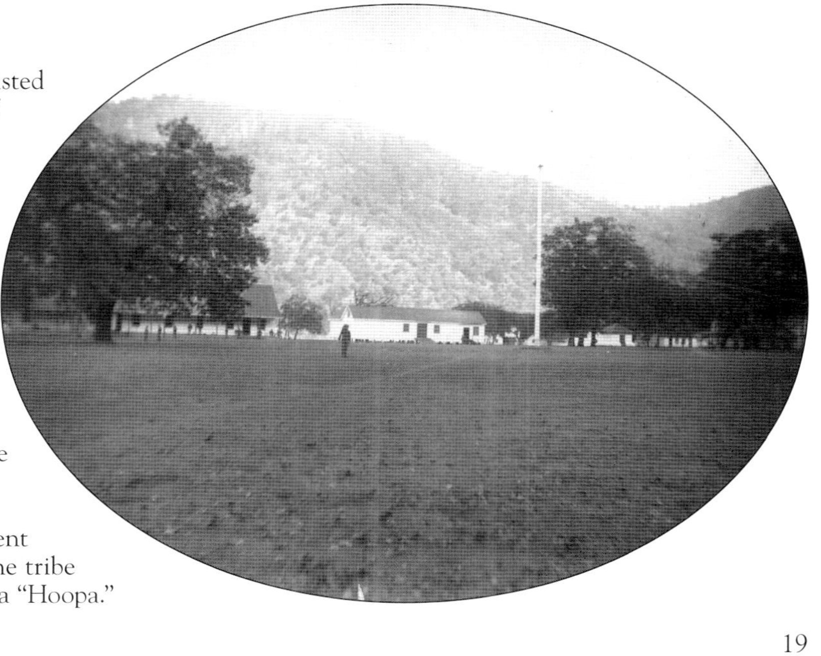

The Hupa tribe resisted removal, the fate of some smaller area tribes, and in 1864 a reservation was established in Hoopa Valley to be overseen by Ft. Gaston, shown here. Individuals from other tribes were forcibly relocated there. The Hupa Reservation remains the largest in California. Current custom is to spell the tribe "Hupa" and the area "Hoopa."

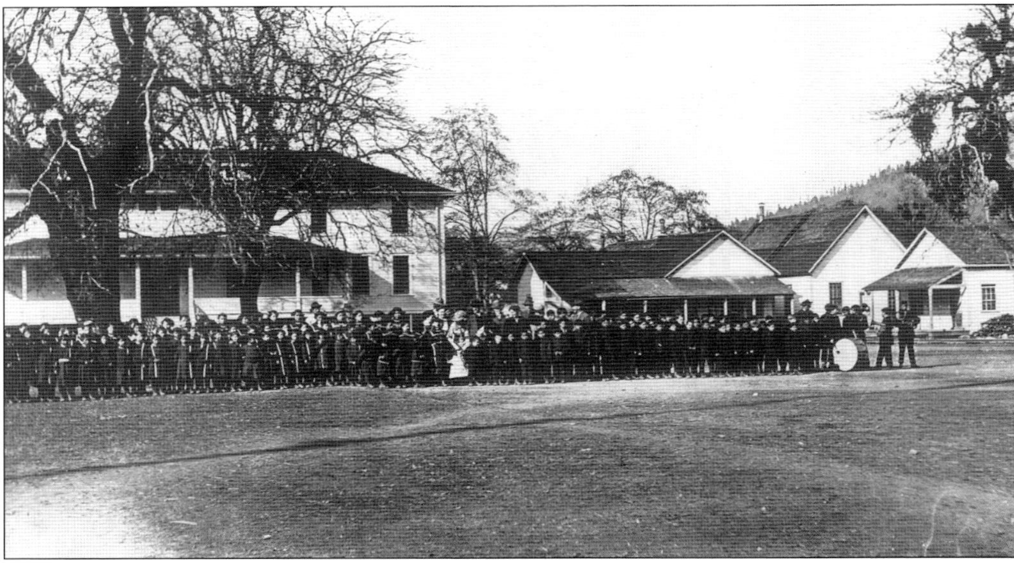

After abandonment by the military in 1893, the Ft. Gaston buildings were used as a boarding school for Indian children. It was photographed here around 1915, although today only two of the original buildings remain. Government policy of forced assimilation involved removing children from their parents, except during summer, making them wear uniforms, and beating them if they spoke their native language or practiced their culture.

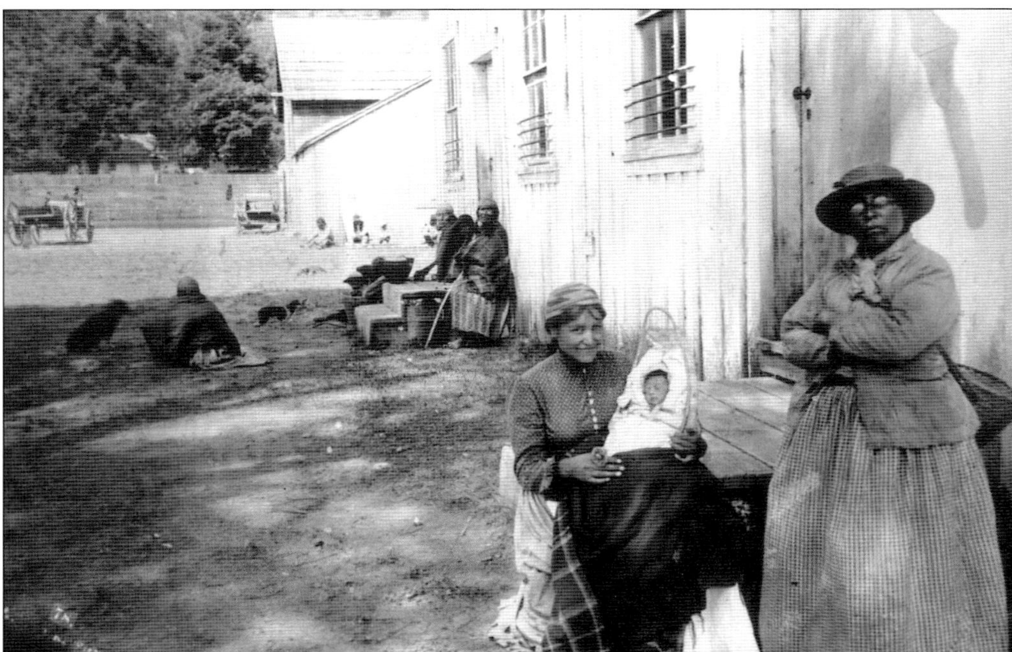

This photograph shows women waiting for government provisions at Ft. Gaston in 1893. Despite the actions of government and settlers, the traditions and pride of the Hupa and other area tribes have survived and strengthened. Where this building once stood is now the site of the Hupa Tribe's Education Center and community college campus.

Two

Gold and Early Settlement

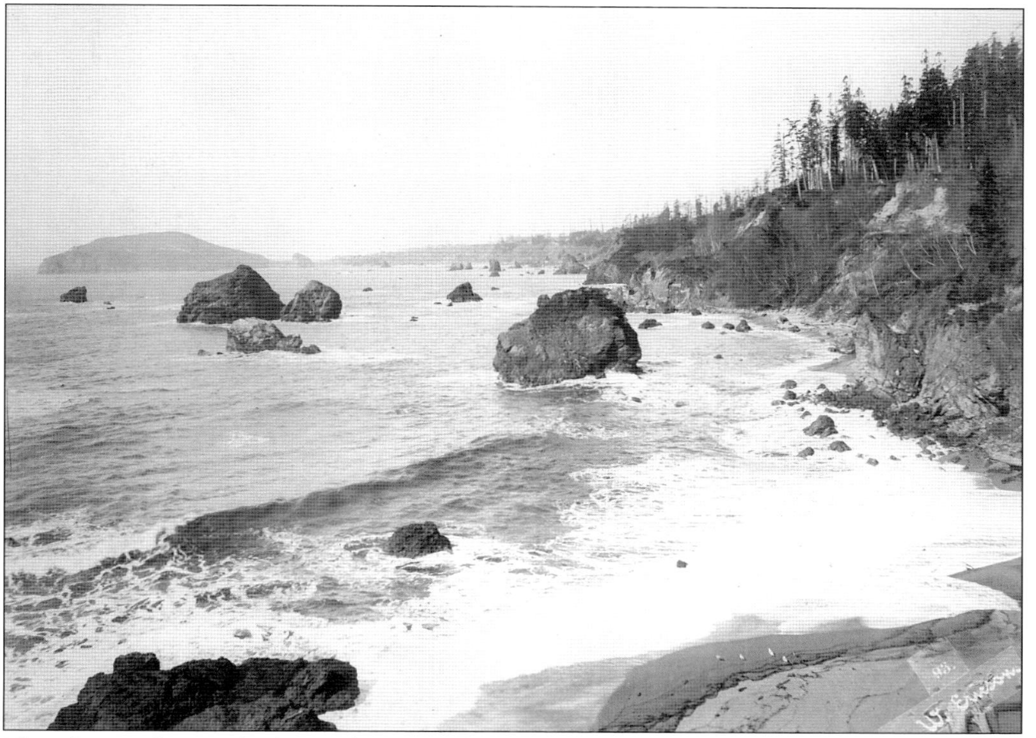

This photo, taken in the late-19th century by local photographer A.W. Ericson, shows the coast south of Trinidad much as it must have looked when the Spanish landed in June 1775. In the distance is Trinidad Head. The Spanish stayed only a few days, taking on fresh water, trading with the village of Yurok Indians, and naming the place Trinidad because it was claimed for Spain on Trinity Sunday.

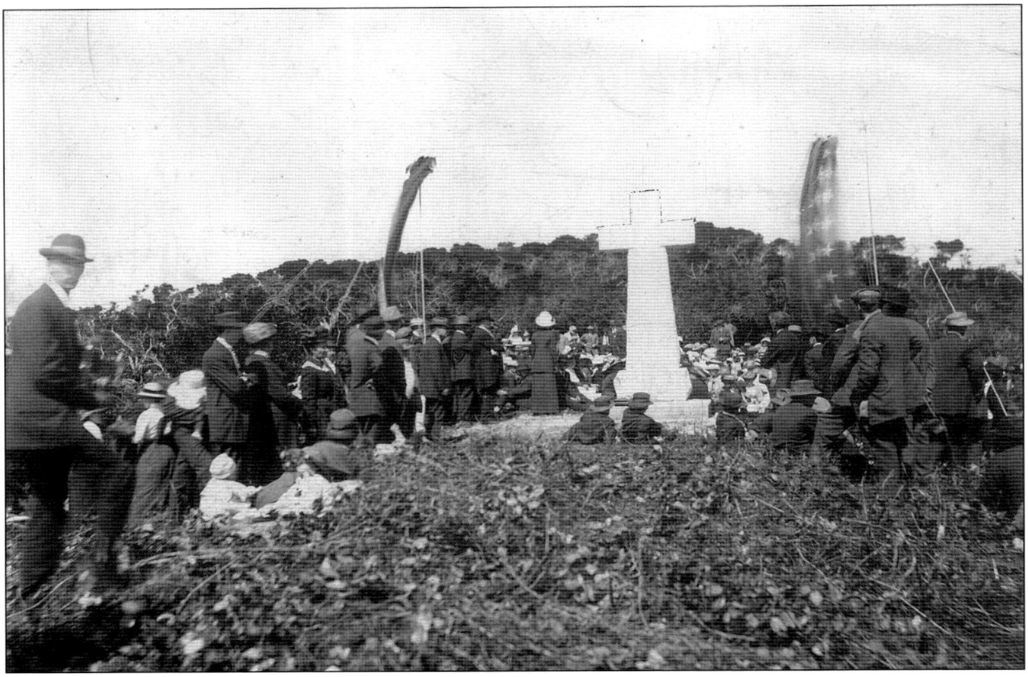

On Sept. 9, 1913, the Club Women of Humboldt County dedicated a stone cross to commemorate the original wooden cross erected in 1775 by the Spanish. It carries the original Spanish inscription, which translates as "Charles III, by the Grace of God, King of Spain."

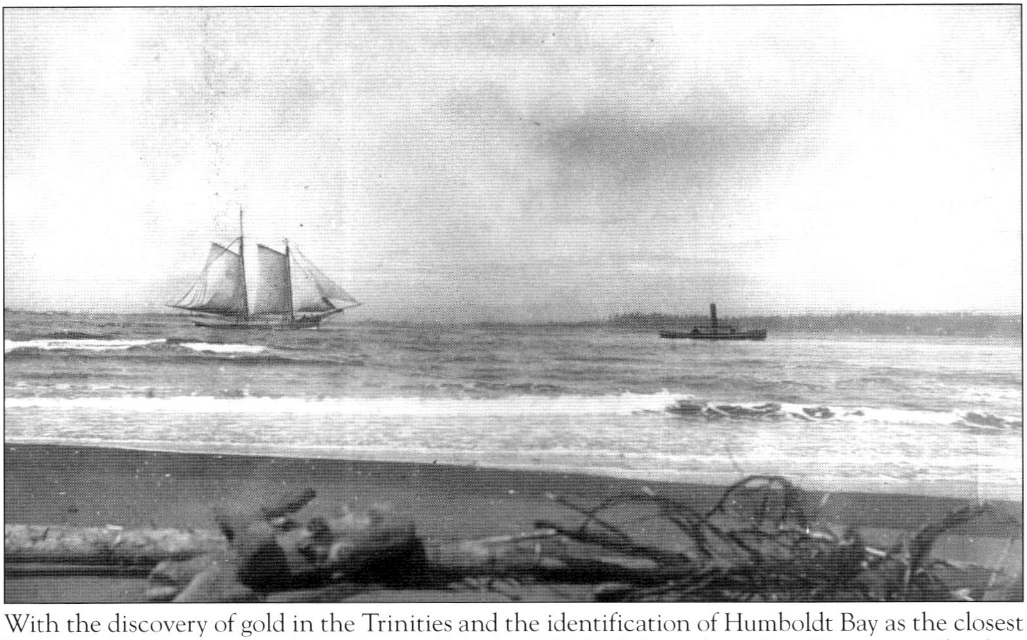

With the discovery of gold in the Trinities and the identification of Humboldt Bay as the closest harbor to the mines, merchants and gold seekers flocked there from San Francisco. This late 19th century photograph gives a good idea of what the bay must have looked like when entered by the first American ship, the *Laura Virginia*, in April 1850.

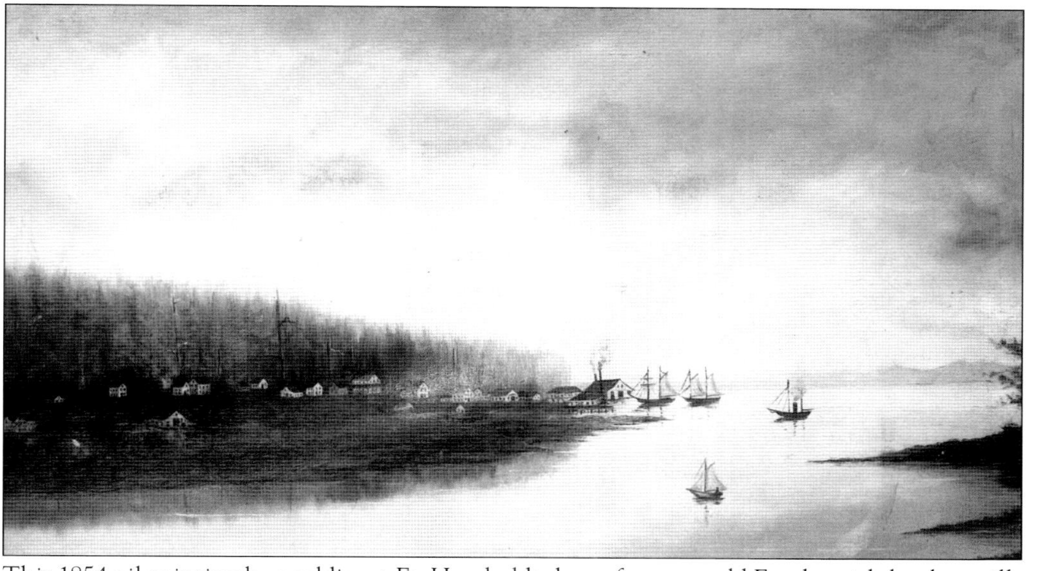

This 1854 oil painting by a soldier at Ft. Humboldt shows four-year-old Eureka with lumber mills already operating on its shores and the redwood and spruce forest already in retreat. The mills shown here are identified as the Smiley Mill, the Muley Mill at the foot of I Street, and the Ryan and Duff Mill located 100-feet east of D Street (destroyed by fire in 1862). Lumber produced at these mills was shipped as far as South America.

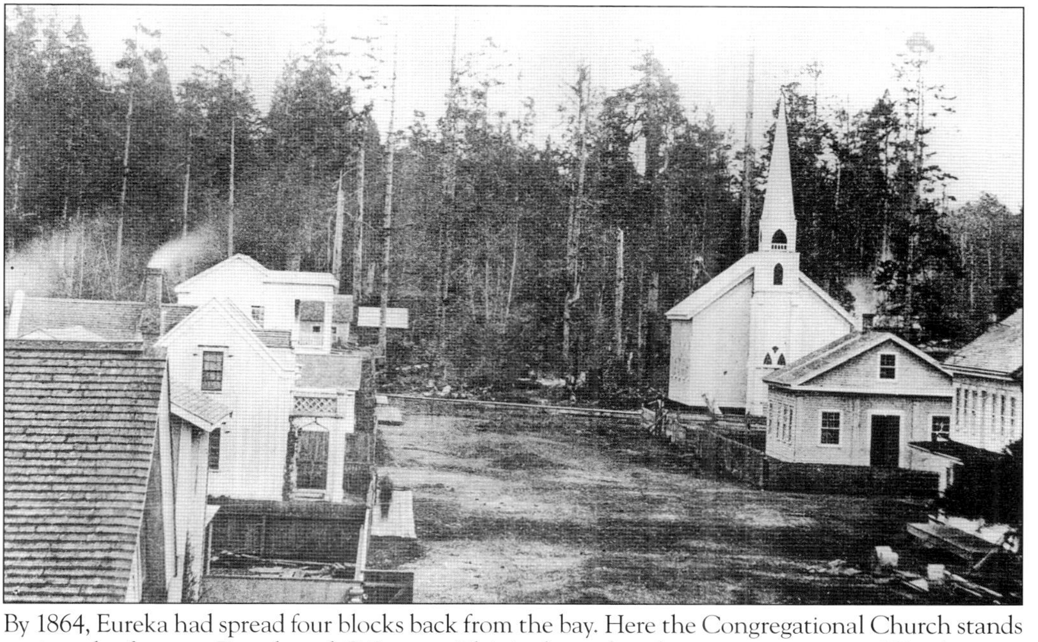

By 1864, Eureka had spread four blocks back from the bay. Here the Congregational Church stands against the forest at Fourth and G Streets. This is the earliest known street scene of Eureka.

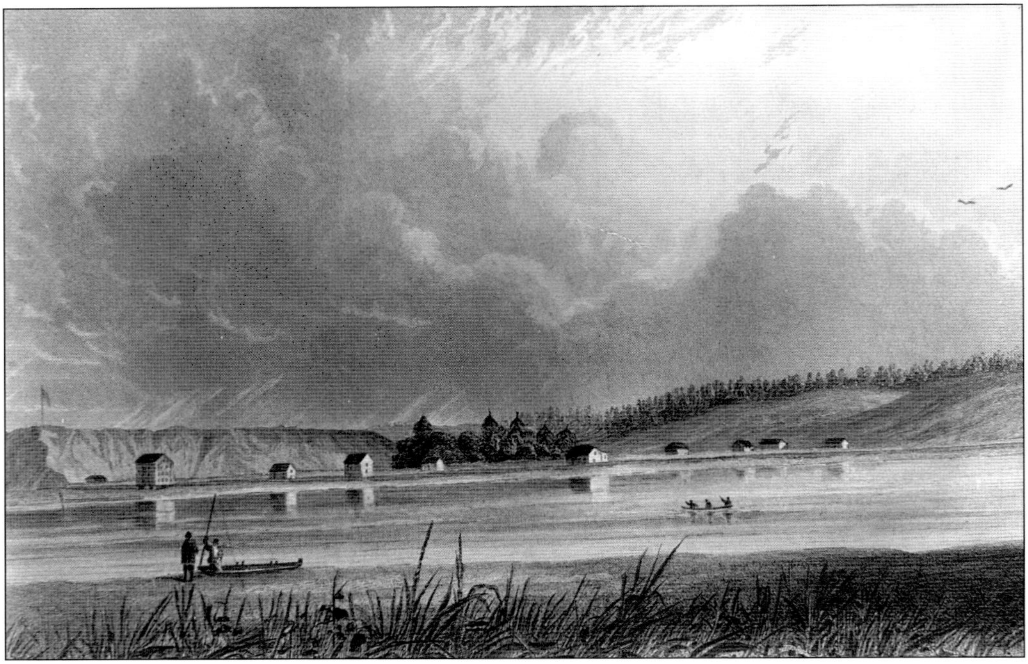

Not all new settlements were as successful as Eureka. Humboldt City, to its south, was also founded in 1850 but within a few years had disappeared. Bucksport seen in this drawing was established between the two and survived longer as a port town. Today both sites are part of greater Eureka. The flag on the bluff shows the location of Ft. Humboldt.

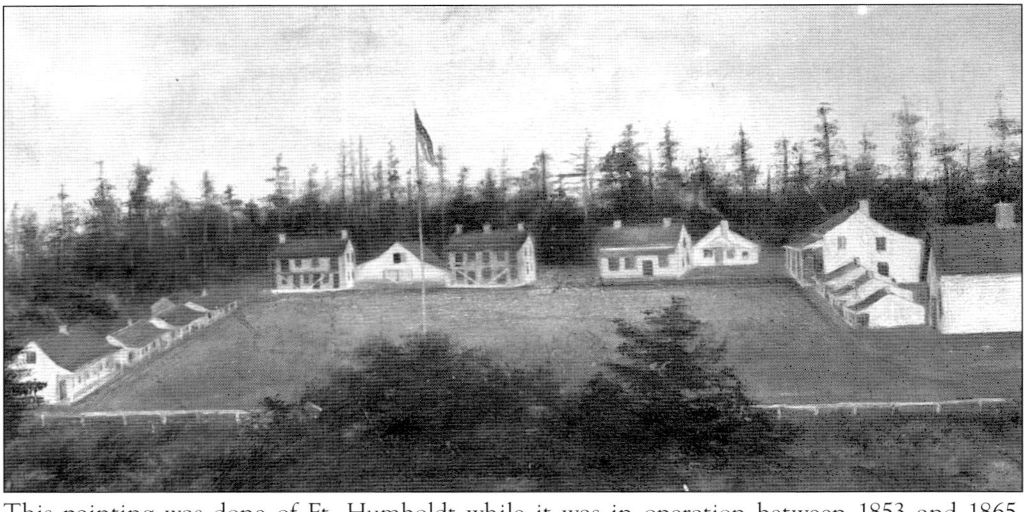

This painting was done of Ft. Humboldt while it was in operation between 1853 and 1865. The fort was founded in an effort to quell the "Indian Wars" and protect the native and settler populations from each other. Its task was made difficult by the size of its jurisdiction, its limited personnel, and the unwillingness of the government to fulfill treaty obligations.

Josiah Simpson was a medical officer second in command at Ft. Humboldt from 1854–1857. During the fort's later years it was involved in forced tribal relocation, and even though given some treatment, many Indians died or grew ill while penned at the fort and the North Peninsula.

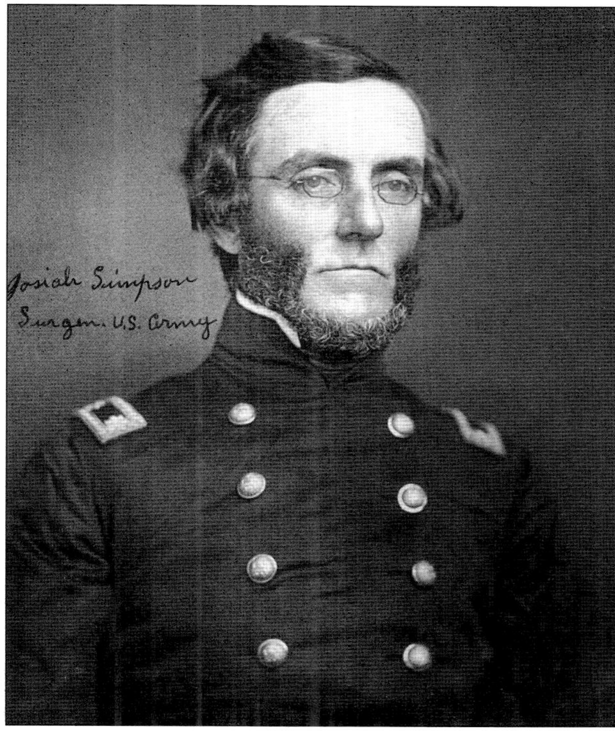

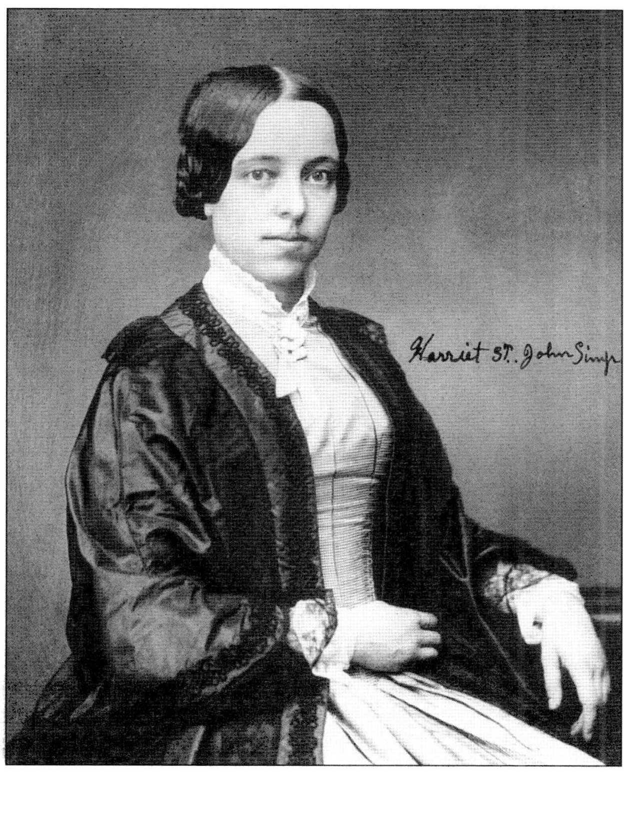

Harriet St. John Simpson, wife of Josiah, was the only woman at Ft. Humboldt when she arrived with her husband, daughter Bridget, and son Johnnie after a voyage in which they all suffered from sea sickness. Another daughter, Mary, was born that year. Her letters home give fascinating details of early Humboldt life, which generally she enjoyed despite complaining of high frontier prices and the cold foggy weather.

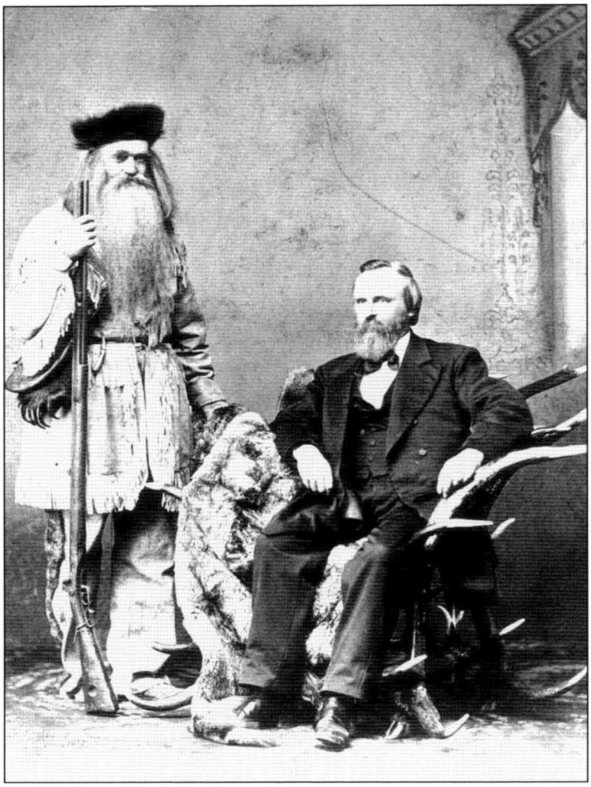

Seth Kinman, Humboldt County's colorful "mountain man" supplied elk and deer meat to the soldiers at Ft. Humboldt, entertained them with stories, and amused all by playing a banjo made from the skull of a favorite mule. He made chairs from elk antlers and presented them to several U.S. presidents including Rutheford Hayes, who was a presidential candidate when presented this chair in 1876. Kinman's buckskin outfit, beaded moccasins, and wooden chest are now in the Clarke Museum collection.

One of the officers posted at Ft. Humboldt and complaining of the isolation and weather was Capt. Ulysses S. Grant. During the mid-20th century, Eureka celebrated this tenuous Civil War connection with its "General Grant Days." In this 1930 photo, Robert E. Lee is played by Harry H Selvage, Abe Lincoln is C. Schwarkoph, and Grant is Eureka barber Ben Shoemaker

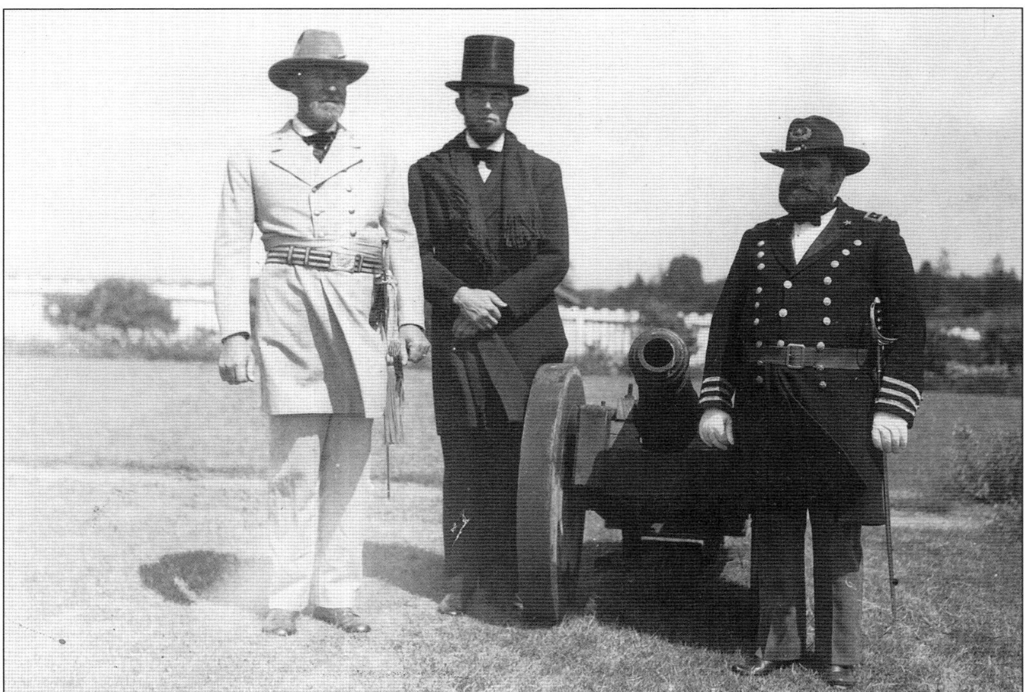

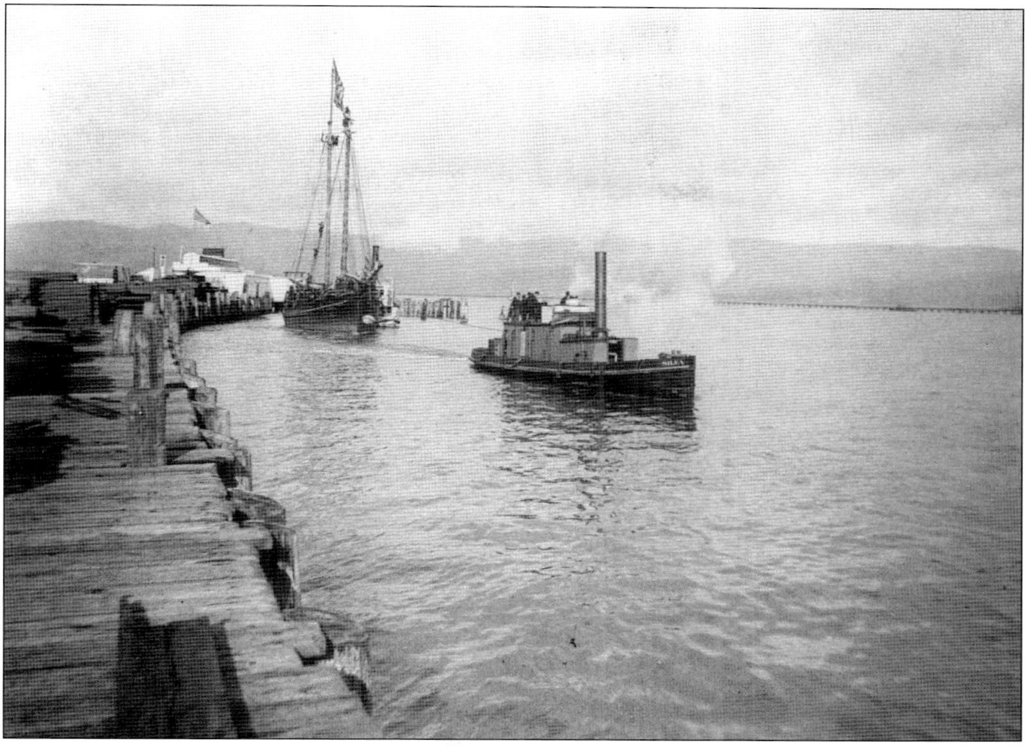

Arcata was well located as a supply port for the mines, but its wide tidal flats meant that long wharfs, one as long as two miles, had to be built. California's first "common carrier" railroad, a horse-drawn car, hauled goods along the Arcata wharf.

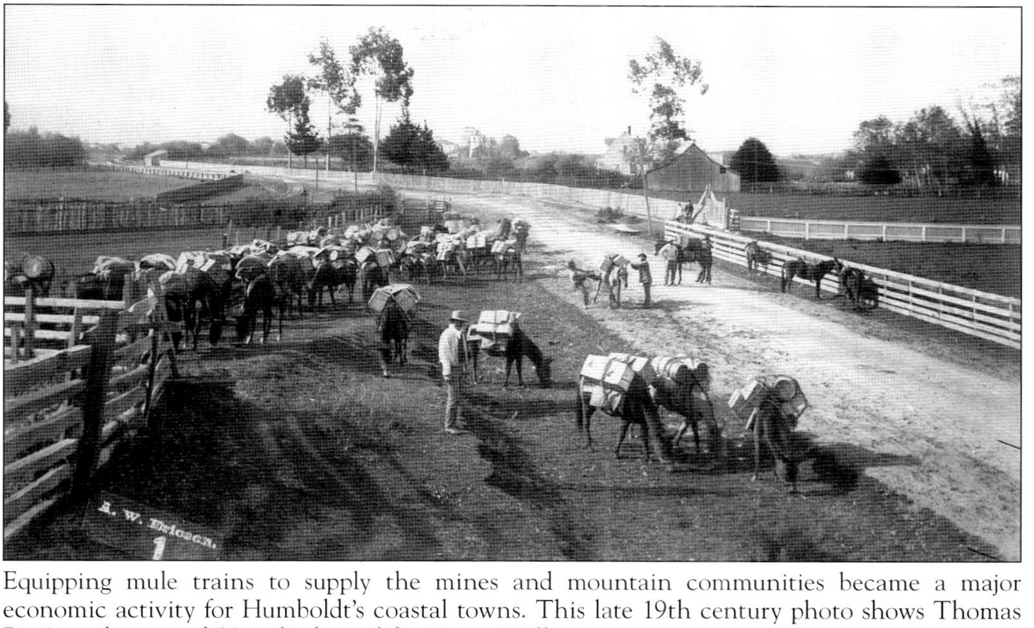

Equipping mule trains to supply the mines and mountain communities became a major economic activity for Humboldt's coastal towns. This late 19th century photo shows Thomas Bair's pack train of 55 mules bound for Hoopa Valley.

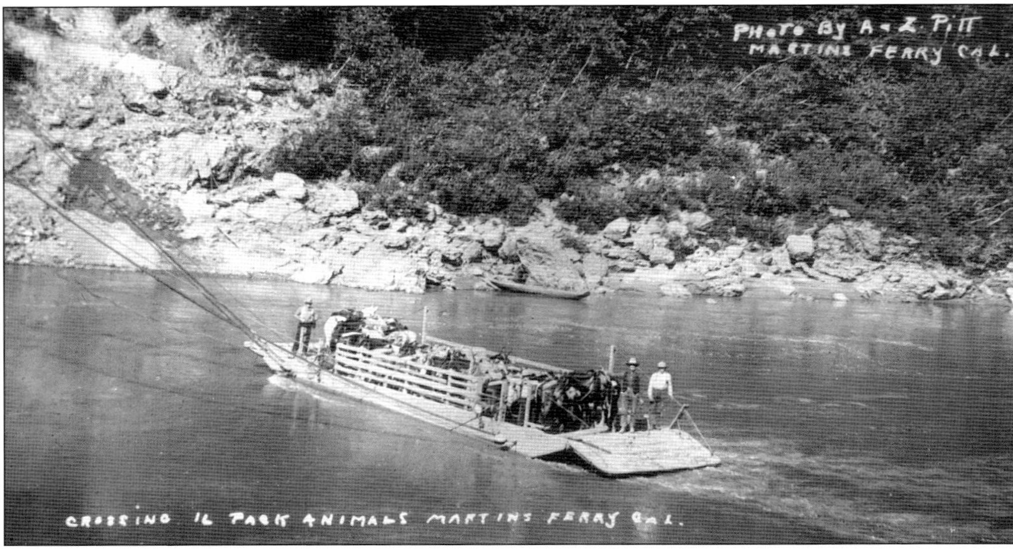

Ferries transported passengers and pack mules across Humboldt's many rivers. Beyond the cable ferry at Martin's Ferry on the Klamath, this photo shows a traditional ferry, a dug-out redwood canoe.

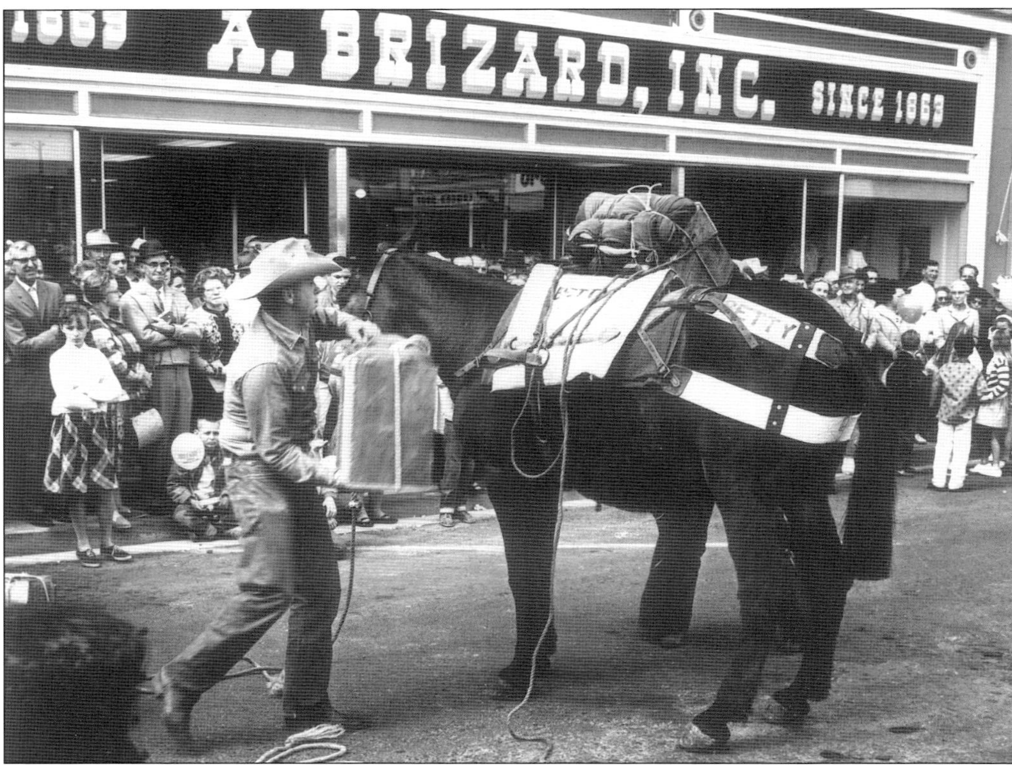

Alexander Brizard founded his general merchandise store in Arcata in 1863. From there his mule trains supplied mountain communities and his branch stores in Hoopa, Willow Creek, Orleans, and elsewhere. Here mule packing is re-enacted in a 1963 centennial celebration.

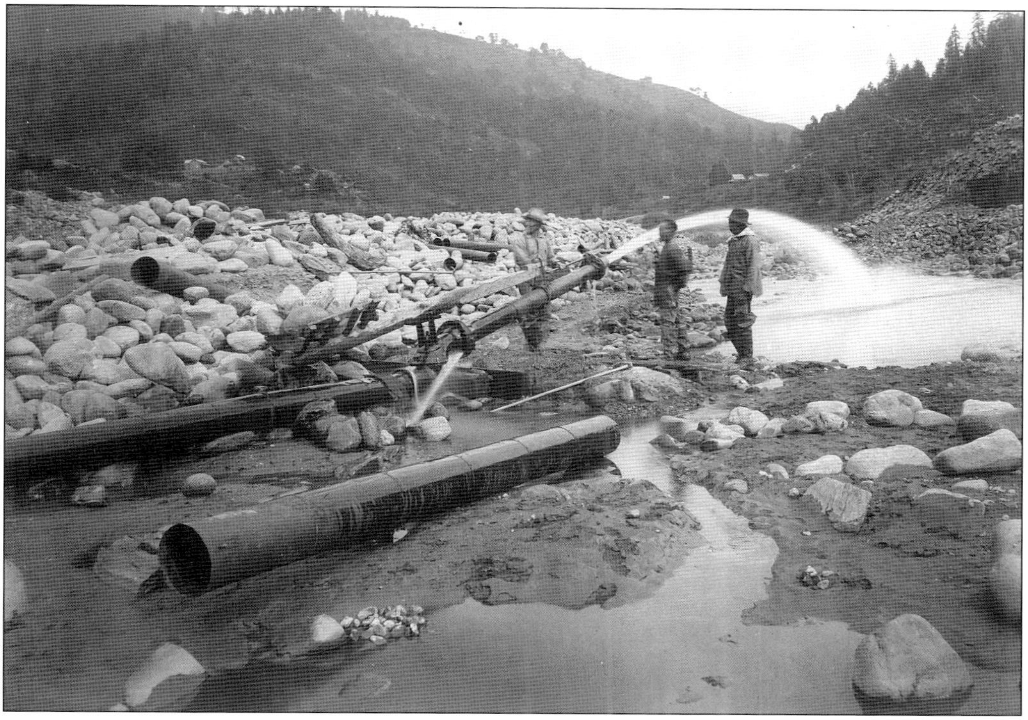

At first, gold miners in the Trinities used gold pans, sluices, and rockers, but soon high powered water cannons, called monitors, were used to undermine banks of river gravel and wash the sand, gravel, and stone through sluice boxes up to a mile long. Whole hillsides were washed away, and soon gravel clogged streams and destroyed native fishing. The miners in this photograph are probably Chinese employed by mine owners.

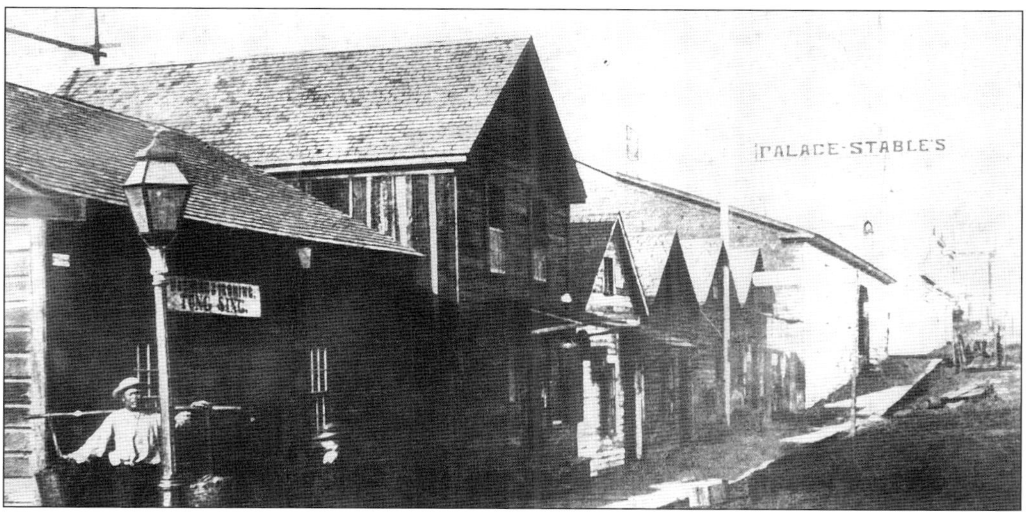

The promise of wealth from California's gold attracted merchants and miners from China. American miners often resented the Chinese who were willing to work for less. In time the towns' resentment grew over cultural differences, economic competition, and the criminal activities of Tongs. Eureka's Chinatown was located between F and E on Fourth Street.

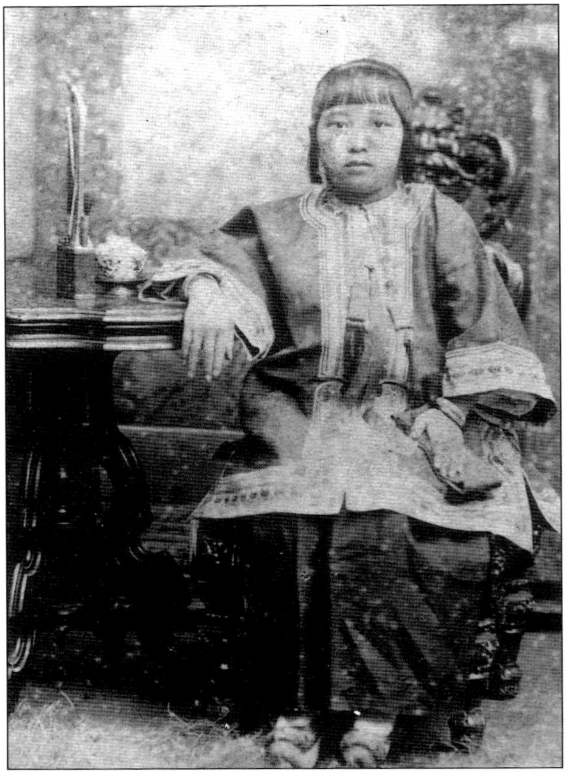

In 1885, a Eureka City councilman was accidentally killed in Tong crossfire. Within days, enraged citizens had herded all Eureka's Chinese onto ships for San Francisco. Within a year, most Asian residents had been driven from Humboldt County. This Eureka girl was photographed shortly before the expulsion. Laws and attitudes prevented Asians from settling in Humboldt County until the late 1940s.

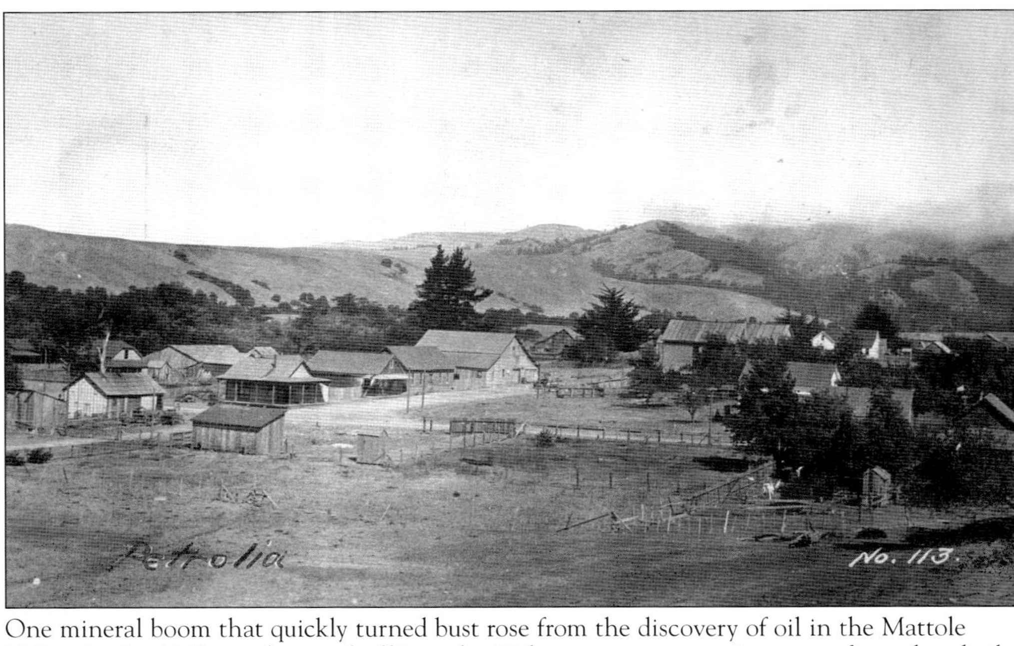

One mineral boom that quickly turned bust rose from the discovery of oil in the Mattole Valley. In the 1860s, and on and off into the 20th century, corporations were formed and oil drilled, but exploitation proved uneconomical. The would-be boomtown of Petrolia developed instead into a quiet farming community.

Three

Humboldt's Red Gold

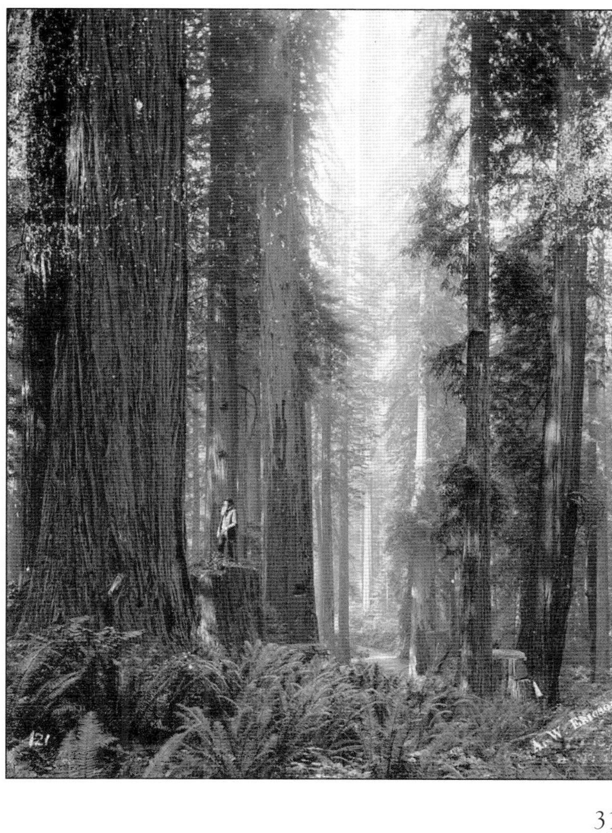

Around a million years ago, Sequoia Sempervirens grew in Europe, Asia, and America. Today they survive only in the narrow fog belt along California's central and north coast and just into Oregon. Resistant to insects and fire, they can live more than 2,000 years and grow to be over 300 feet tall. Early explorers and settlers were awed by the majesty of Humboldt's redwoods.

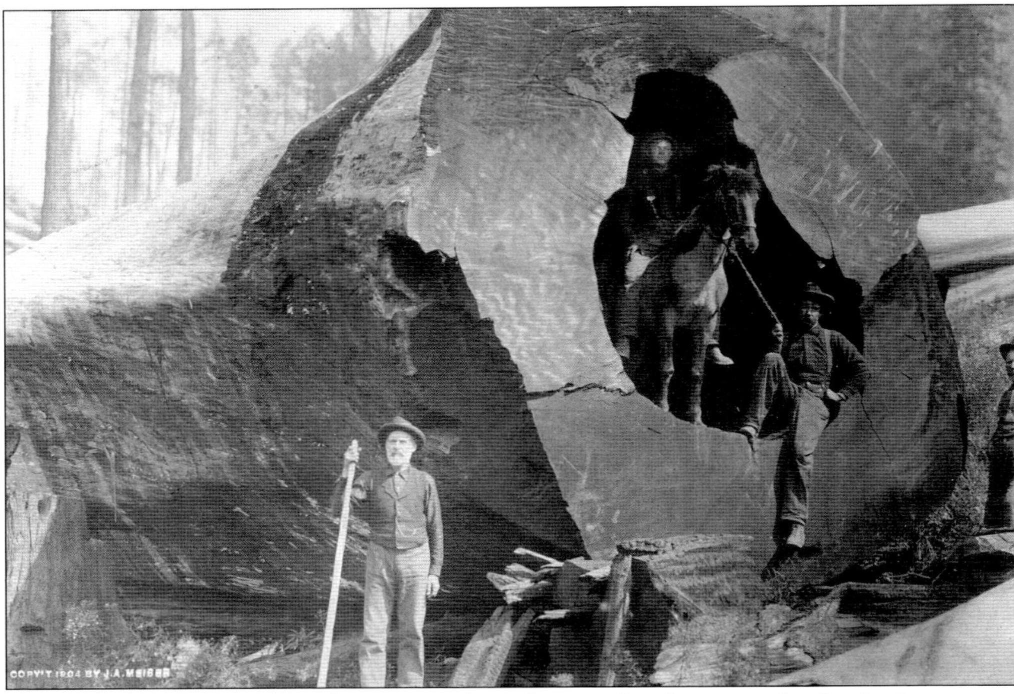

Posing on or in giant redwood stumps to show their size has been popular for the last century and a half.

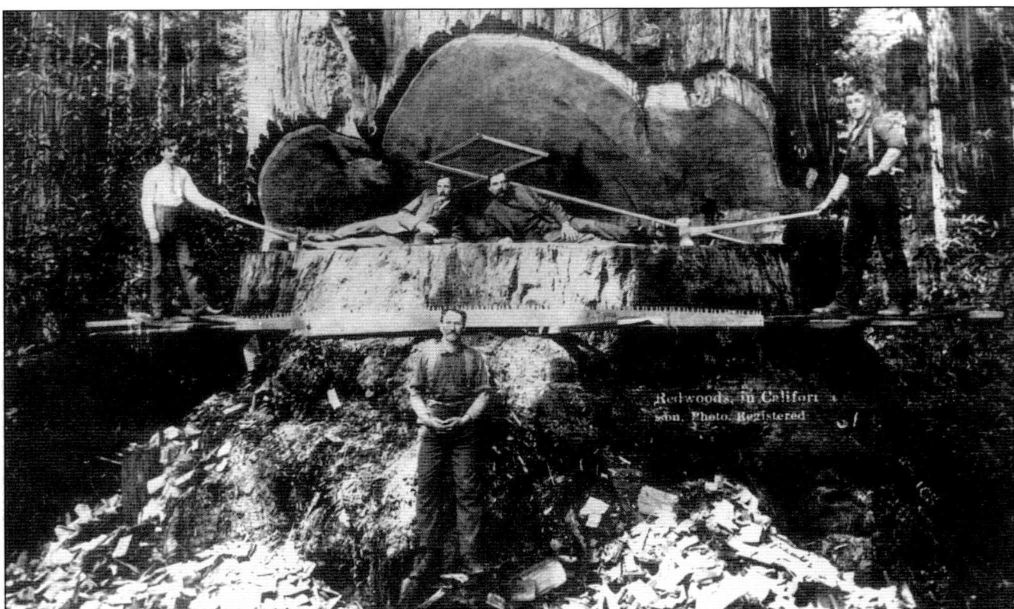

The economic role of Humboldt's "red gold" soon became apparent. Lumbermen flocked here from around the country and the world. Tools and techniques had to be adapted to match these giant trees. Using axes, cross-cut saws, and wedges, it took days to make an undercut which was then back-cut to bring the tree down.

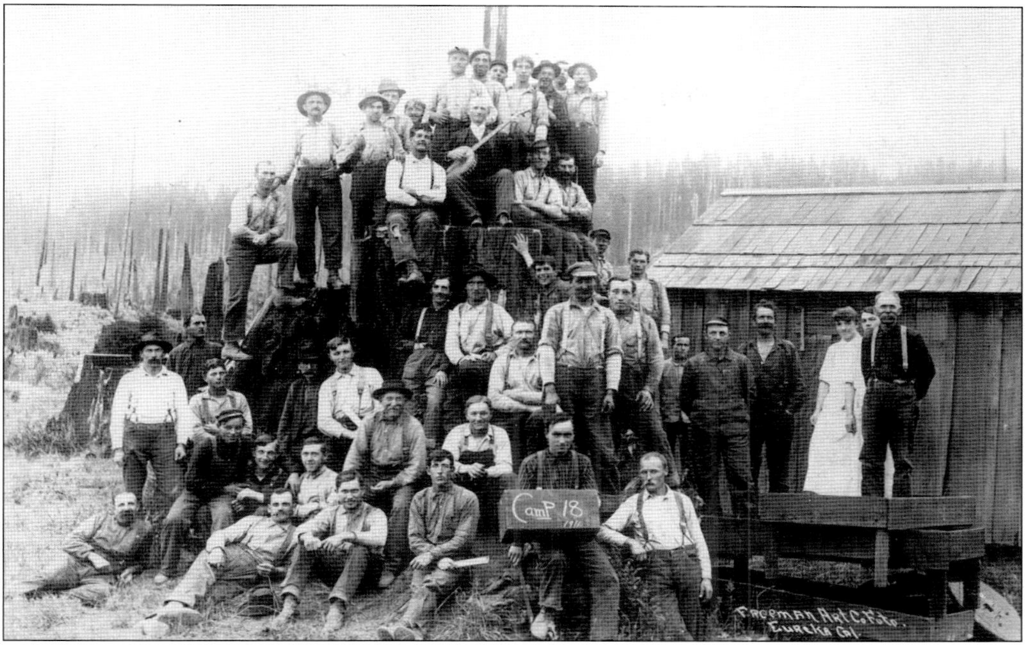

Lumber camps moved inland as forests were cut. Here the woods crew at a camp strikes a typical group pose for the photographer.

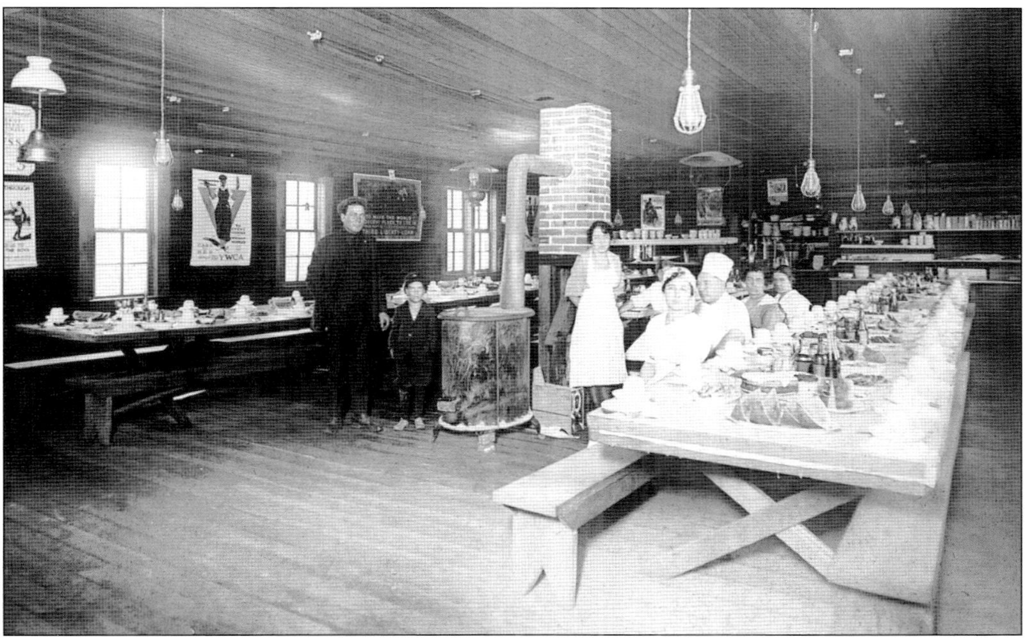

Lumber camps and mills housed and fed many employees, mostly single men, and the cookhouse was legendary for good food and plenty of it. This cookhouse, pictured around 1918 judging by the World War I posters, is typical. Note how plates and cups are set out ahead of time upside down to keep off flies and dust. The former Hammond Lumber Company's Samoa Cookhouse is now a public restaurant serving in the "lumber camp style" and is the last of its kind still in operation.

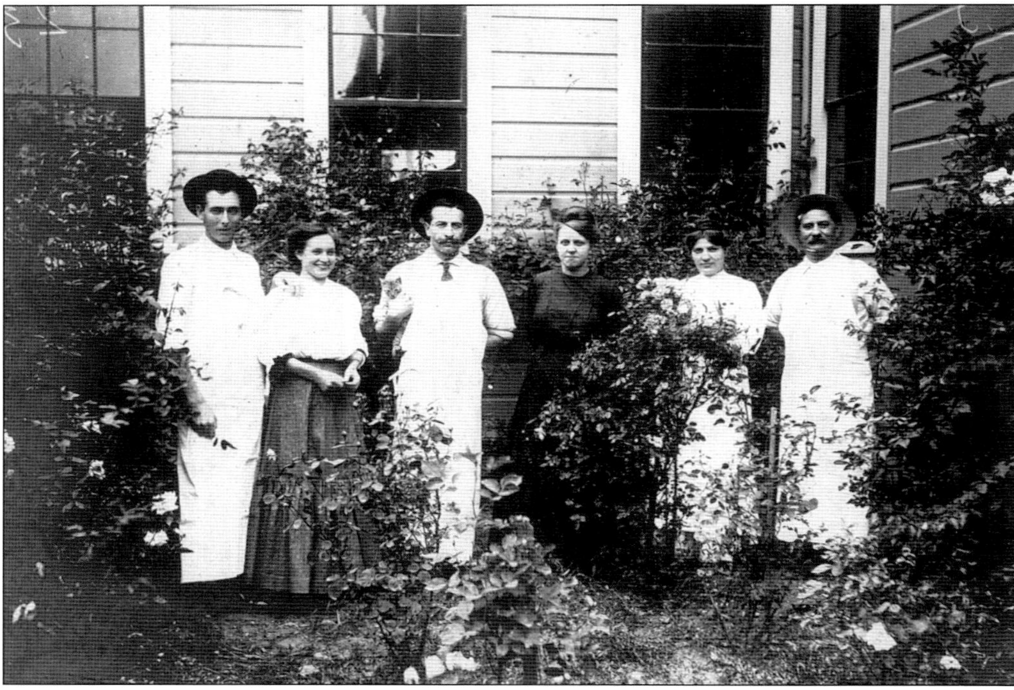

The cookhouse staff at the Korbel Mill poses in the building's garden. Note the kitchen kitten being held by the third man from the left.

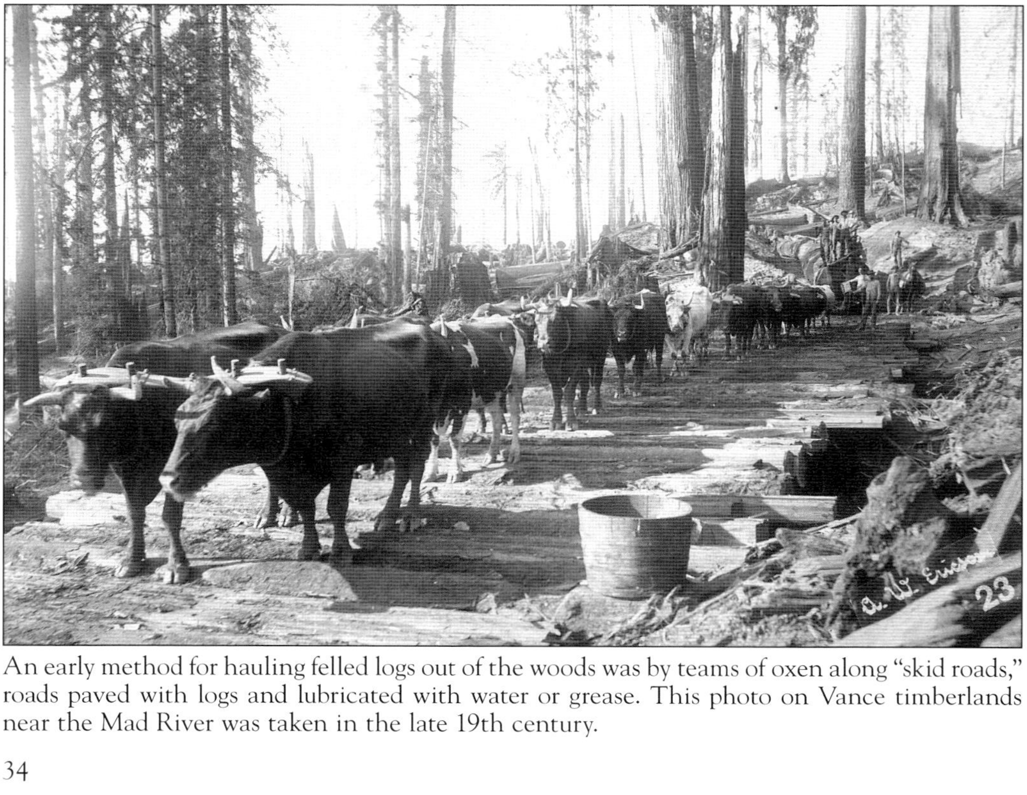

An early method for hauling felled logs out of the woods was by teams of oxen along "skid roads," roads paved with logs and lubricated with water or grease. This photo on Vance timberlands near the Mad River was taken in the late 19th century.

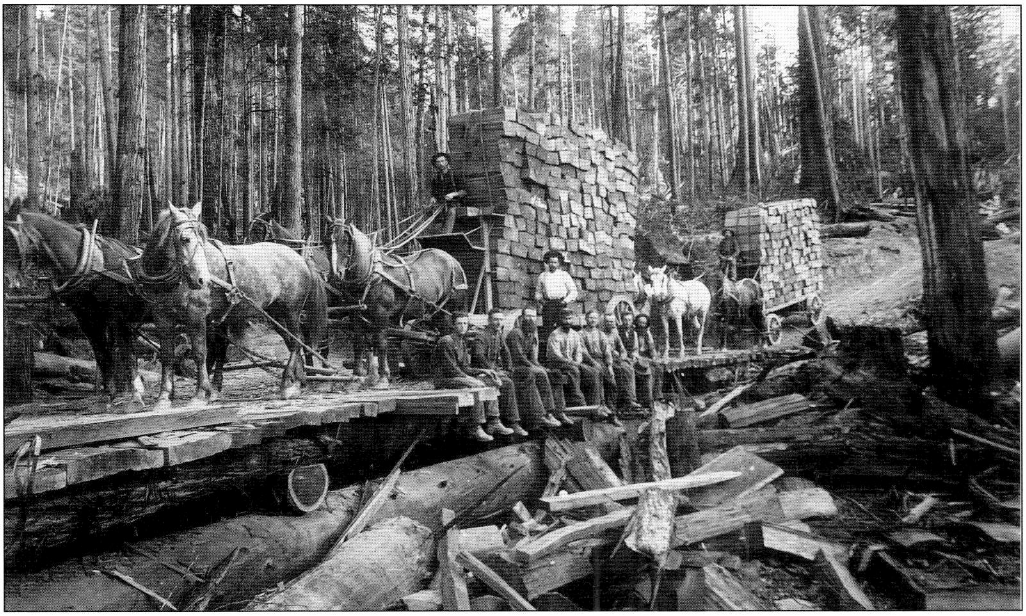

This photograph is identified as Ole Hanson's bolt crew near Freshwater, 1891. The front driver is Simon Frazier; the back driver, Charly Calson. They are hauling blocks of redwood salvaged from a cut-over area to a shingle mill.

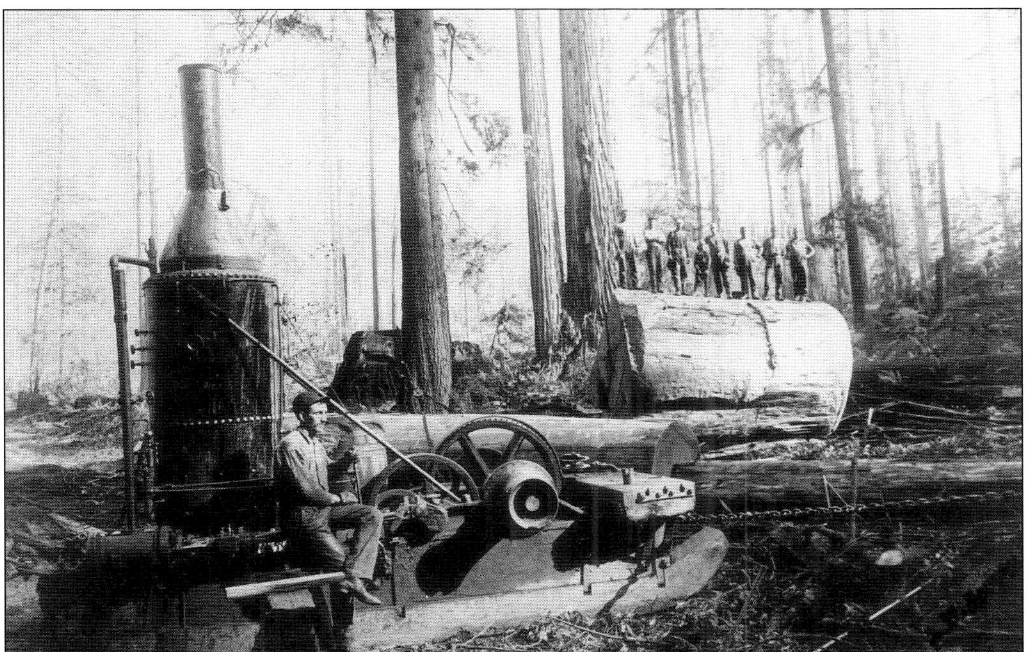

Animal power was replaced by the "steam donkey," an early-1880s invention of Humboldt lumberman John Dolbeer, a partner of William Carson. Usually a series of donkeys was set up. Once a log was dragged to one donkey, the cables were attached to the next donkey and the log dragged further until it eventually reached the railroad or river.

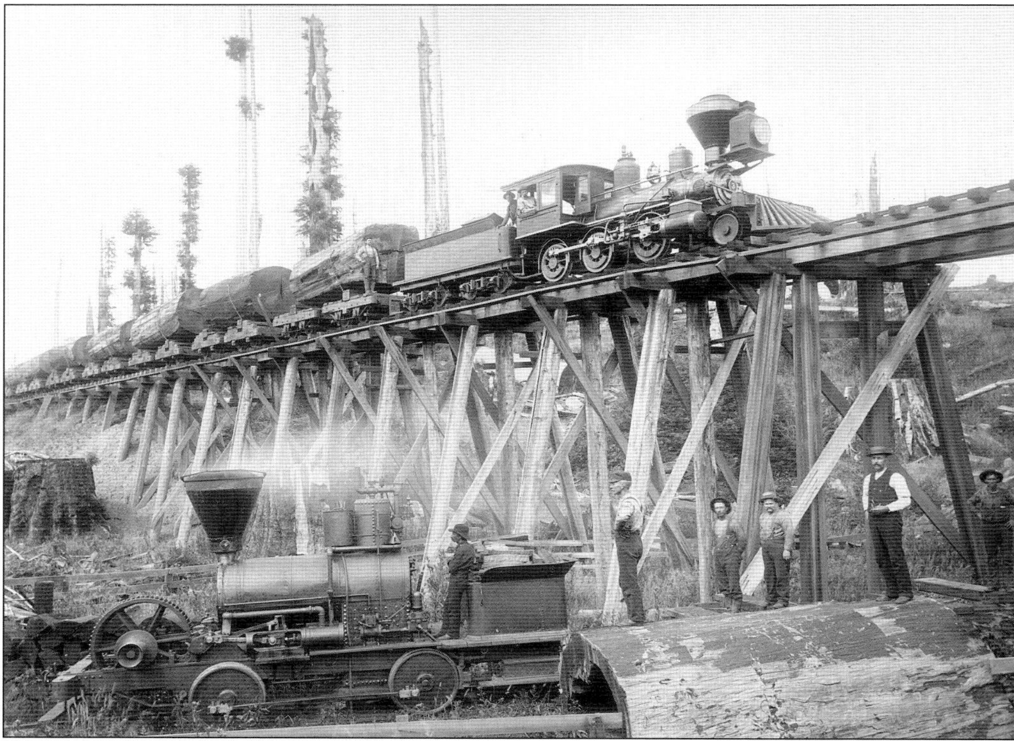

By the 1870s, lumbering operations had moved far inland and trains were beginning to be used to haul out the logs. This often required massive trestles to be built over ravines. Logging trains continued operation in some areas until the early 1960s.

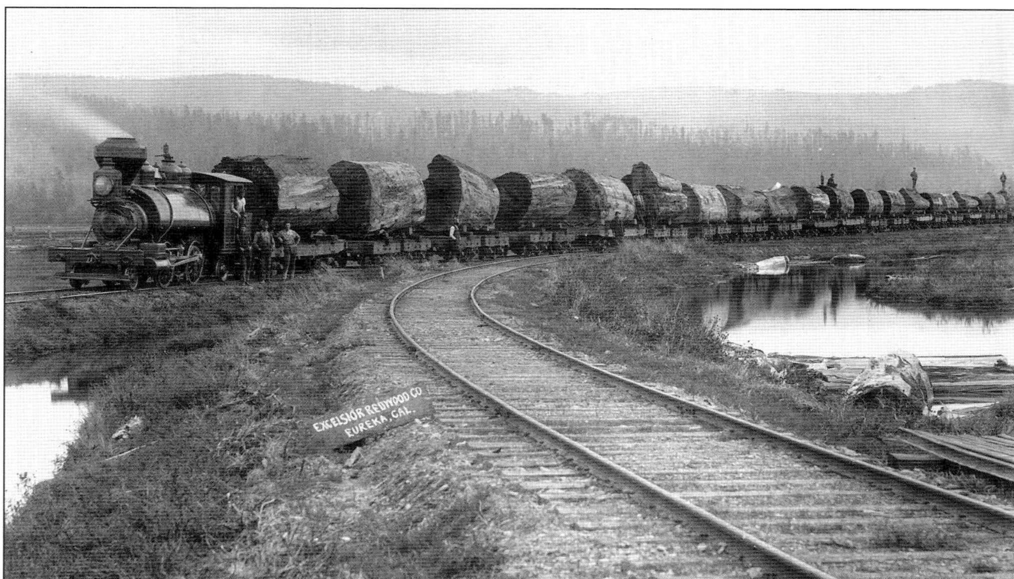

Most of the early rail lines in Humboldt County were built and operated by the lumber companies. This late-19th-century photo of an Excelsior Redwood Co. train was taken near Eddyville.

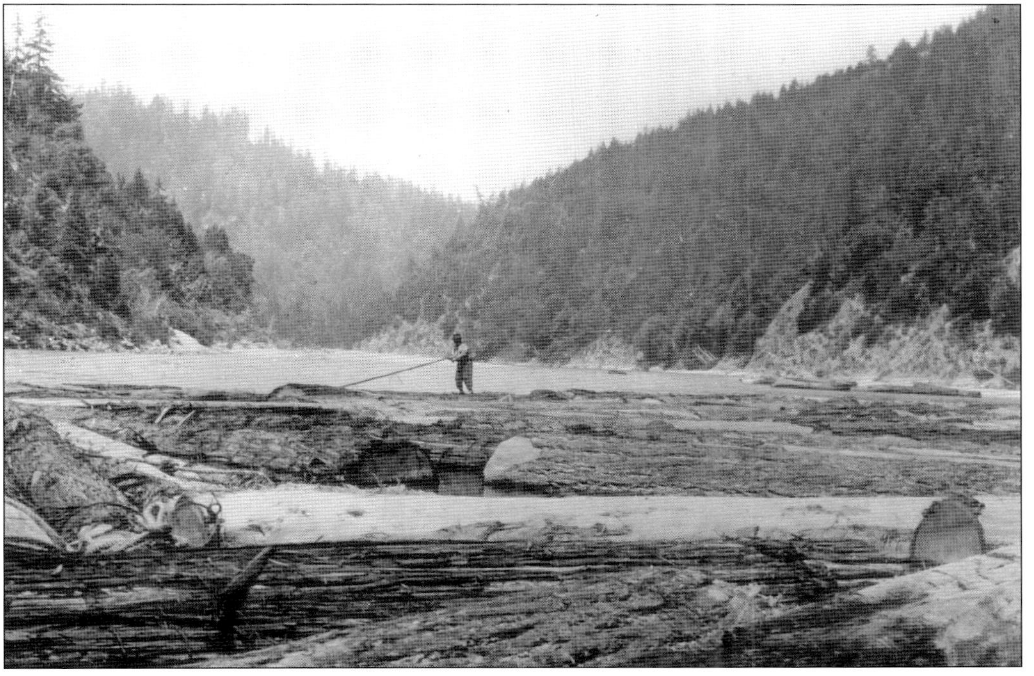

Once hauled to a large river, logs were dumped in and floated to mill or port. Log rolling was a skilled and dangerous occupation. This picture of floating cedar logs was taken on the Klamath River in 1926.

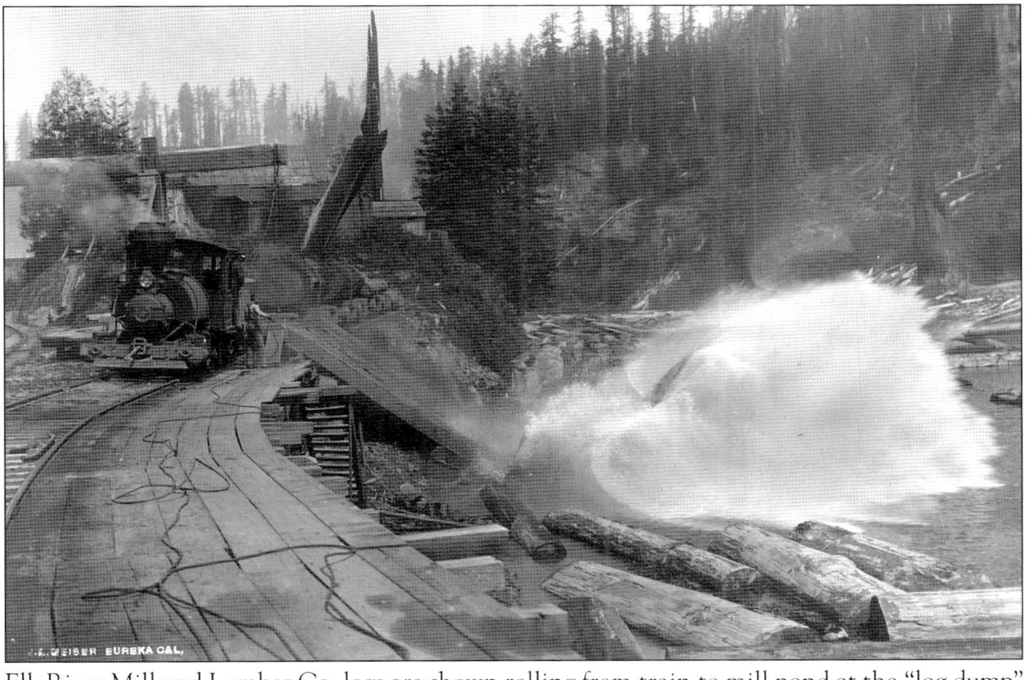

Elk River Mill and Lumber Co. logs are shown rolling from train to mill pond at the "log dump" at Falk around 1905.

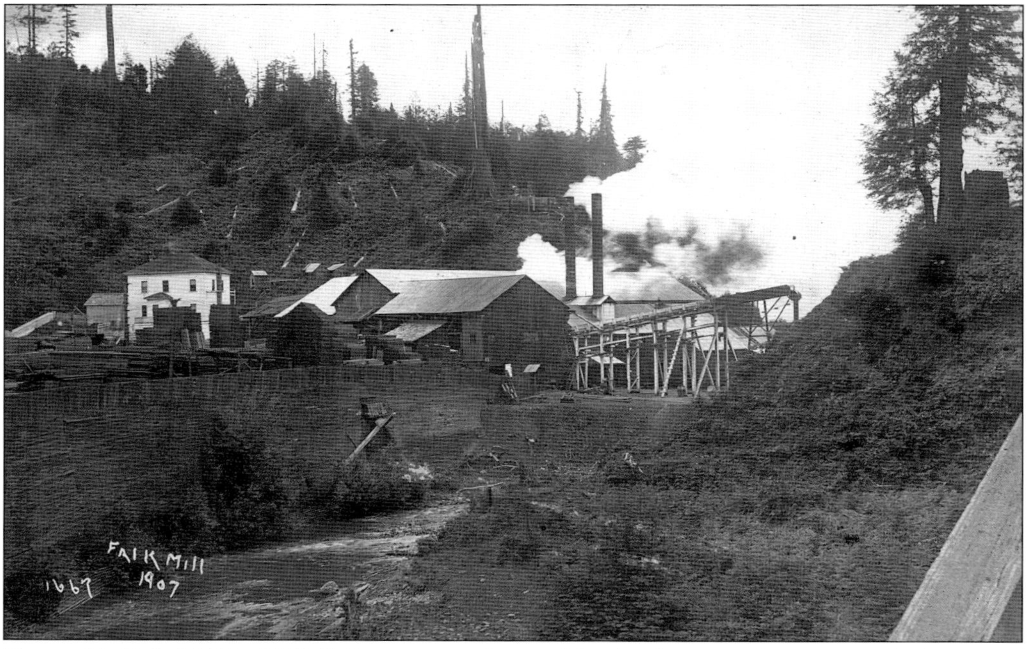

Pictured is Falk Mill in 1907. Falk was one of many Humboldt towns that grew with the rise of the lumber industry and disappeared during one of the industry's downturns. The mill ceased operation in 1937 and soon the town site was largely deserted. After years as a "ghost town" most of the buildings were destroyed, but interpretive trails have now been developed at the site.

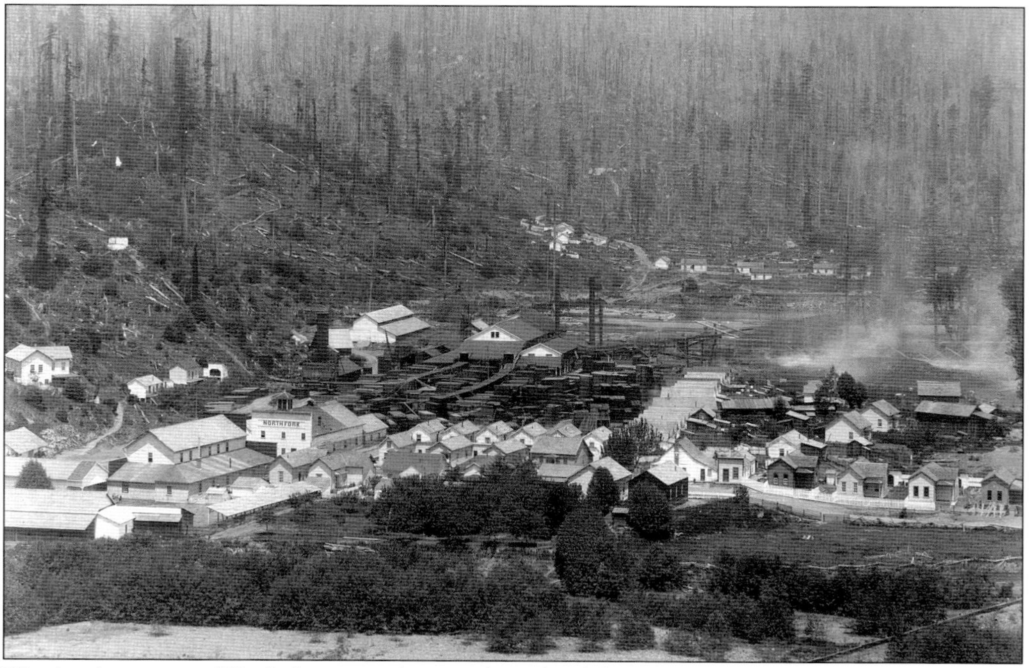

The lumber town of Korbel was on the North Fork of the Mad River. The Mad River received its name in 1849 because of an argument on its banks among the early Gregg Party.

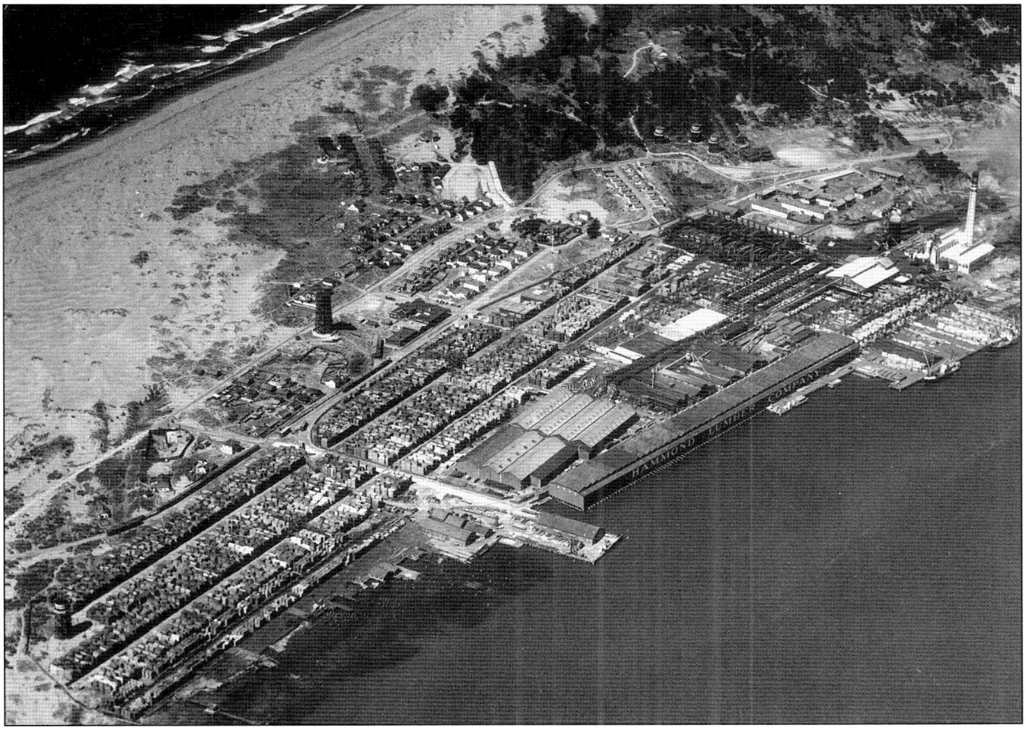

As time passed, some milling operations became very large. This aerial photograph taken in 1931 shows the Hammond and Little River Redwood Co. plant at Samoa. The steamers *Tillamok* and *Tiverton* are loading at the dock. Humboldt Bay is on the right and across the narrow North Peninsula the breakers of the Pacific Ocean are seen on the left.

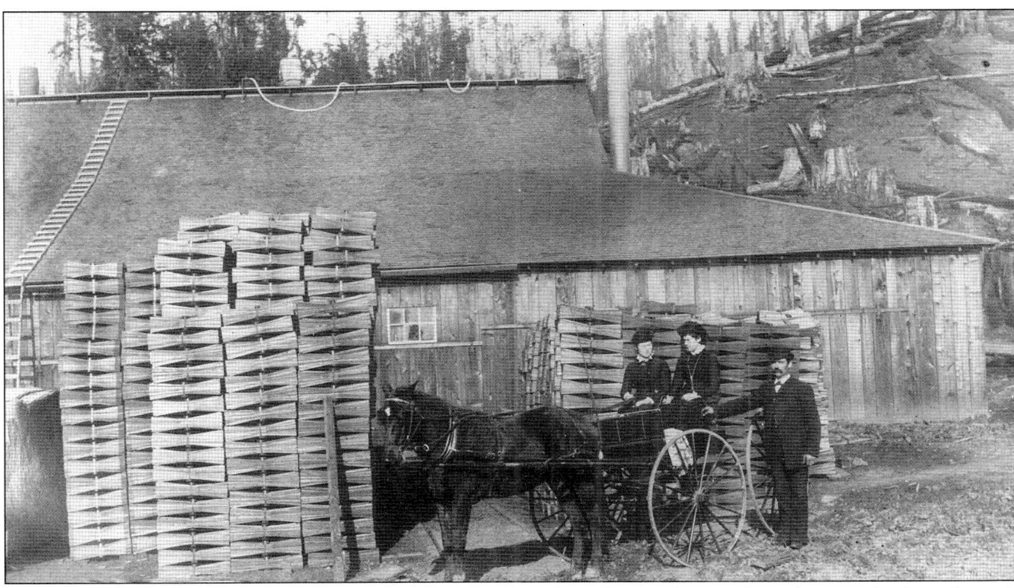

Humboldt redwood was also milled into shingles.This photo shows shingles stacked and ready for market at a shingle mill east of Arcata.

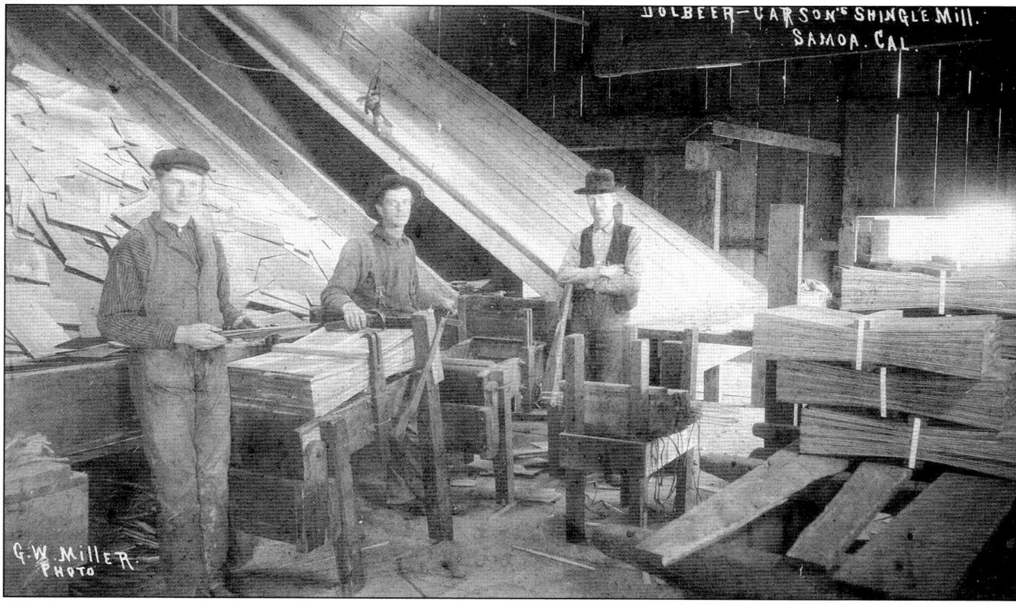

Workers pose inside the Dolbeer-Carson Shingle Mill on Humboldt Bay.

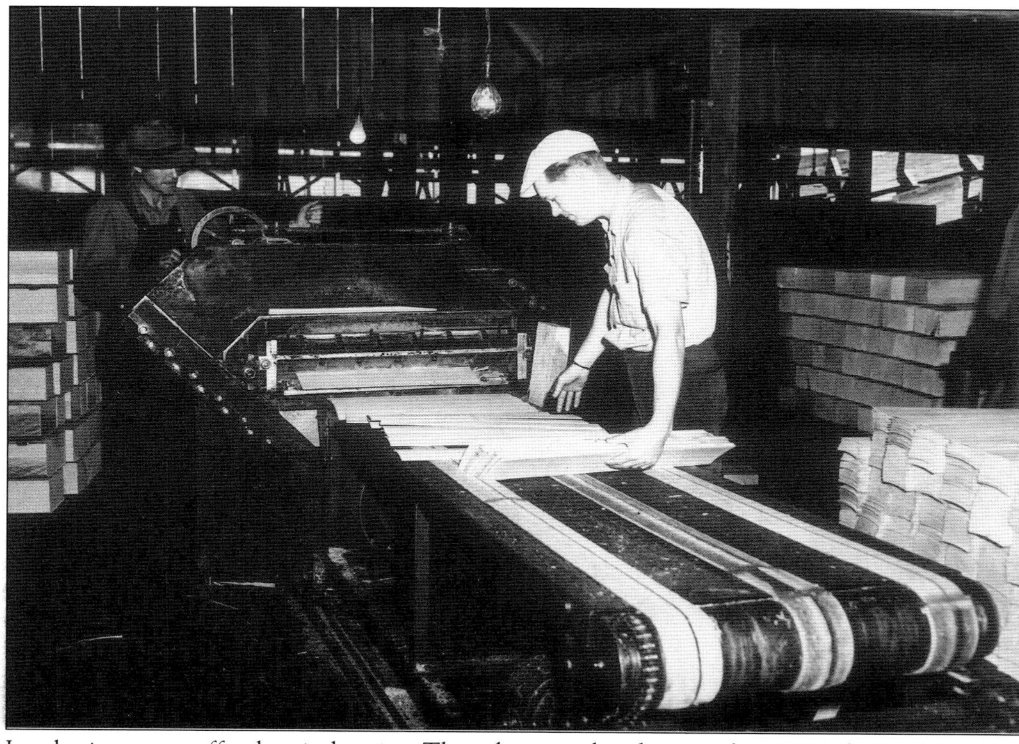
Lumbering spun off other industries. This photograph taken in the 1930s shows slats being cut at Arcata's California Barrel Co. for making wire-bound vegetable crates that were used in shipping California lettuce and celery. These crates could be shipped from the factory flat in large quantities and then quickly assembled.

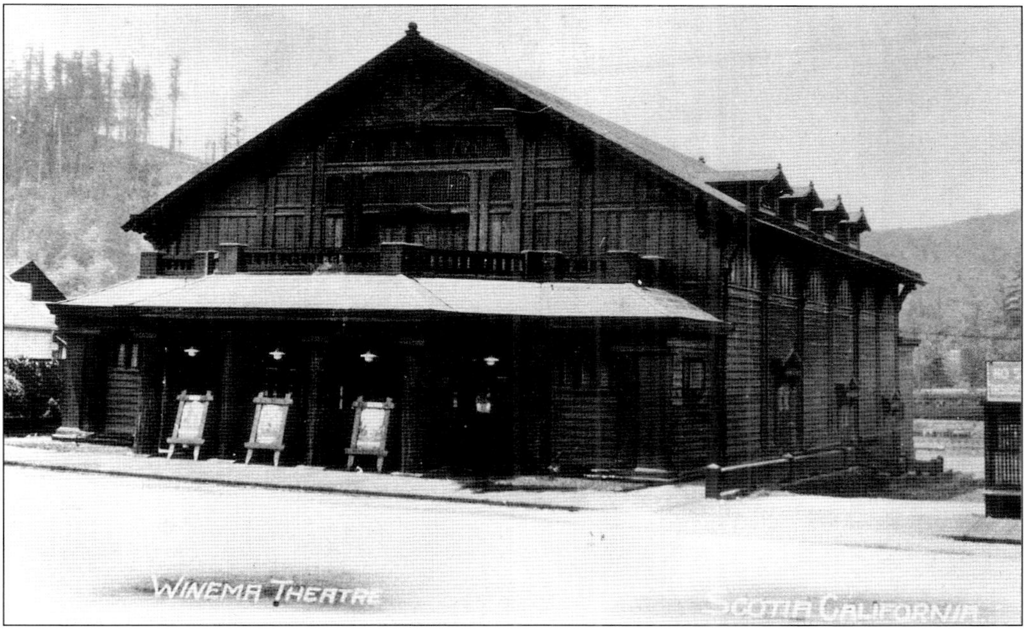

Several Humboldt towns began as company towns where lumber companies took paternal care of their employees—providing housing, shops and entertainment. In 1925, the Winema Theater was the pride of the Pacific Lumber Company's town of Scotia. Today, Scotia is the last lumber company owned town in California.

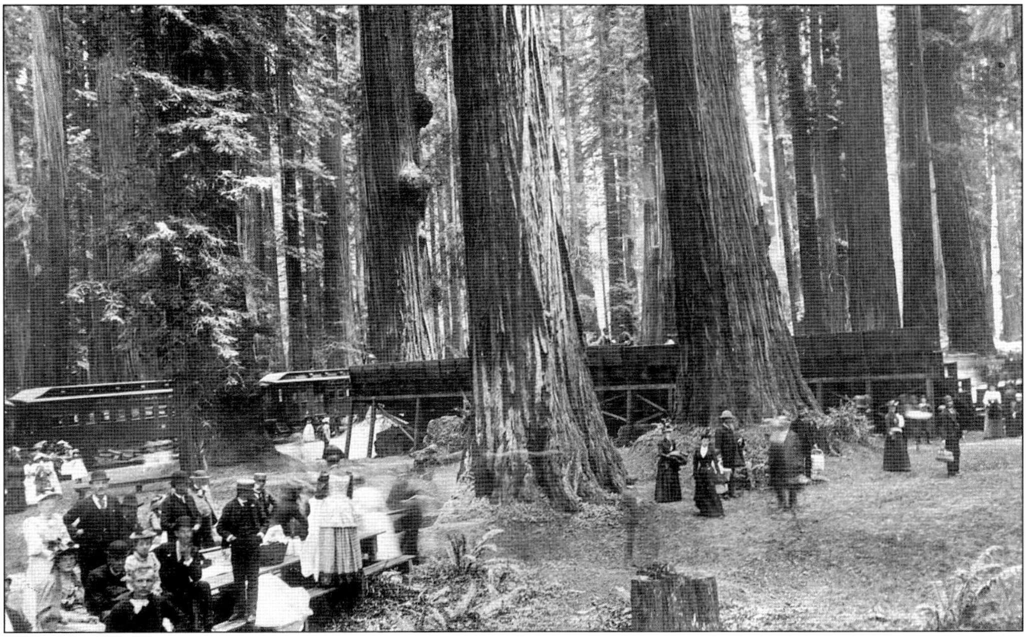
This photograph from the 1890s shows a picnic at Scotia's ball park.

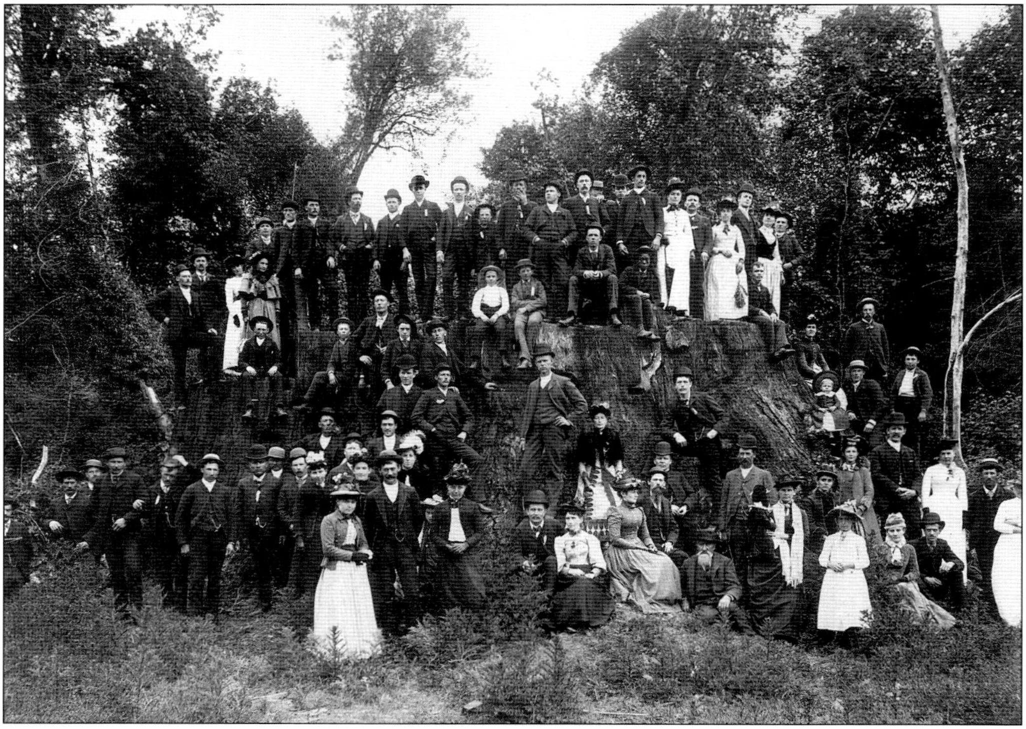

Posing for photographers on large stumps was typical for outings in logging areas. This photo was taken in the 1890s on the North Fork of the Mad River near Korbel.

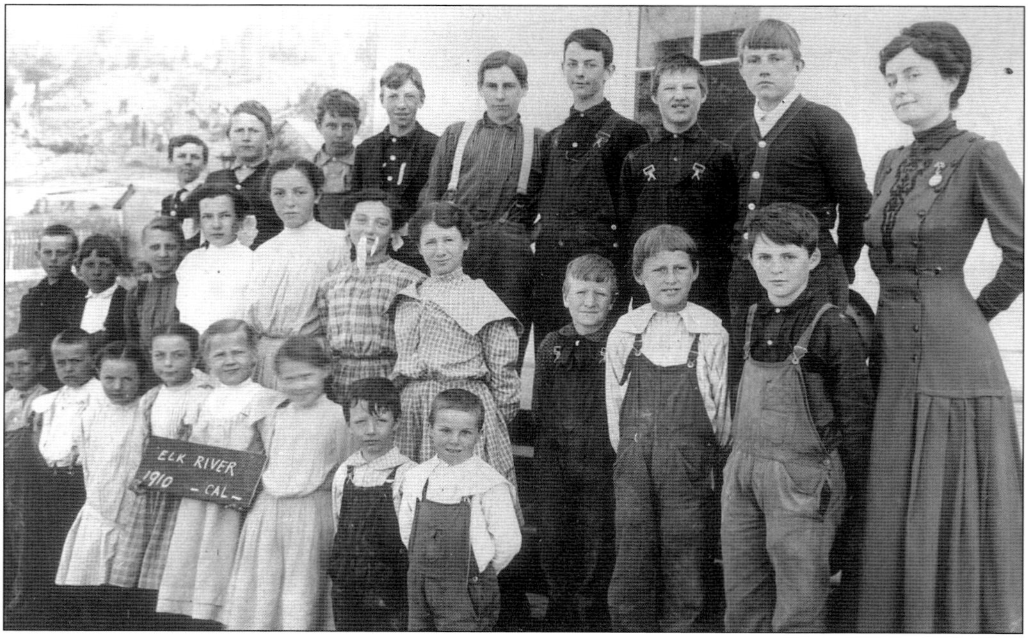

Logging-based communities supported churches, stores, and schools. In 1910, a single teacher taught all ages at the Elk River Schoolhouse. Note the logged hillsides in the background.

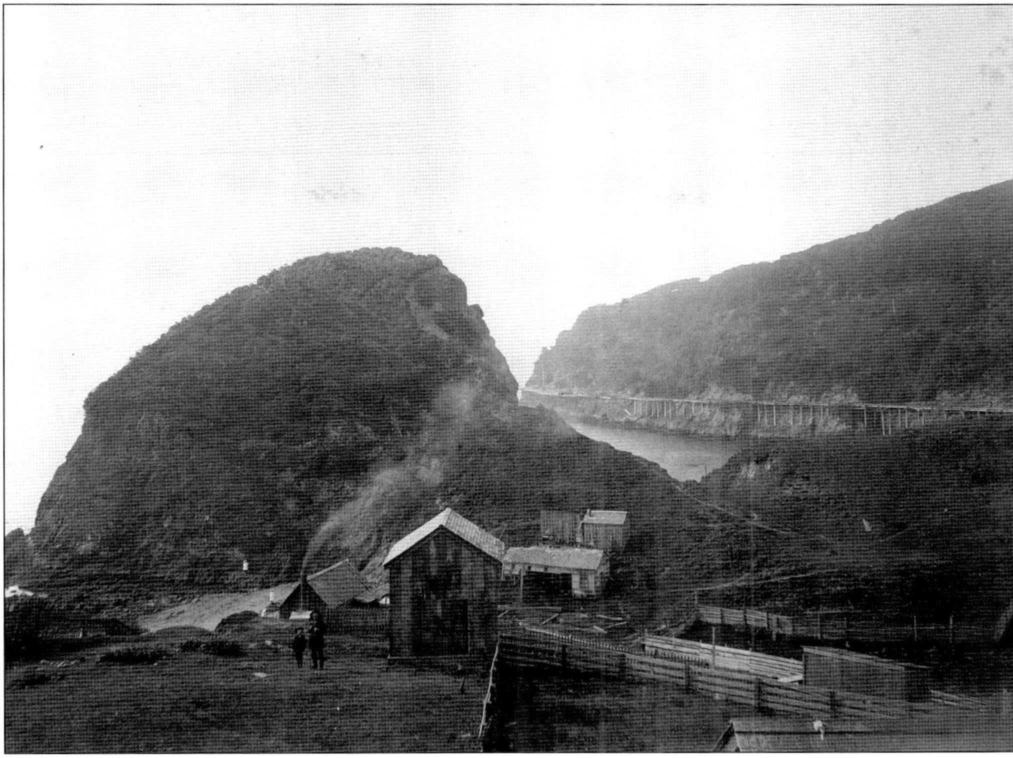

Although founded to supply the mines, by the 1880s Trinidad was largely a lumber port. The trestle built along Trinidad head served to bring lumber alongside ships moored at the wharf.

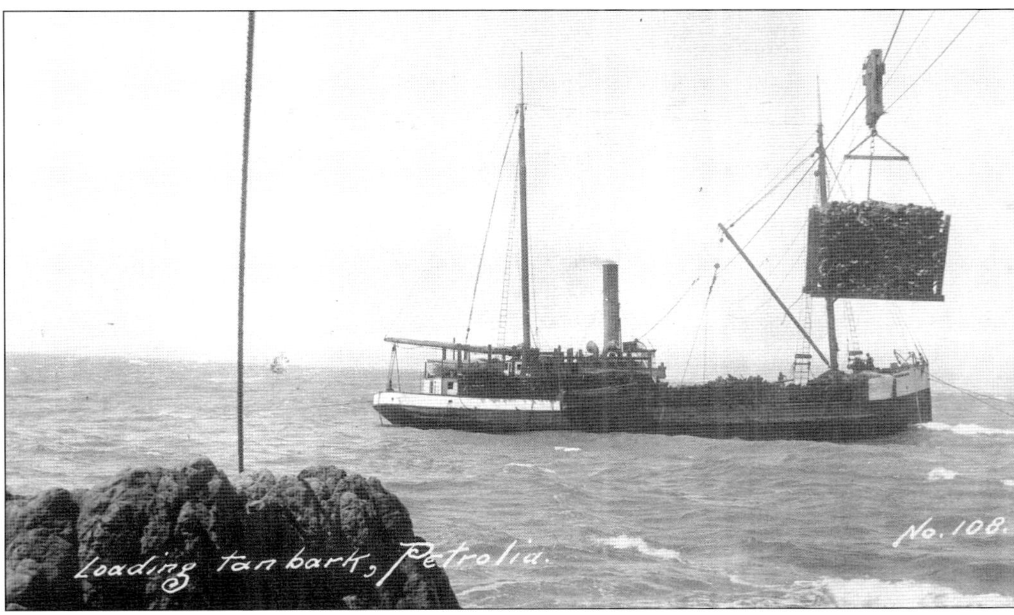

Tanbark from the Mattole Valley was loaded by cables onto off-shore ships such as this steam schooner.

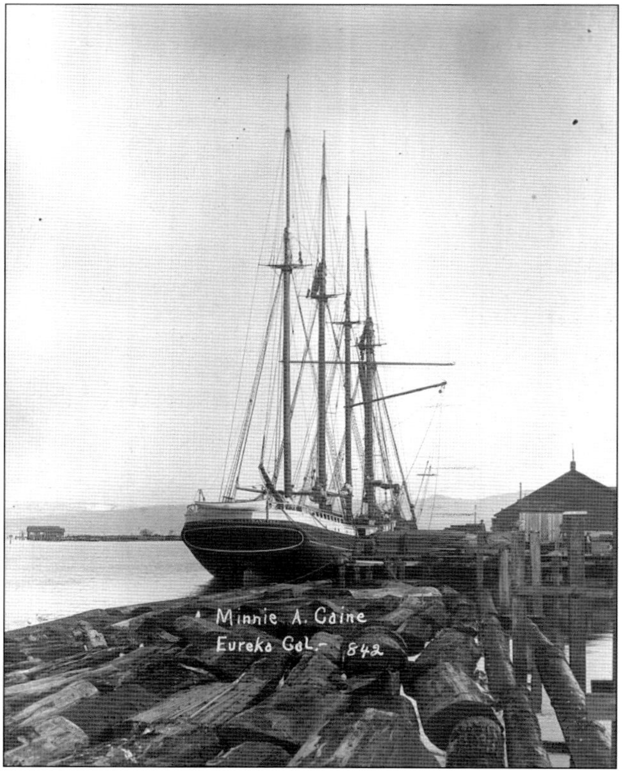

Humboldt Bay was a harbor deep and protected enough to be ideal for lumber loading. Here the *Minnie Caine*, a four-mast schooner, takes on lumber at the Excelsior Mill at the foot of C Street in Eureka. Successful early mills were located adjacent to wharfs for direct access to shipping.

From the tower of his mansion, William Carson and his successors could look over the Dolbeer-Carson lumber yards in the heart of Eureka and all the way to the harbor entrance.

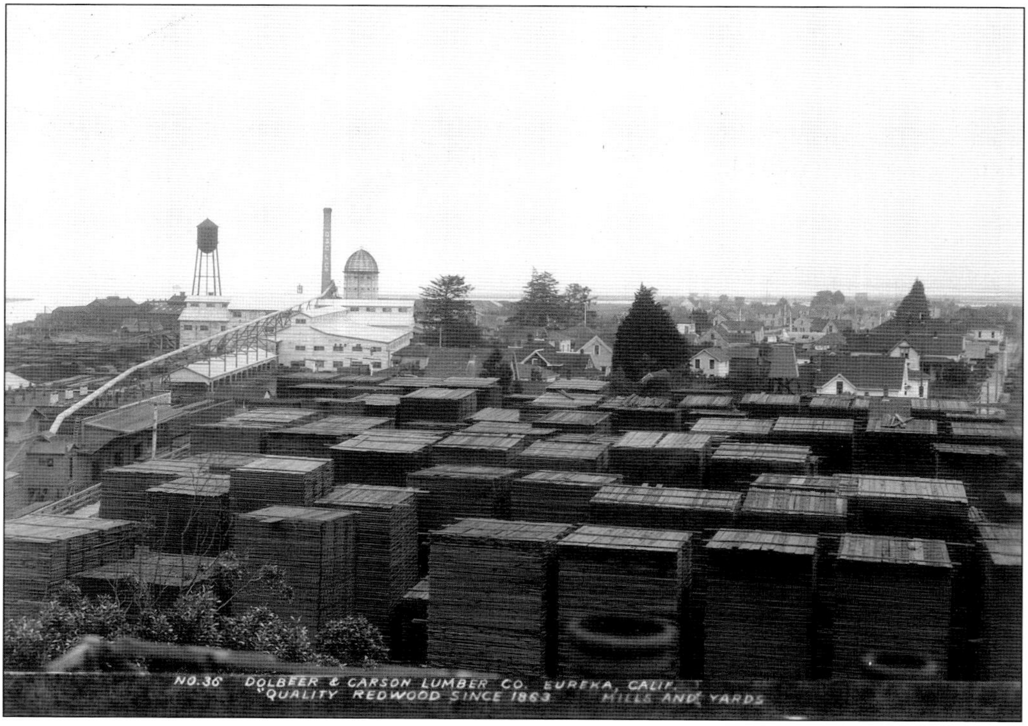

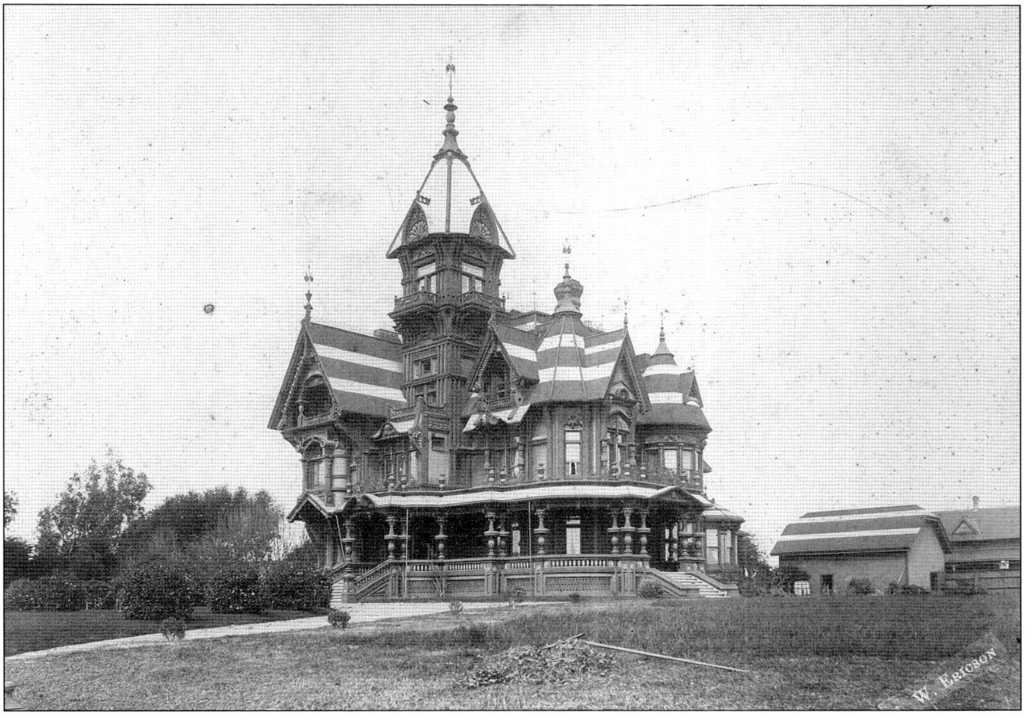

During a depression in the lumber industry, William Carson kept one hundred of his workers employed building his family's mansion. Completed in 1885 after two years' construction, it is now the most photographed Victorian house in America. It was sold by the family in 1950 and since then has been the private Ingomar Club.

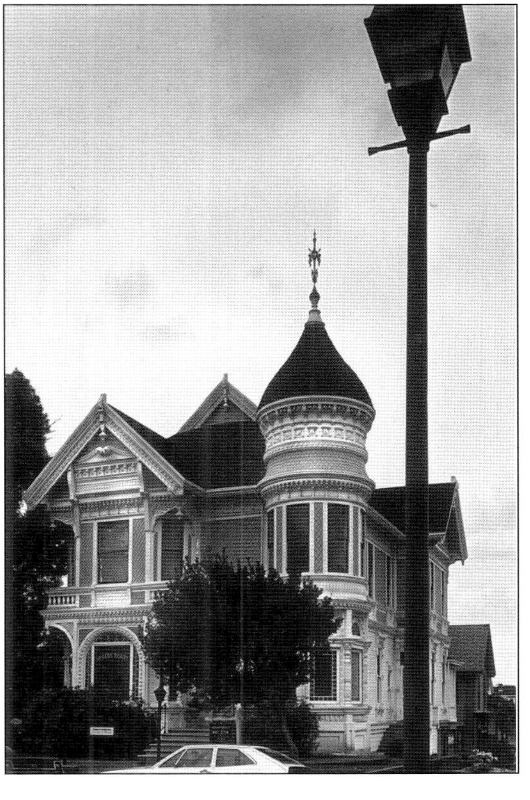

Across the street from his mansion, William Carson built a second mansion as a present for his son, Milton, who married in 1889. The "Pink Lady" is an outstanding example of Queen Anne/Eastlake architecture. This and hundreds of other Victorian homes serve today as major tourist attractions for Humboldt County.

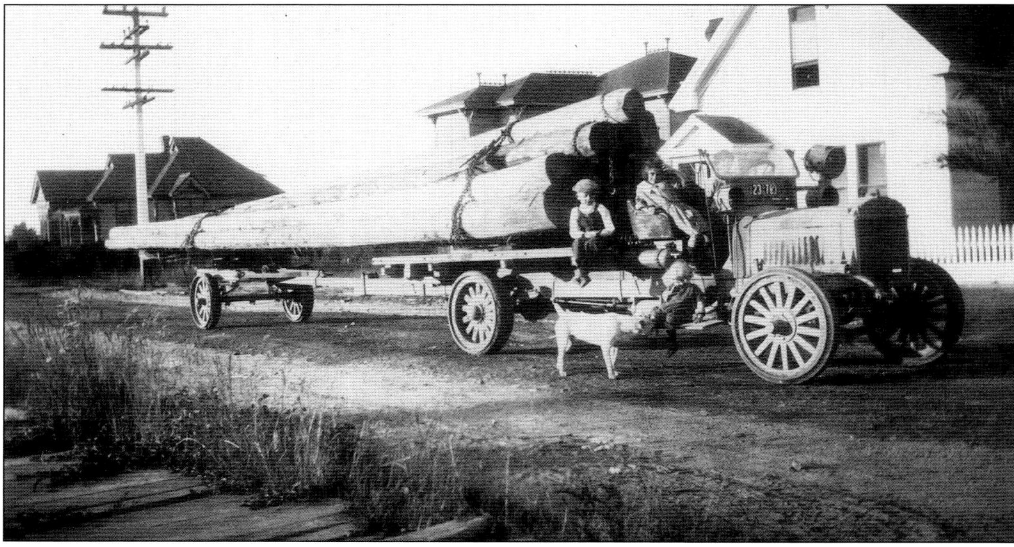

Redwood and other lumber was put to many local uses. Here utility poles are about to be installed in Eureka around 1915.

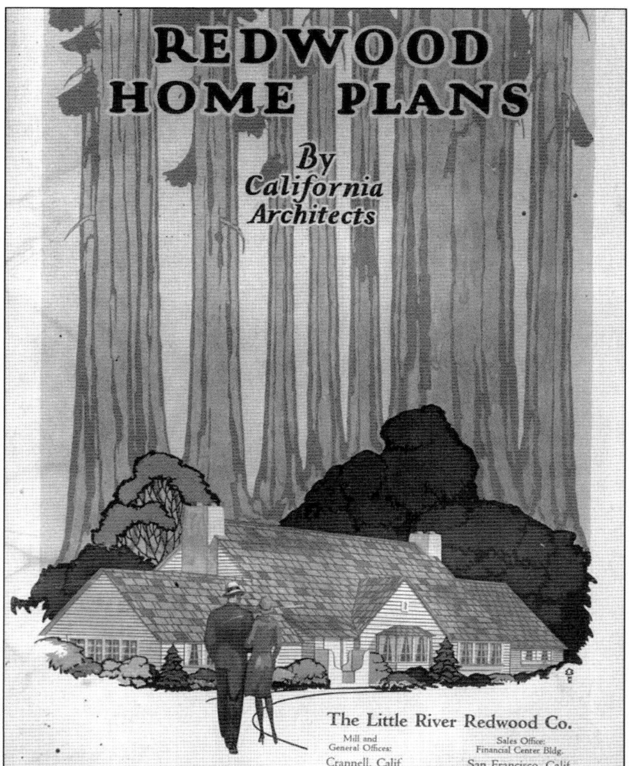

From the 1850s on, Humboldt redwood was in demand around the world, and was shipped to Latin America, Asia, and Europe. The Little River Lumber Co. promoted its architectural use in this 1927 booklet.

Four

LIVELIHOOD FROM THE SEA

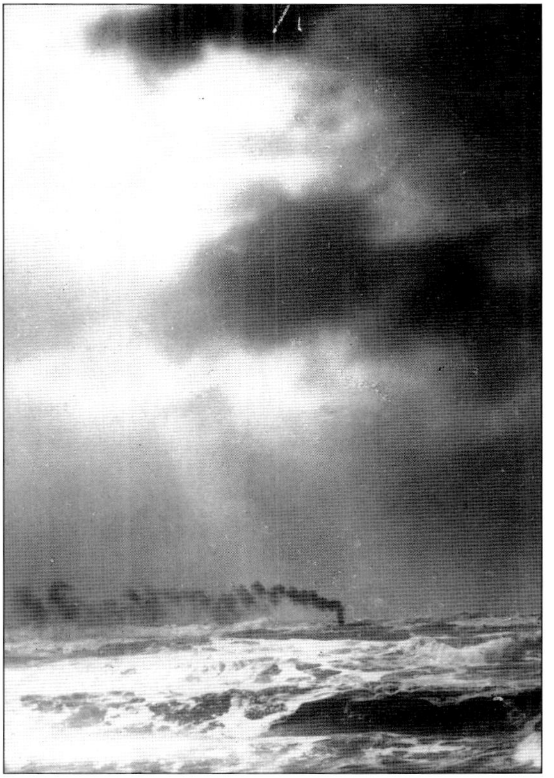

Breaking waves over a sandbar across Humboldt Bay's narrow entrance channel initially delayed discovery of the bay and continued to make entrance difficult. Here a steamer "crosses the bar" in heavy seas.

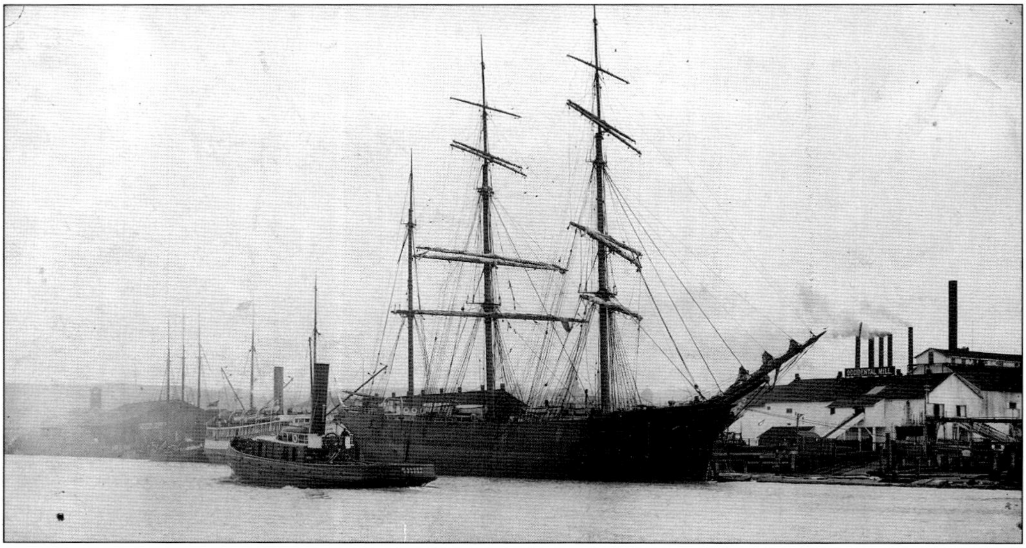

In the 19th century, sailing ships frequented Humboldt Bay bringing passengers and goods and leaving with passengers and lumber. Here a bark has moored at Eureka's Occidental Mill to take on a cargo of lumber while the tug *Ranger* passes by. Such pilot boats were necessary to guide ships in and out of the treacherous harbor entrance, which to this day is considered the most dangerous on the West Coast.

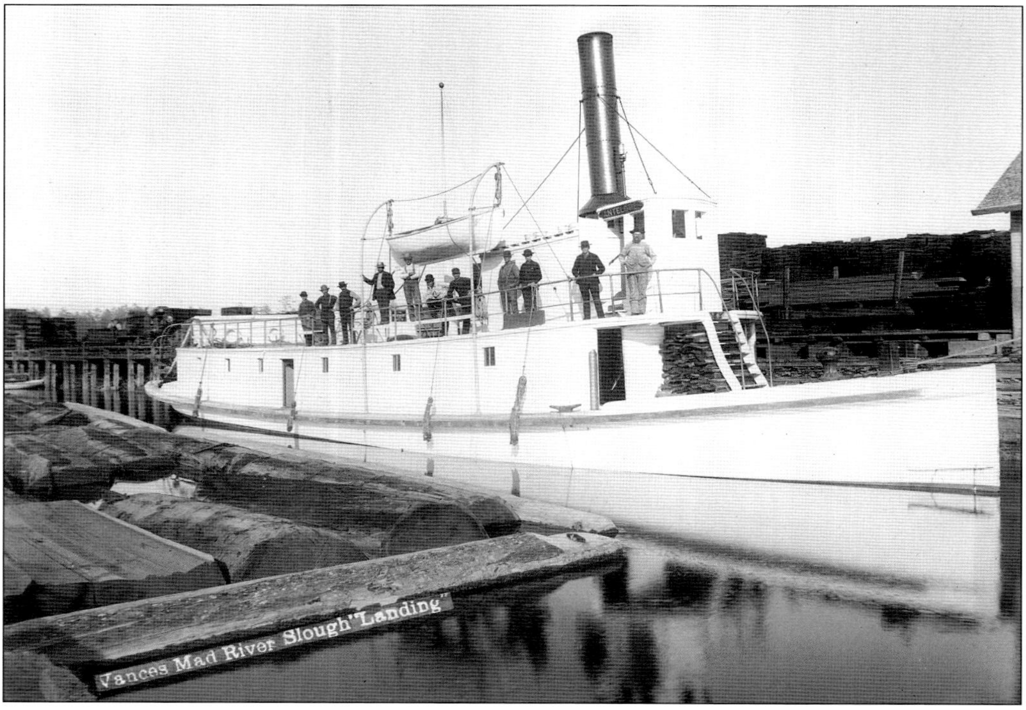

Steam replaced sail, but lumber remained a major cargo since California redwood was in demand around the world. Here the Coggshall Launch and Towboat Company's stern-wheeler *Antelope* waits for business at the Mad River slough landing for Vance's Mill.

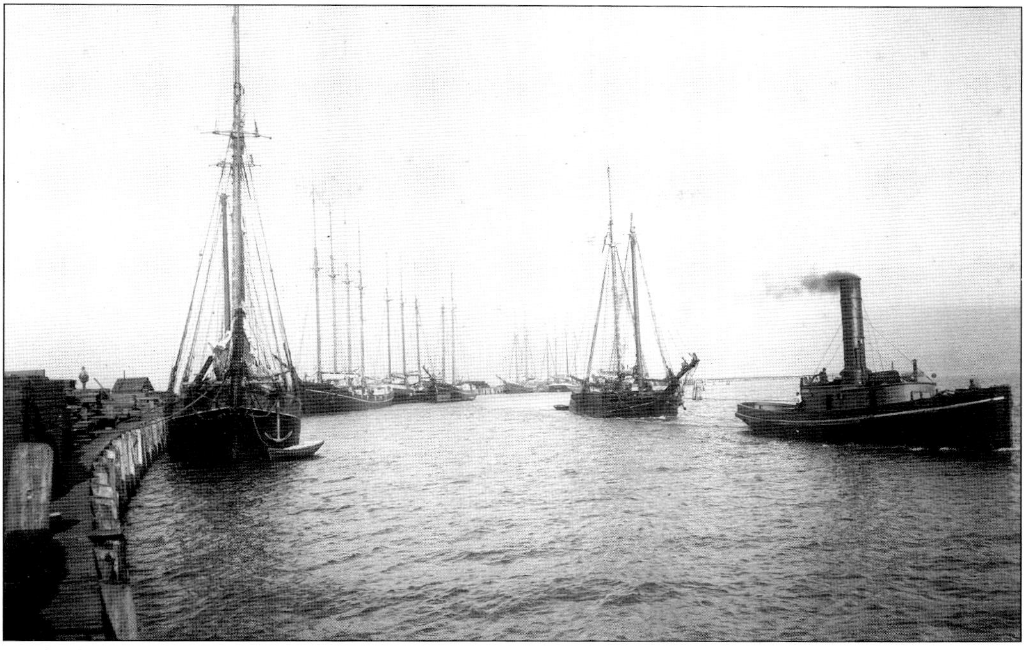

In the late 19th century, the Arcata Wharf was a busy place. These schooners are identified as *Letitia*, *Esther Buhne*, *R.W. Bartlett*, *Eva*, *Western Home*, *Mary Buhne*, *Robert and Minnie*, *Laura Pike*, *Neptune*, and *Hayes*. Some of these names reveal that H.H. Buhne, who in 1850 was the first pilot to enter Humboldt Bay, remained active in area maritime life.

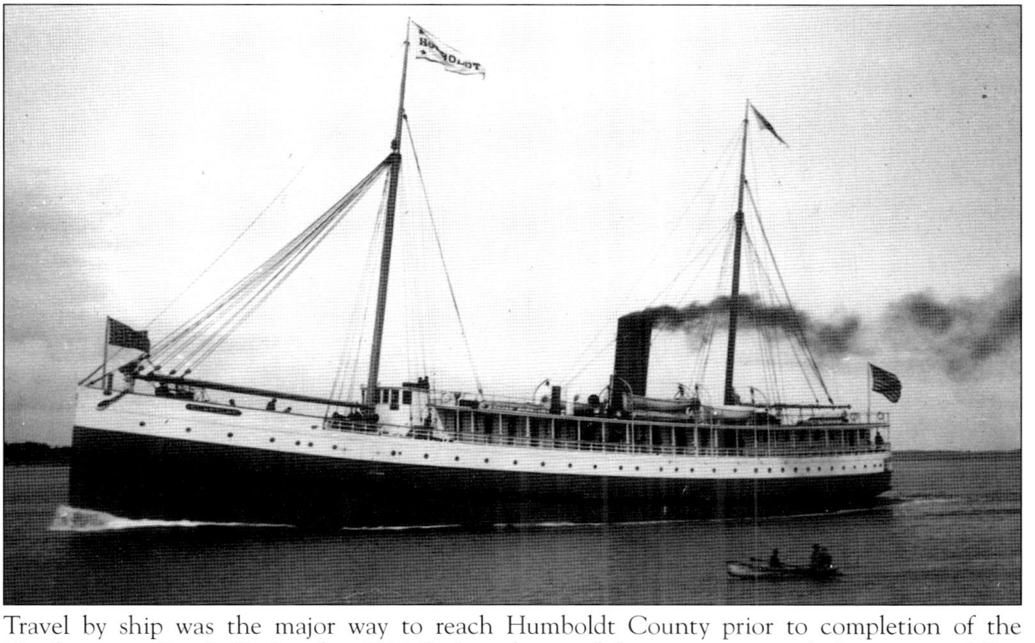

Travel by ship was the major way to reach Humboldt County prior to completion of the Northwestern Pacific Railroad in 1914. Sailing ships and then steamers regularly connected San Francisco and other West Coast ports with Eureka. Here the steamer *Humboldt* enters the bay around 1895. The arrival of steamers in port was always a big public event.

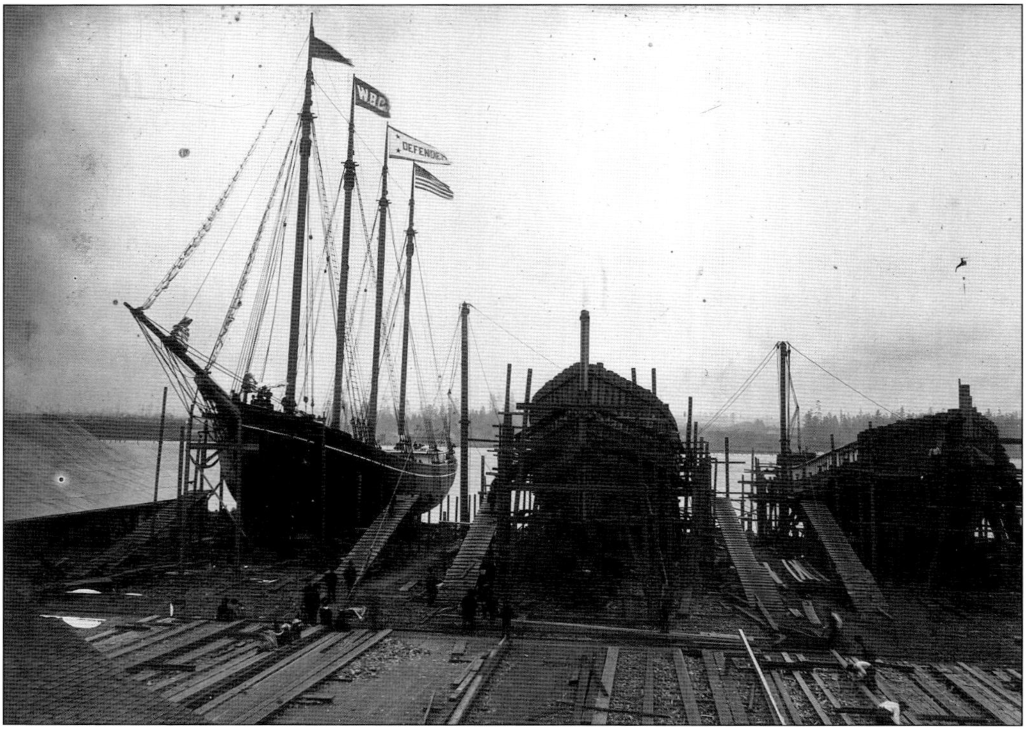

The abundance of lumber and the thriving commerce of Eureka's early gold rush days quickly sparked the shipbuilding industry. Here at Fairhaven's Bendixsen shipyards, the *Defender* is being prepared for launch.

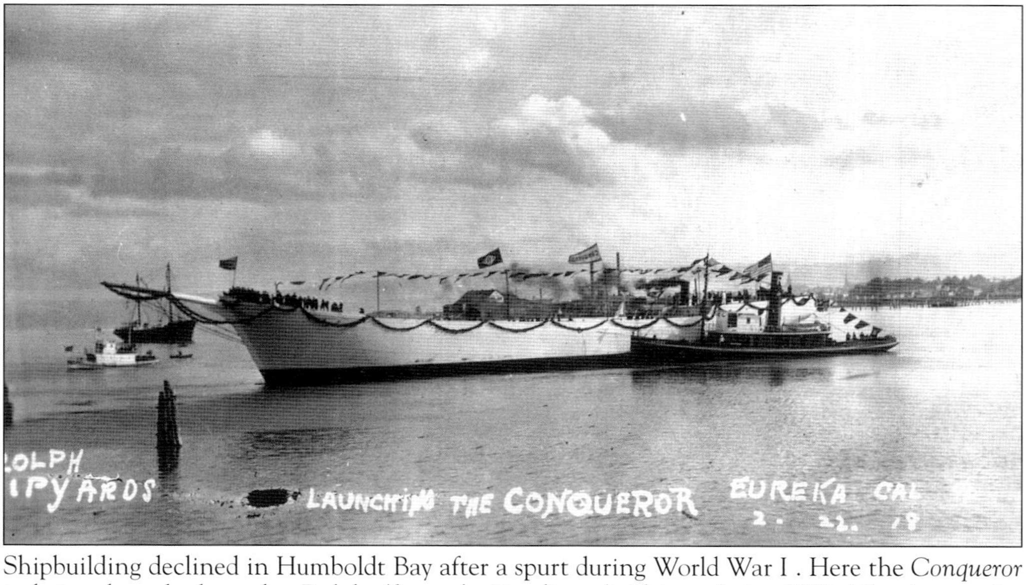

Shipbuilding declined in Humboldt Bay after a spurt during World War I . Here the *Conqueror* is being launched at the Rolph (formerly Bendixsen) Shipyards in 1918. The last major shipbuilding occurred at the Chicago Bridge and Iron Company yards at Fairhaven during World War II.

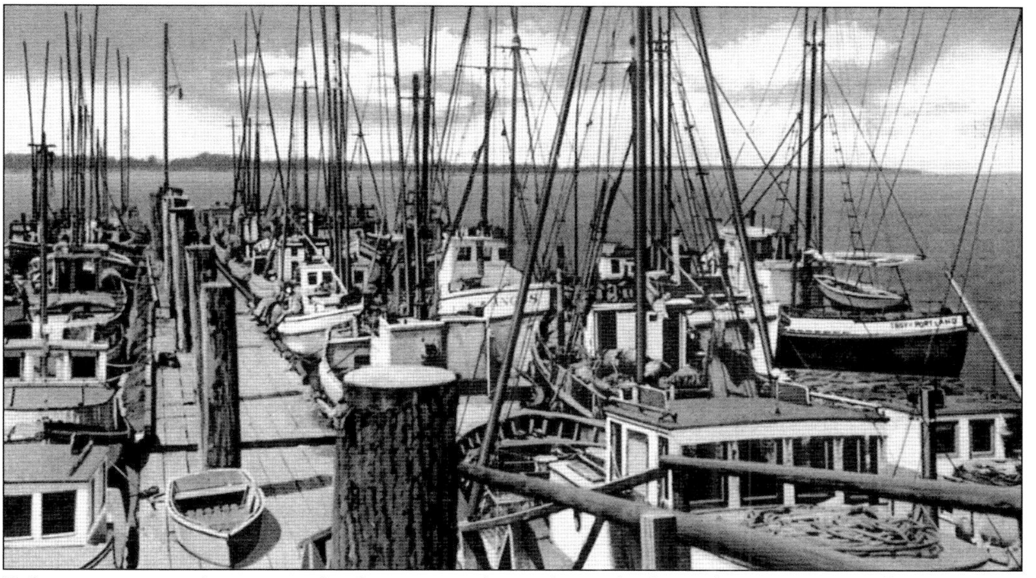

Fishing was a supplementary food source to the early settler but it became especially important to Humboldt's economy once the railroad connection allowed fish to be sent quickly to San Francisco area markets. Humboldt and Trinidad bays became busy fishing ports as shown in this early-20th-century postcard of Humboldt Bay's fishing fleet. The importance of commercial fishing continues today.

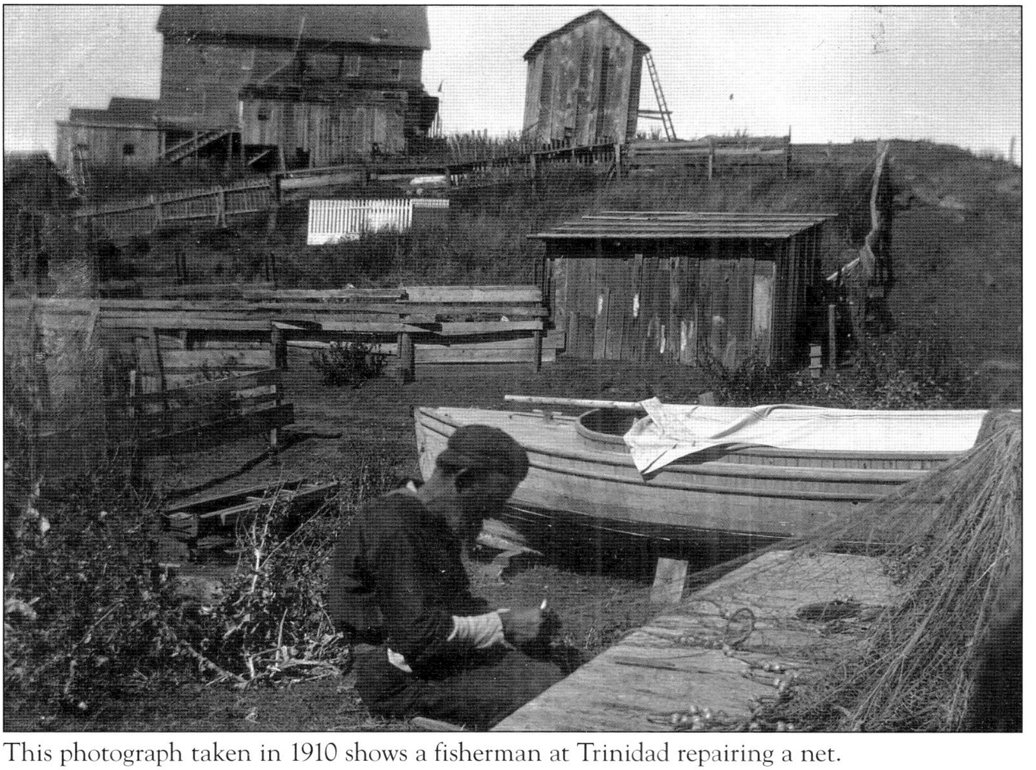

This photograph taken in 1910 shows a fisherman at Trinidad repairing a net.

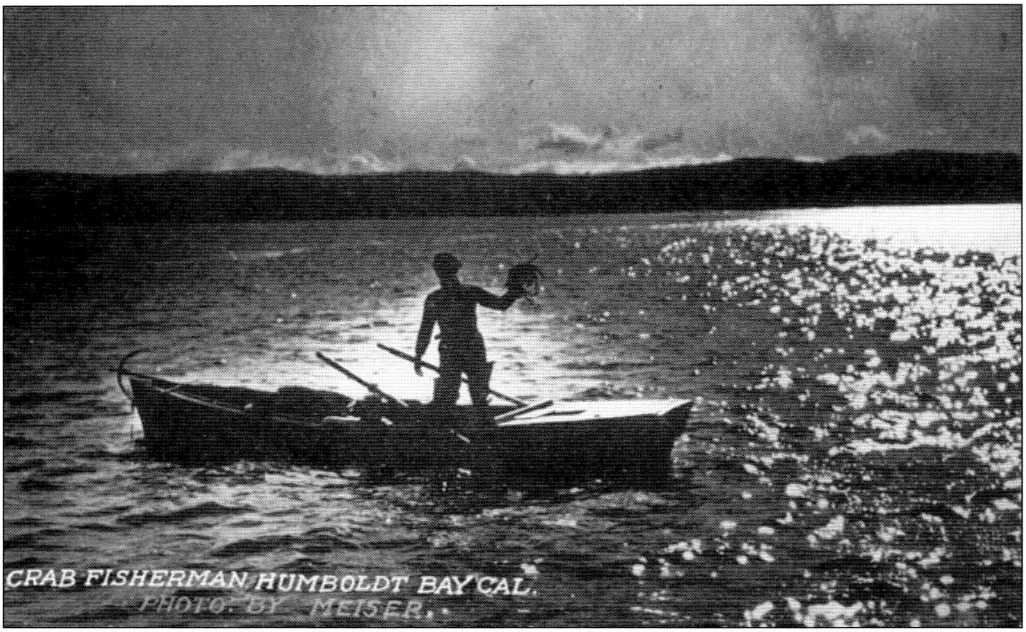

Crabs were favored by coastal Indians and also became important to the diet and economy of Humboldt's settlers. During the winter, many boatloads of dungeness crabs are still brought in for export and for local tables.

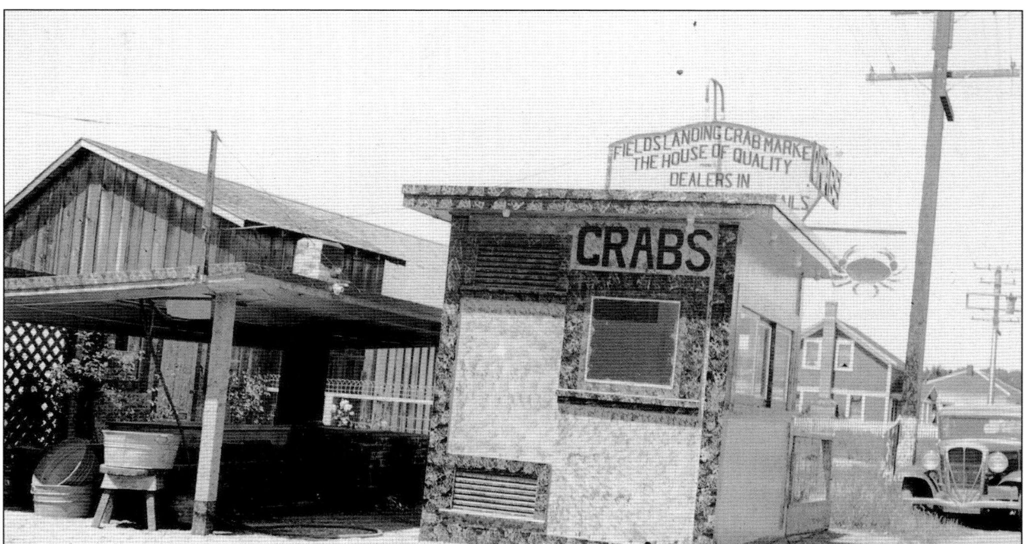

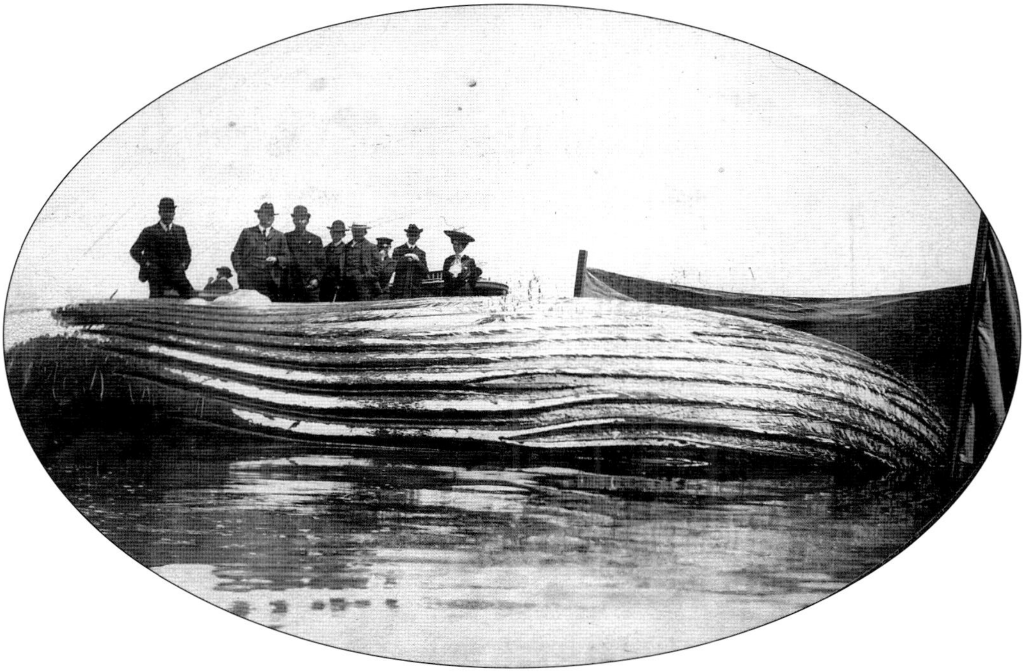

On and off, whaling was carried on from Trinidad and Humboldt bays. This turn-of-the century photograph at Trinidad shows that, as with large trees, whales were something to be posed beside.

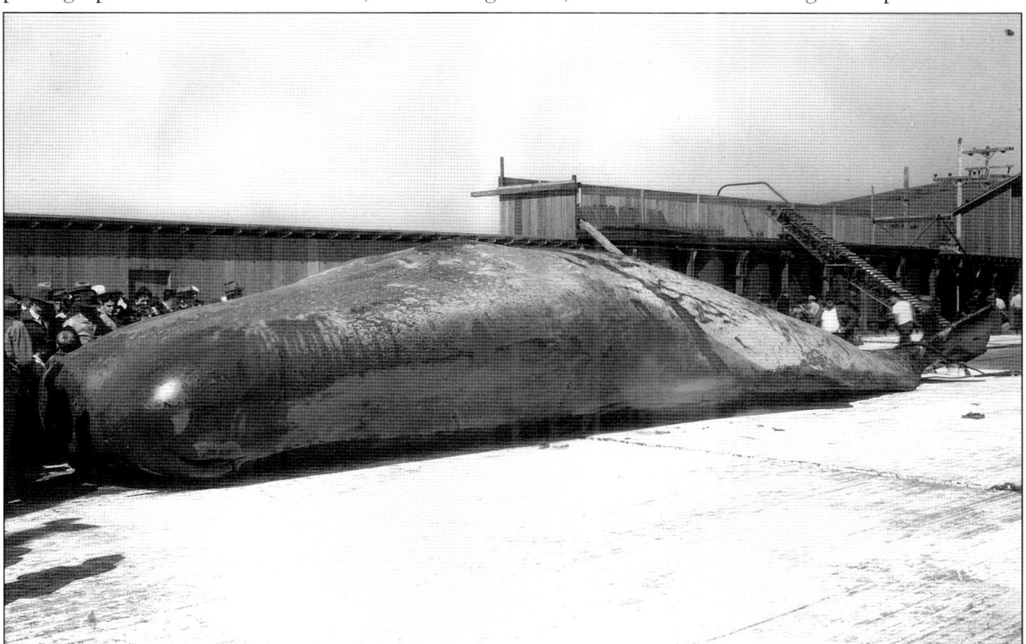

The whaling station at Fields Landing, south of Eureka, where this sperm whale was brought, was the last to be established on the West Coast. It closed in the early 1950s. Bone was taken, oil rendered, and the rest dried for chicken feed.

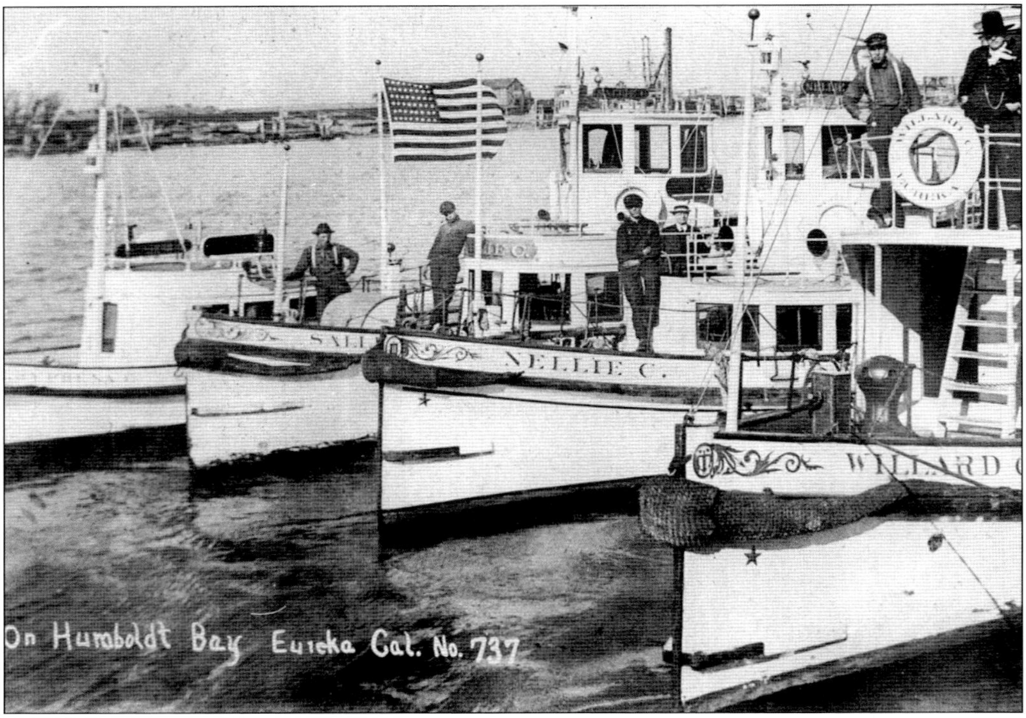

Until the Eureka/Samoa bridge was completed in 1971, ferryboats carried mill, dock and shipyard workers to sites around the bay while also transporting shoppers, goods and excursion takers. This early 20th century photo shows the Cousin's fleet of ferries. The Nellie C. later became the Madaket which has been in continuous service since 1910 and still gives sightseeing cruises on Humboldt Bay.

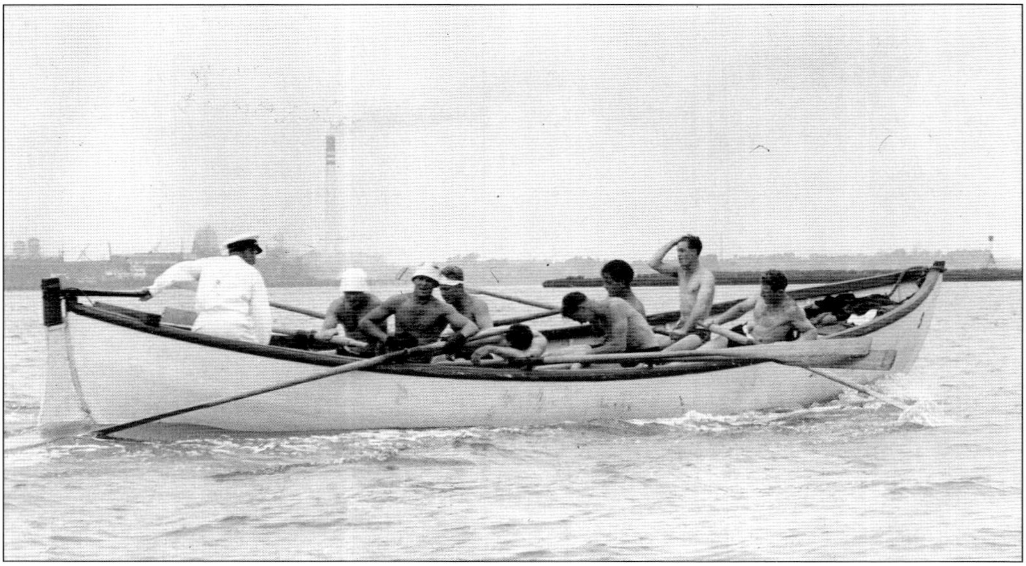

Humboldt Bay has also been an important center for recreation. Here Sea Scouts are just finishing a race on the bay. Hammond Lumber Mill at Samoa is seen in the background.

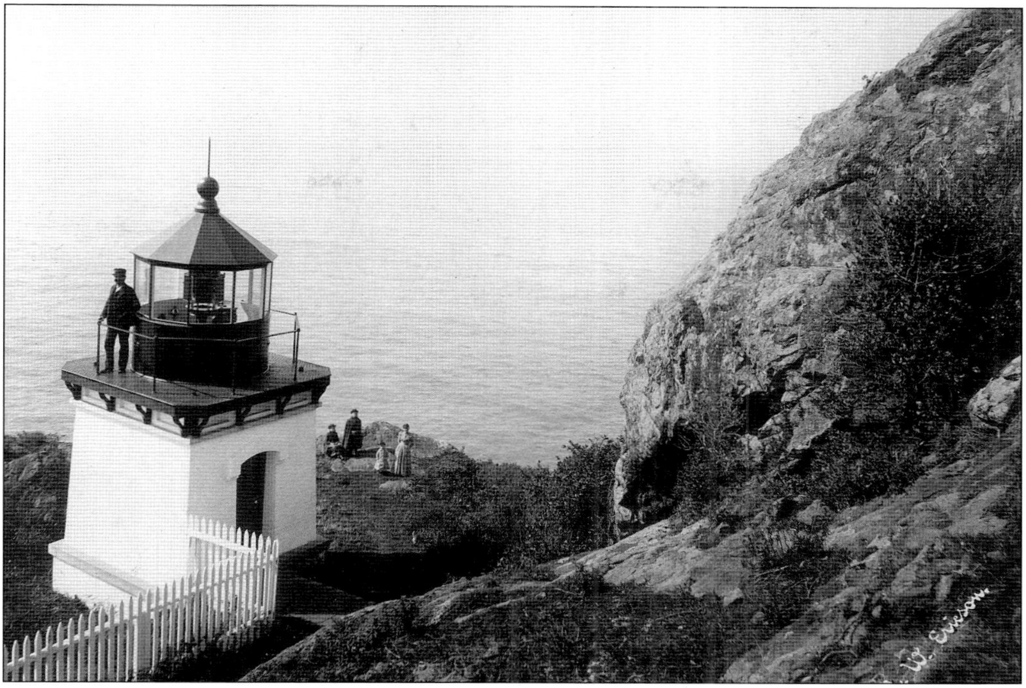

The Humboldt coast, with its fogs, rocks, and dangerous currents, was hazardous for shipping. Five lighthouses were built along Humboldt's stretch of coast with two more just to the north in Del Norte County. On calm days, the Trinidad light made a pleasant seashore excursion.

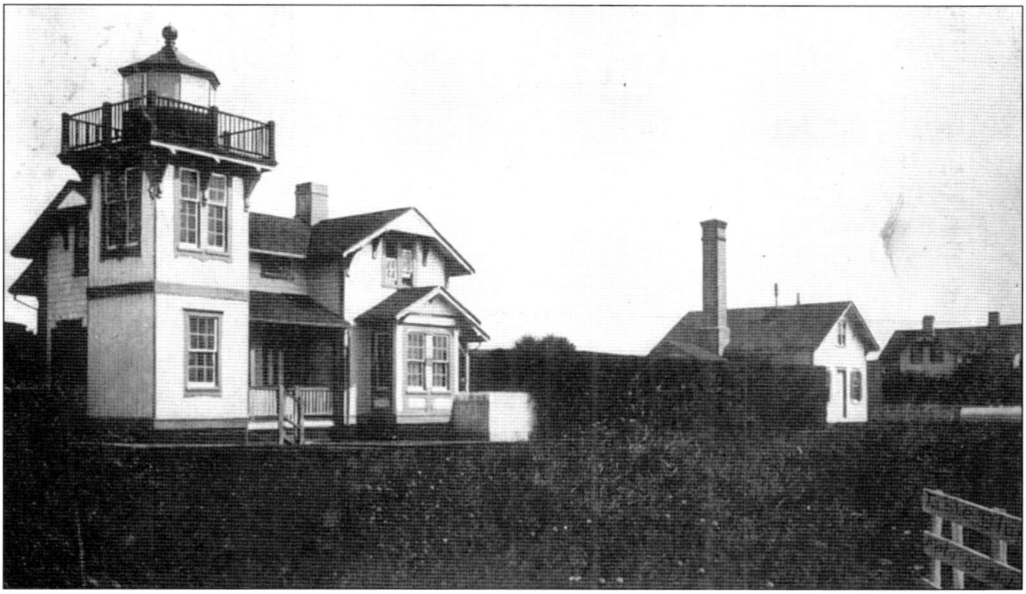

Table Bluff, an aptly named rise at the end of Humboldt Bay's South Spit, housed a light from 1892 to the 1950s. Afterwards, the lighthouse was moved to Woodley Island where it now serves as a beacon for tourists. It's multifaceted lens is displayed at the Humboldt Bay Maritime Museum, which is located on Eureka's First Street within sight of this redwood tower.

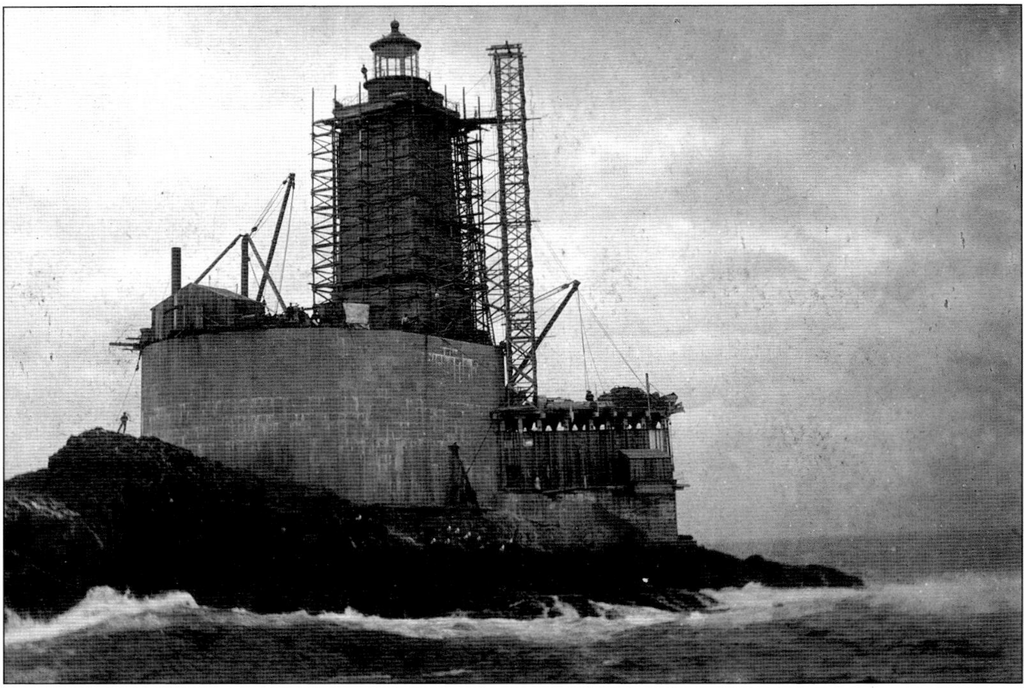

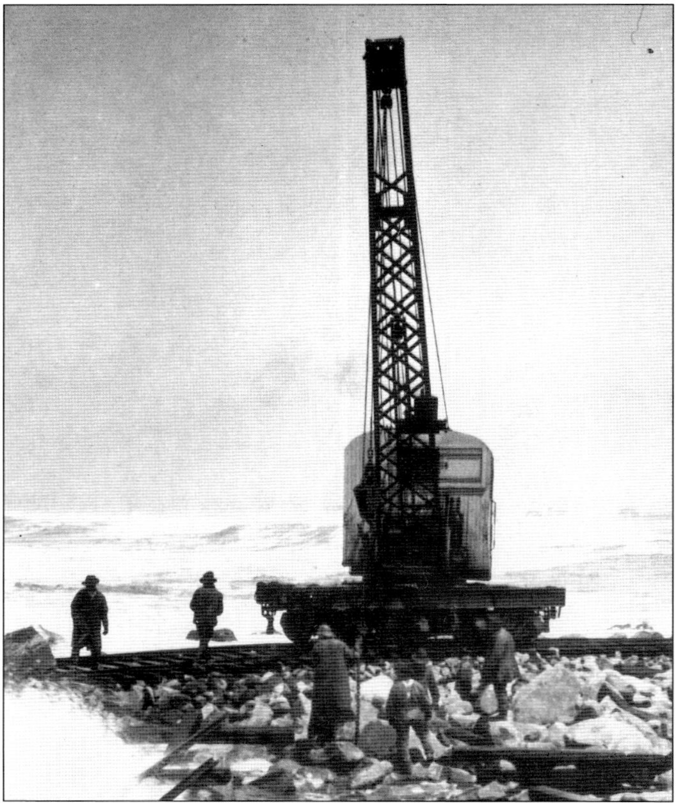

This photograph taken by H.H. Buhne around 1890 shows the construction of St. George lighthouse in Del Norte County, just to the north of Humboldt. It was built of granite from the Mad River.

From the late 19th century on, stone jetties have been built and rebuilt at the entrance to Humboldt Bay in an effort to control the meandering channel .

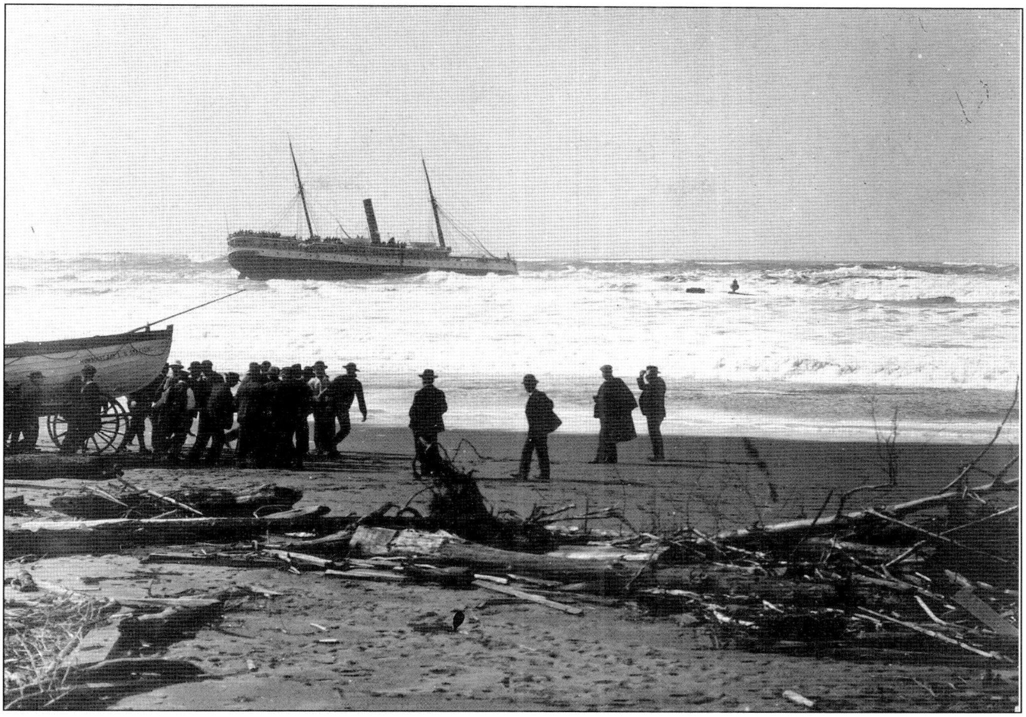

The hazards of Humboldt's coast made for a number of notable wrecks. The *Corona* was wrecked off the North Jetty in 1907 due to erroneous instructions given the helmsman.

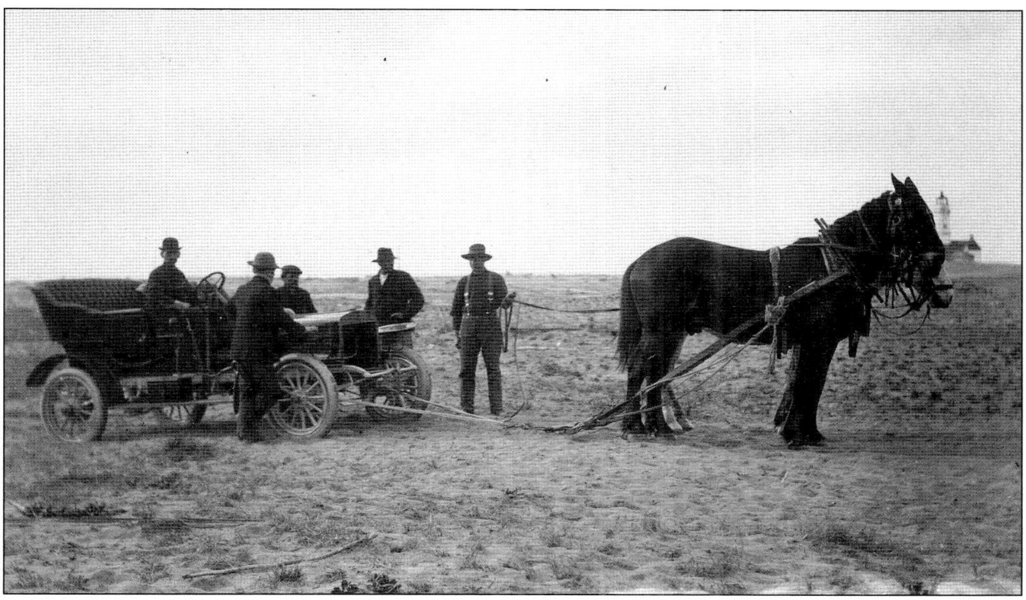

F.W. Smythe of Eureka was expecting delivery of his new car by ship. But after the wreck of the *Corona*, it had to be dragged onshore and across the sand by horse. The Humboldt Harbor lighthouse, abandoned since 1892, can be seen in the background.

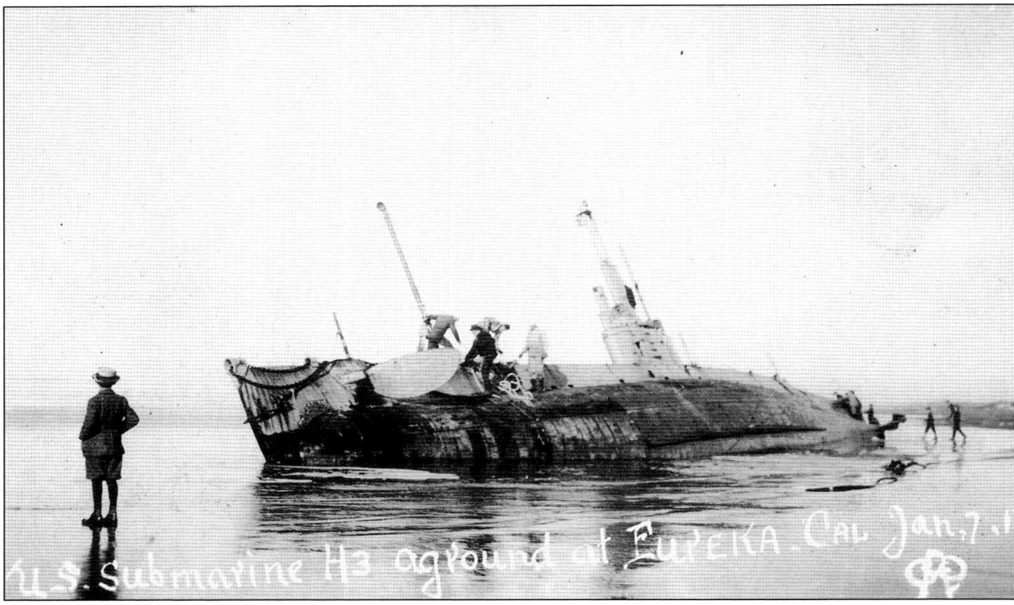

In December 1916, the U.S. submarine *H3* became lost in the fog and was beached off Samoa.

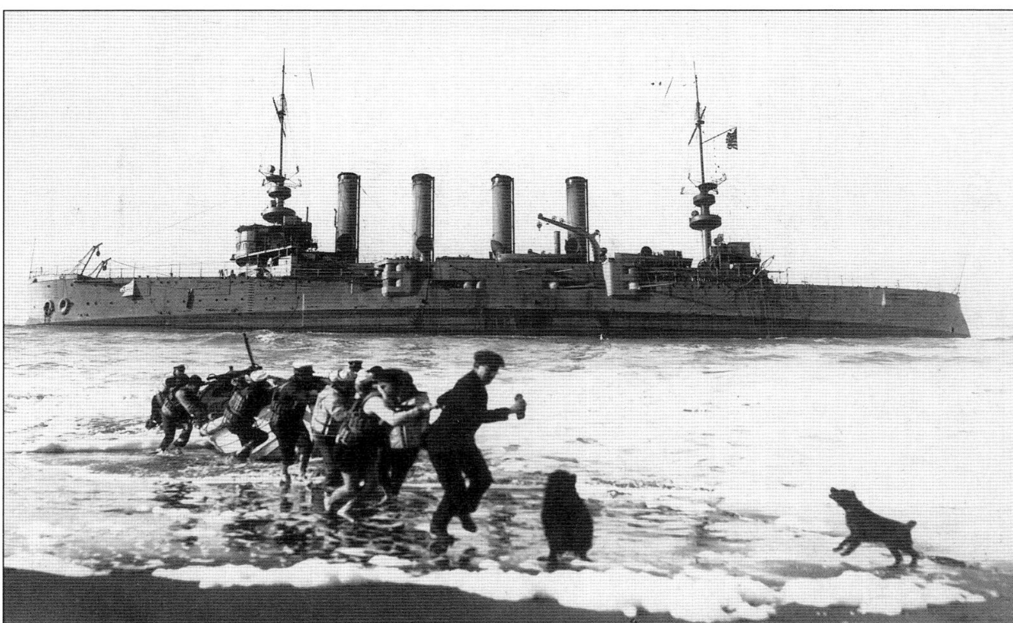

In an attempt to free the submarine, the cruiser *U.S.S. Milwaukee* was also beached. All but one of its crew were saved, but the ship was left to salvagers and local souvenir hunters. Its rusted skeleton can still be seen offshore at very low tides. This disaster was considered the worst peacetime loss the U.S. Navy had suffered up until that time.

Five

Farming and Rural Communities

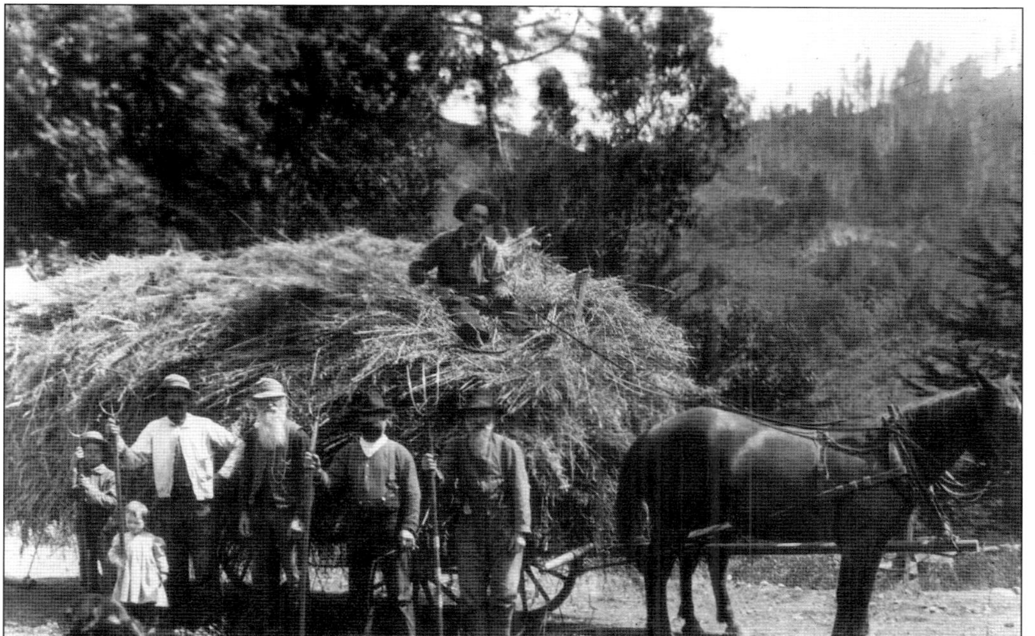

Humboldt County's mountainous terrain is crossed by numerous rivers. Near their mouths, the occasionally flooding rivers leave rich silt upon bottomlands that are ideal for farming. Here hay is gathered around the turn of the last century in bottomlands along the Eel River near Ferndale.

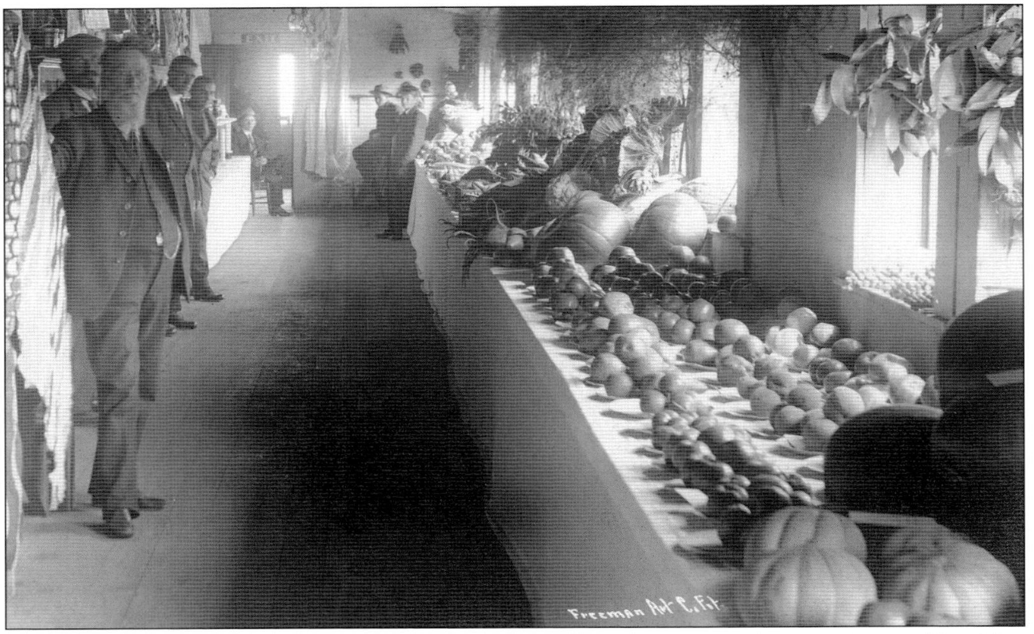

Humboldt's year-round moderate climate proved excellent for growing fruits and vegetables. The area became particularly known for its fine apples, which were shipped by the barrelful to San Francisco. The best of the best are displayed at an early-20th-century county fair.

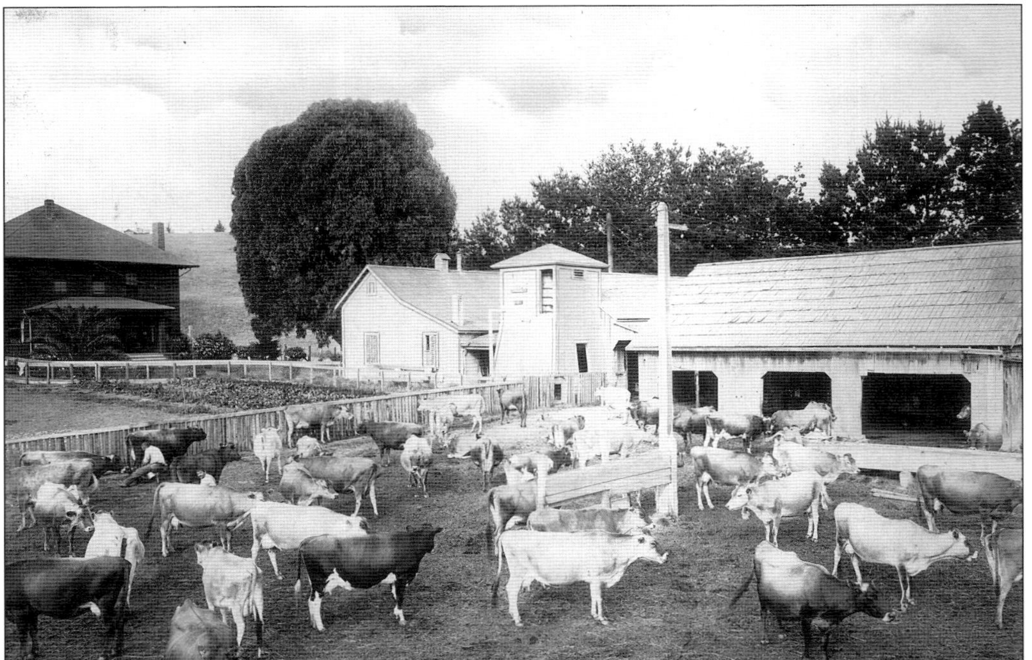

Dairy farming became preeminent in Humboldt County once nutritious new grasses were introduced in the 1880s. This early-20th-century dairy farm has a typical large farmhouse, vegetable garden, and water tower.

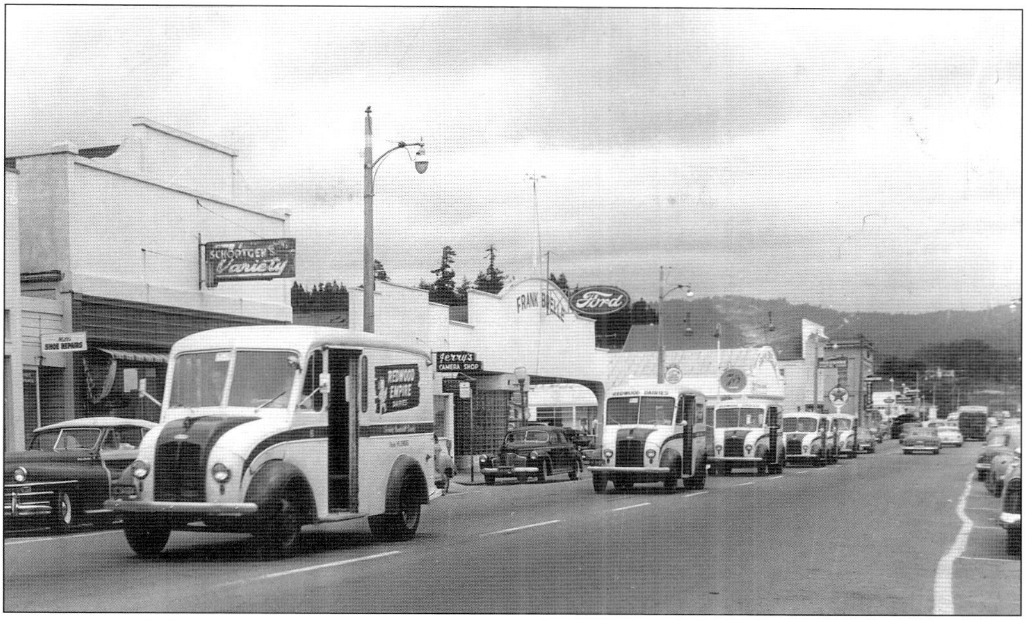

A number of dairies sprang up in the western part of the county, most eventually joining cooperatives. Processed products such as butter, cheese, and powdered milk became valuable exports while the locals also enjoyed fresh, locally produced milk. This 1950s photograph shows the morning milk delivery fleet of Fortuna's Redwood Empire Dairies.

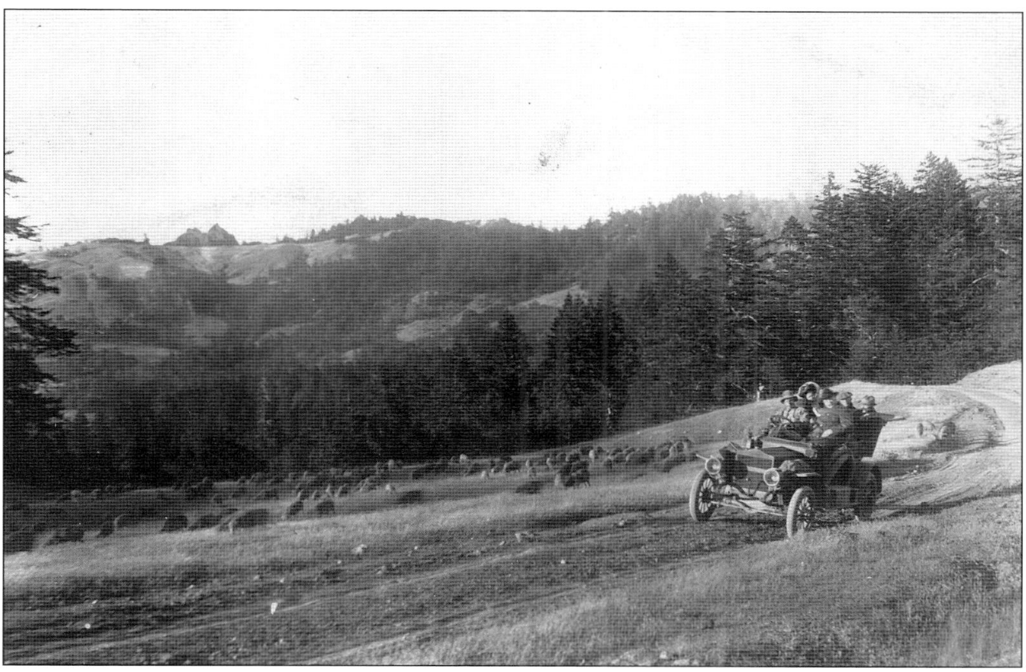

Free range cattle were part of Humboldt's landscape for this auto excursion on the old "overland" stage road from Willits to Shively around 1910. Numerous cattle and sheep brands were registered during Humboldt County's first few decades

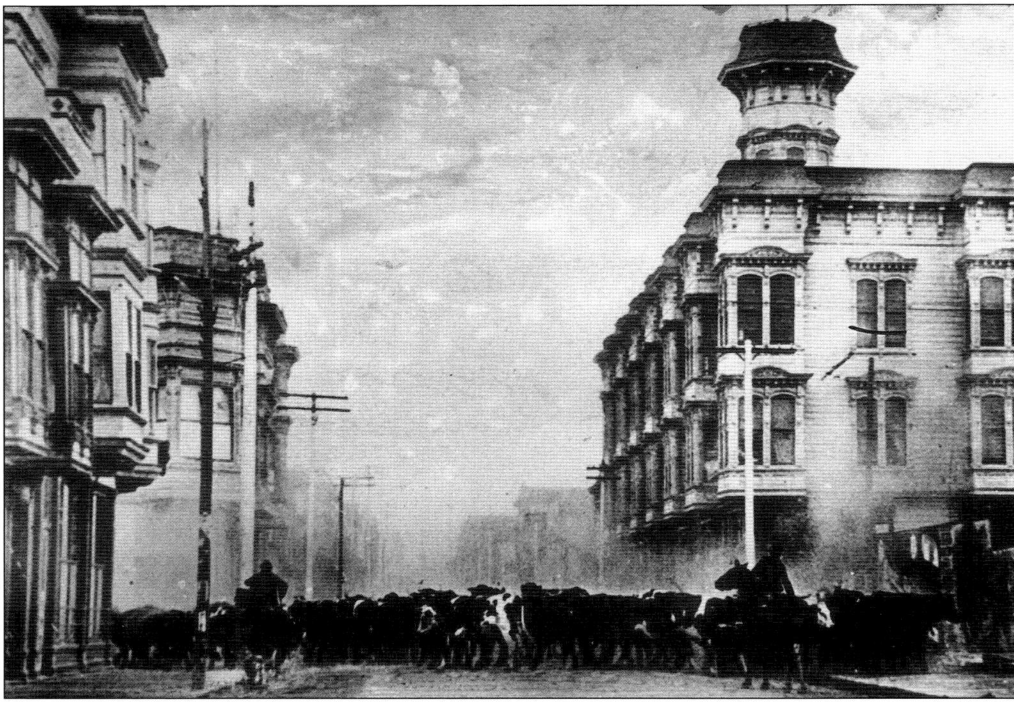

Cattle are being driven through downtown Eureka in the late 19th century. The Eagle House Hotel on the left is still in operation.

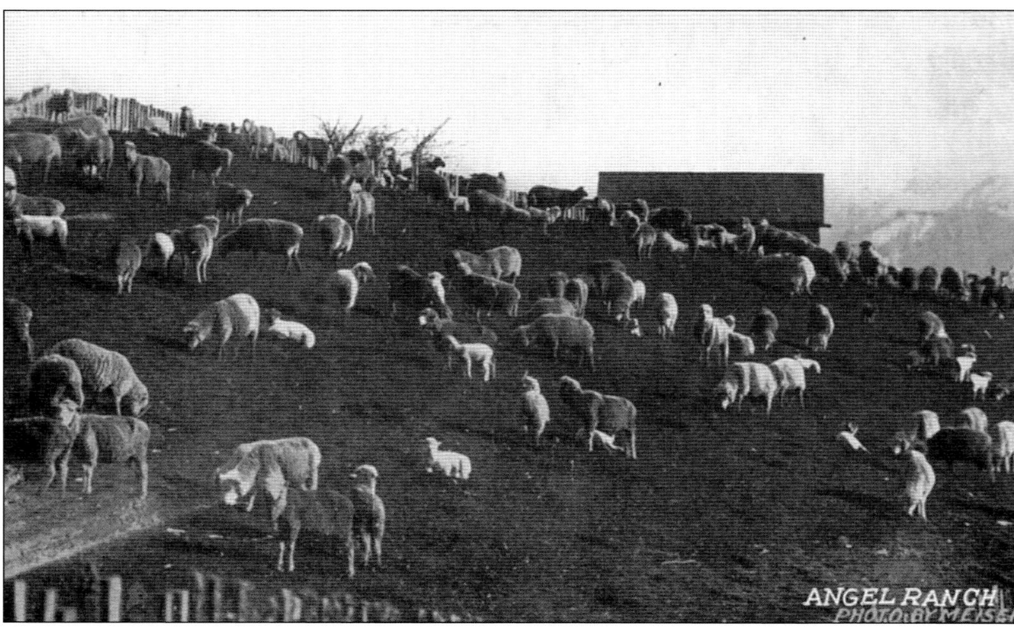

The climate and grasses in Humboldt's hills were ideal for raising sheep with long thick wool. Here sheep graze on the Angel Ranch, owned by Jacob Zehndner, above Korbel, in the early 20th century.

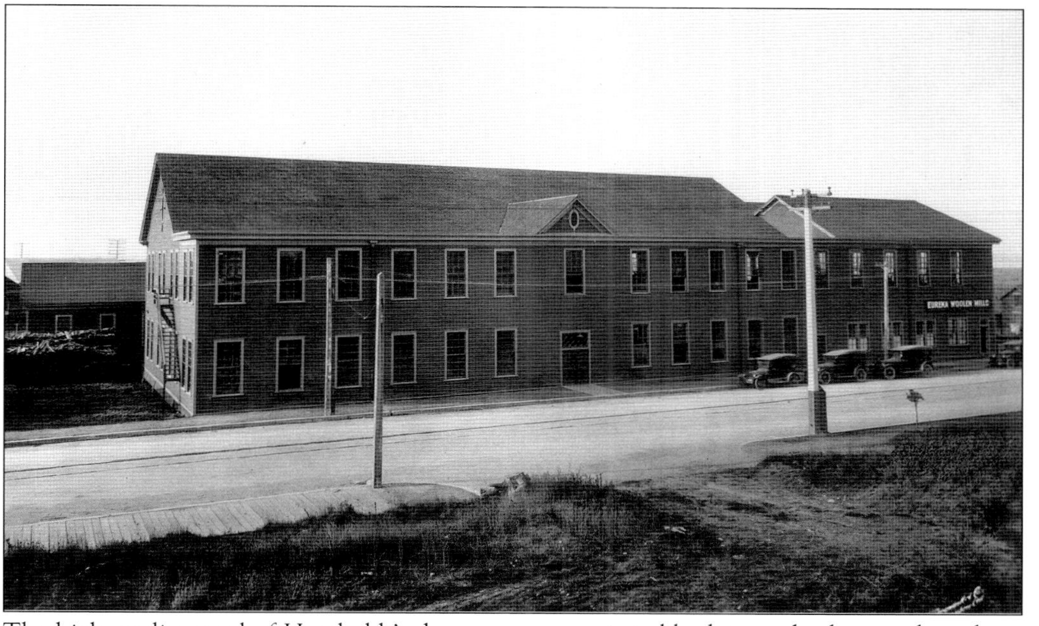

The high quality wool of Humboldt's sheep was woven into blankets and other wool products at the Eureka Woolen Mill on Broadway (where Walgreen's Drug Store is now located). The mill operated between 1904 and 1950 and supported approximately 150 employees. Note the streetcar track in the foreground of this 1923 photograph.

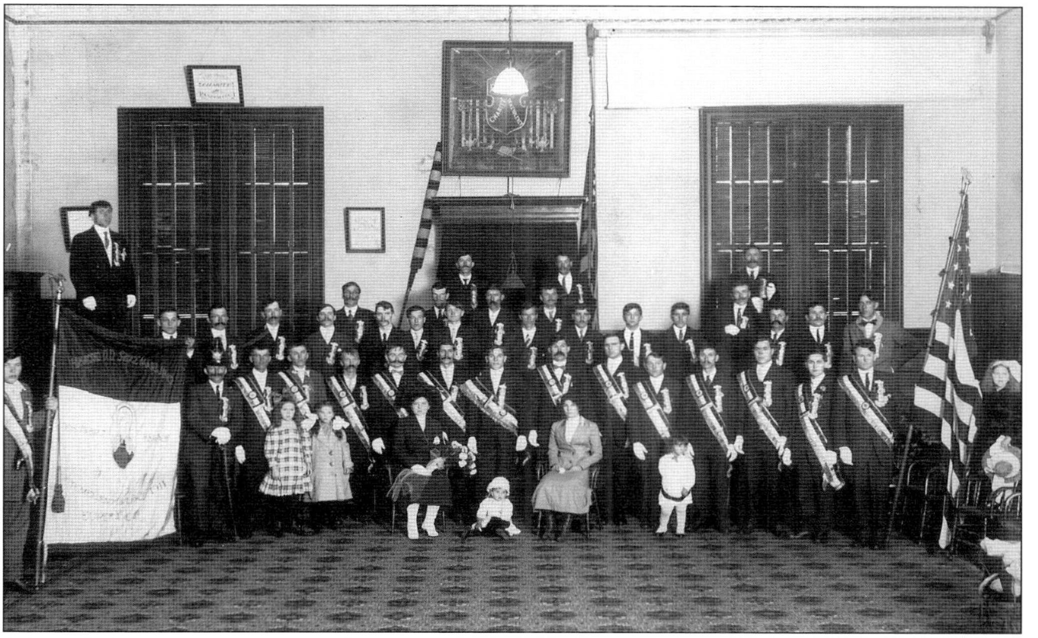
Political disruption in late-19th-century Europe sent immigrants of many nationalities to America. Portuguese, Italians, Scandinavians, Swiss, Croatians, and others brought their farming skills to Humboldt County. This 1911 photograph shows a gathering of the local Croatian Society.

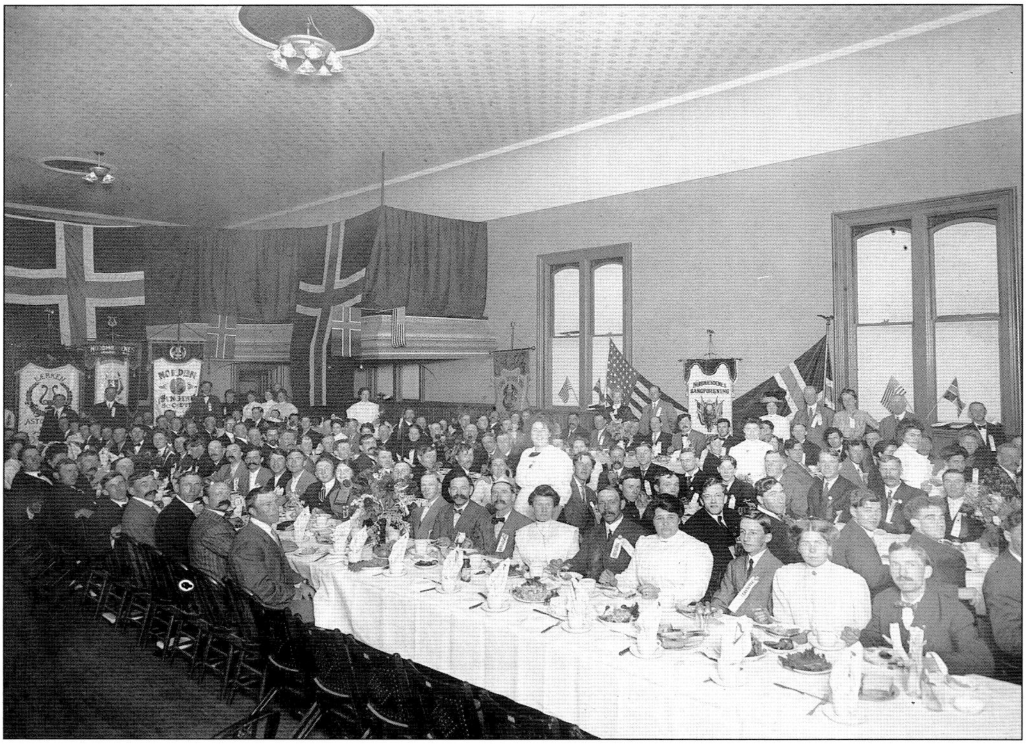

Most nationalities had their support groups to help ease the transition into American life by providing charitable support, social activities, and a chance to speak in one's native tongue. Here Humboldt's Norwegian Society meets for a grand banquet.

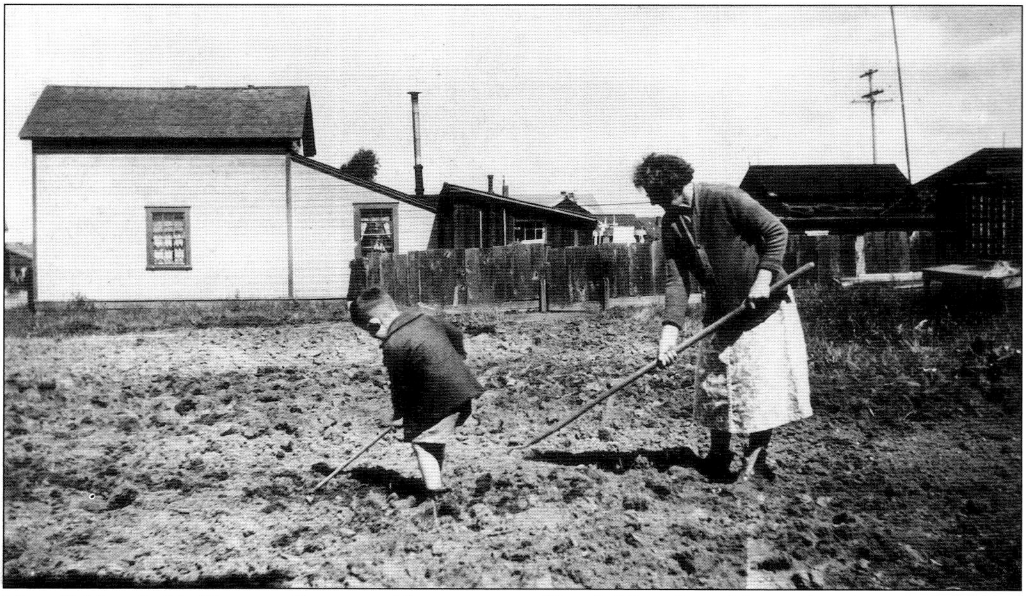

Not all Humboldt "farming" required large tracts of land. Here Josie Howard and a young helper work on a Eureka Victory Garden in 1942.

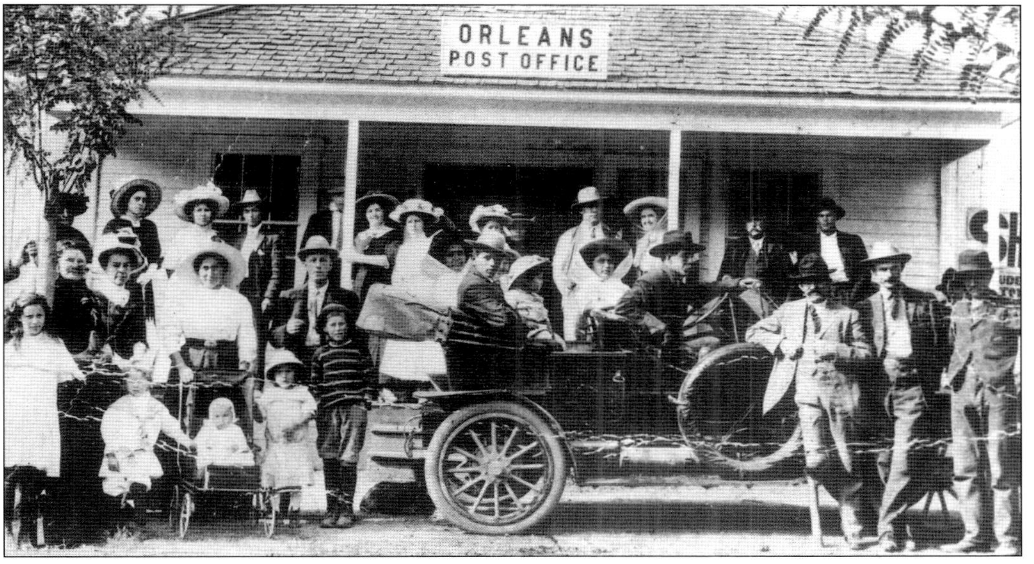

Orleans is upriver on the Klamath in Karuk territory. This photograph was taken around 1910 at the post office, the heart of many small communities. Orleans was the principal mining town within the county and today is an outdoor outfitting center and the focus of many small farms that supply produce for Eureka's and Arcata's Farmers' Markets.

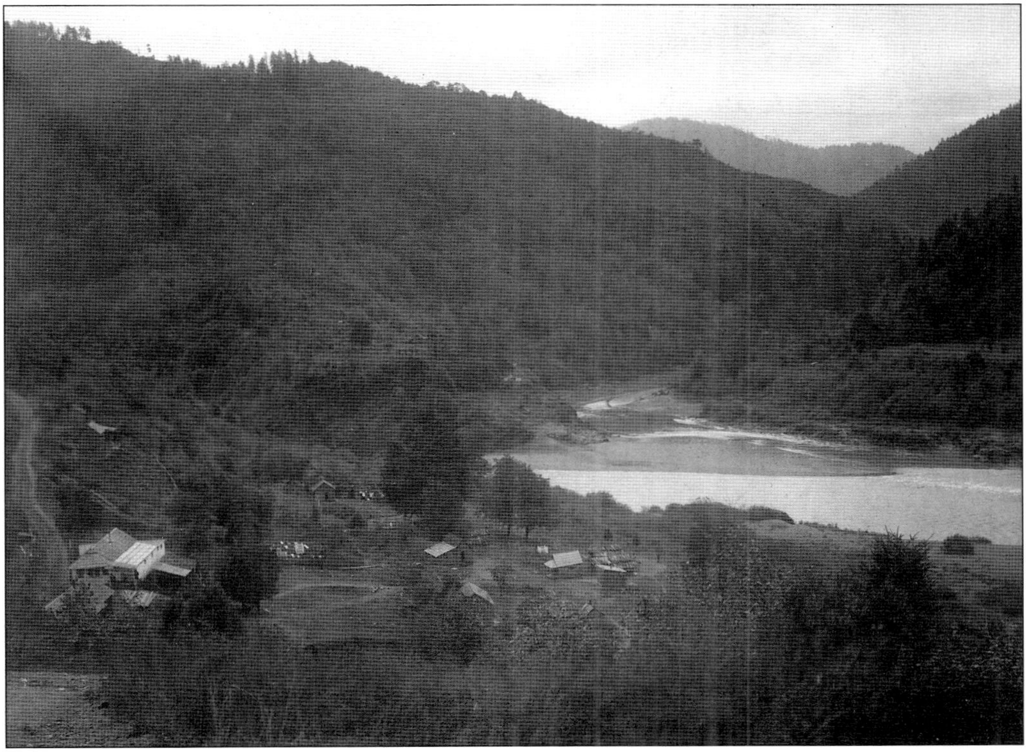

Weitchpec is at the confluence of the Trinity and Klamath Rivers, in Yurok territory. This early-20th-century photograph shows some traditional plank houses among the later buildings.

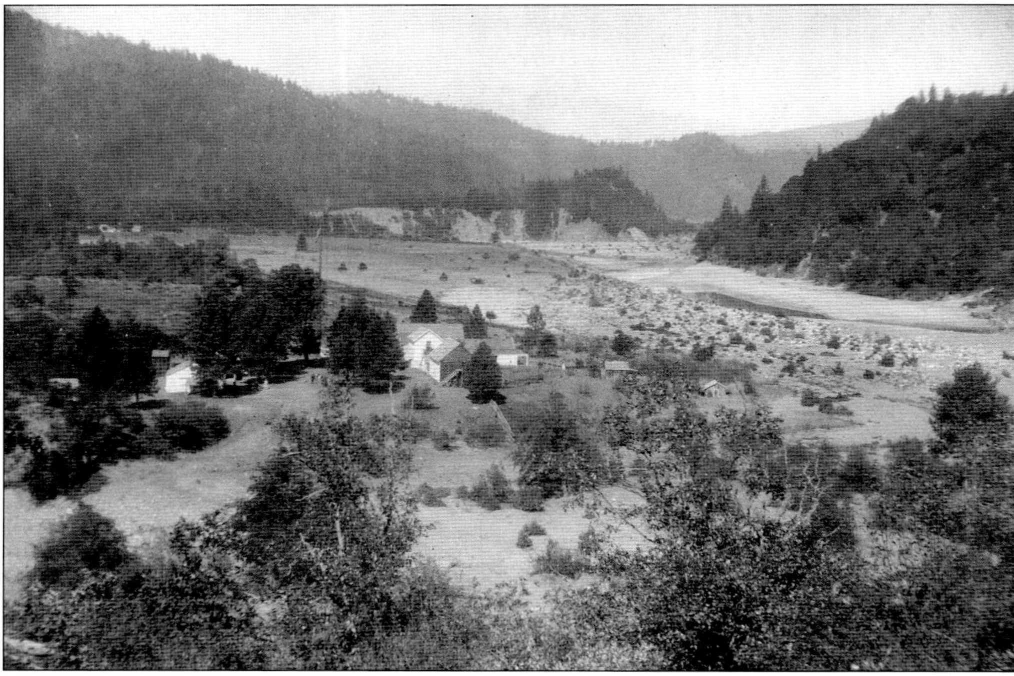

Willow Creek, just south of the Hoopa Reservation, is where the main route between the Sacramento Valley and Humboldt's coast (now Highway 299) meets the Trinity River. Auto travel on this route was not possible until the 1920s. Today this small community is known primarily for its association with legendary Bigfoot.

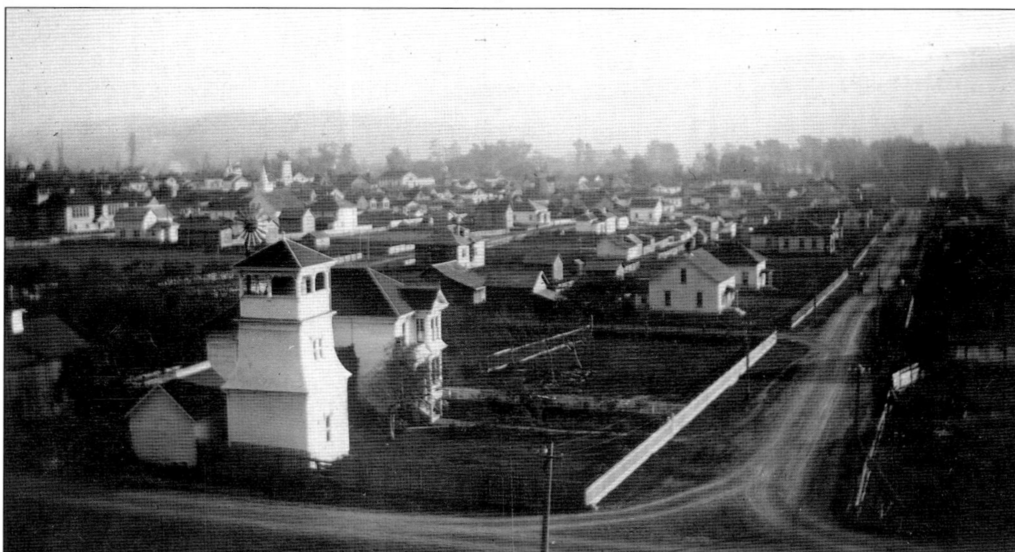

When the town of Blue Lake was founded in 1871, it was situated on a lake that had been left by an earlier flood of the Mad River. By the time this photo was taken in the early 20th century, the lake had almost dried up. The tank in the Tower (foreground) was filled by a treadmill operated by a dog. It was part of the Fountain house. Both house and Tower remain to this day.

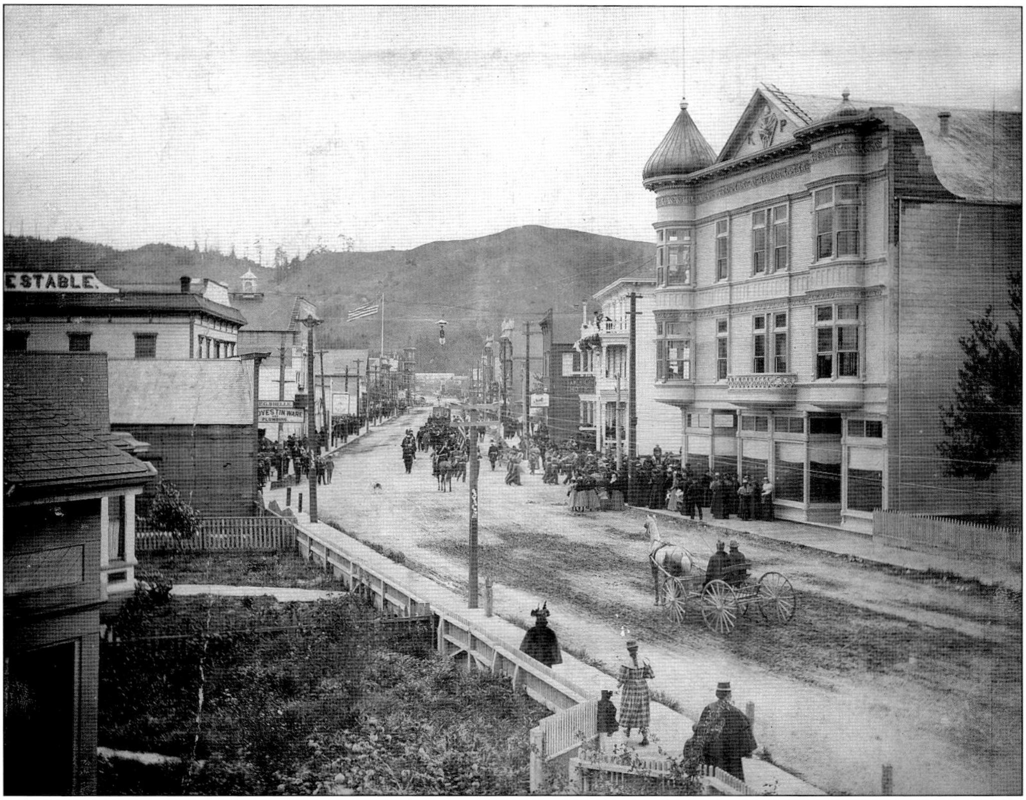

In the 1890s, Ferndale saw this parade down Main Street. The town grew wealthy, largely from dairy farming in the rich bottom lands of the Eel River. Today its elegant Victorian homes and commercial buildings make Ferndale a major tourist attraction and movie location.

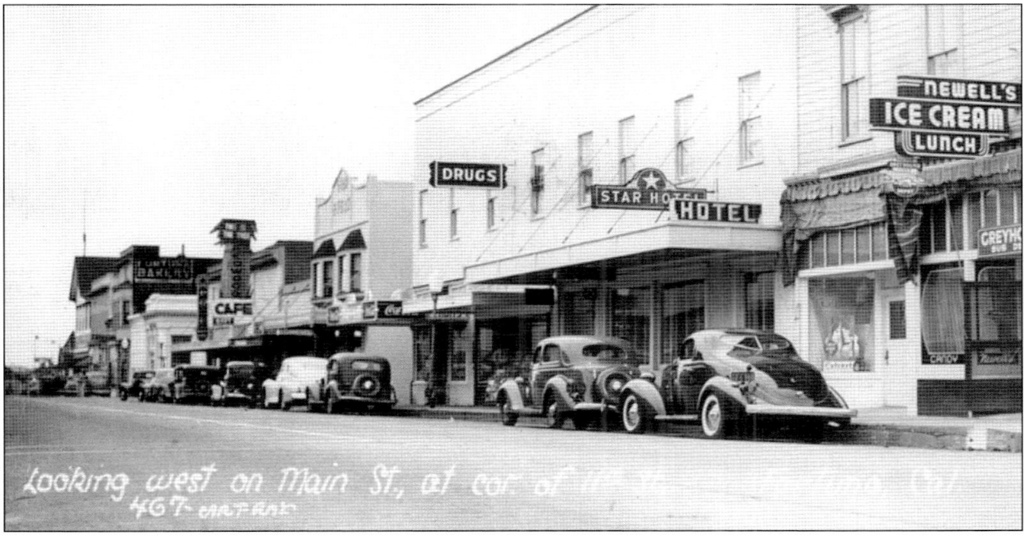

Fortuna, east of Ferndale, based its prosperity on farming, timber, and rail connections. Its typical "small town" Main Street, seen in this 1930s photograph, is still evident today.

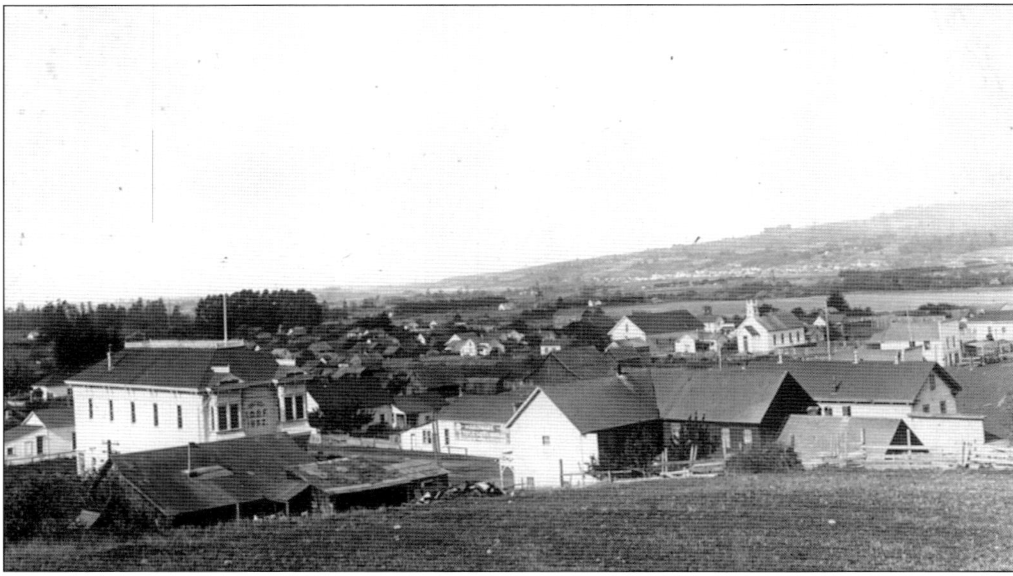

Rohnerville, southeast of Fortuna, was once a railhead and the more important of the two. But the routing of the main rail line south through its neighbor led to Rohnerville's decline. Note the large building belonging to the Odd Fellows, which, along with other benevolent fraternal organizations, was a major social force in many Humboldt towns in the 19th and 20th centuries.

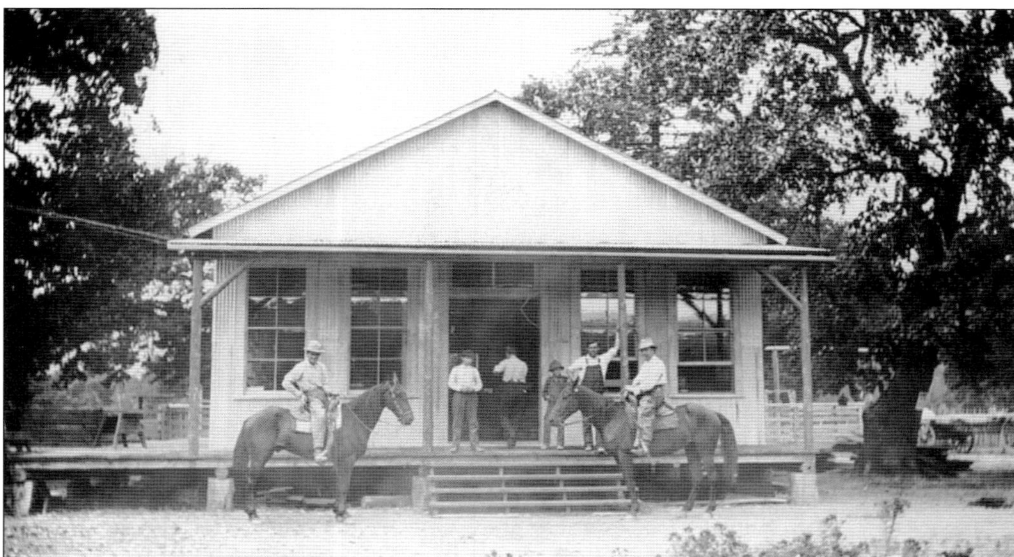

In smaller towns, the general store was the focal point where people gathered to talk and to see and be seen. This photograph of the Helmke store at Ft. Seward was taken around 1914.

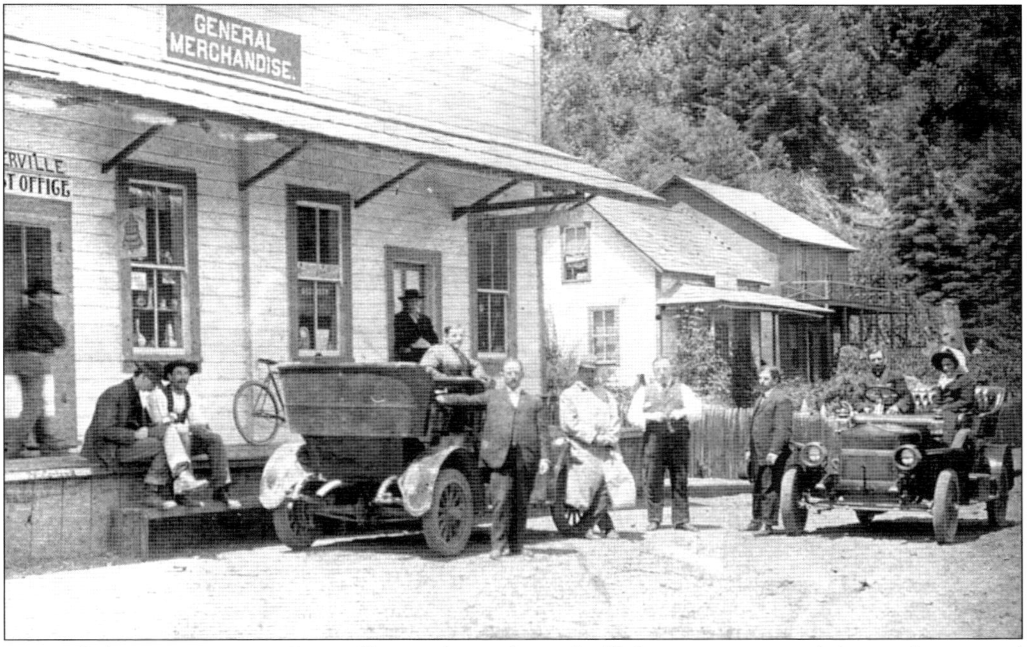

Around the same time at Dyerville, residents showed off their new automobiles at the general store and post office. For years, this building was a polling station for the surrounding area, but it was carried away by the 1955 flood.

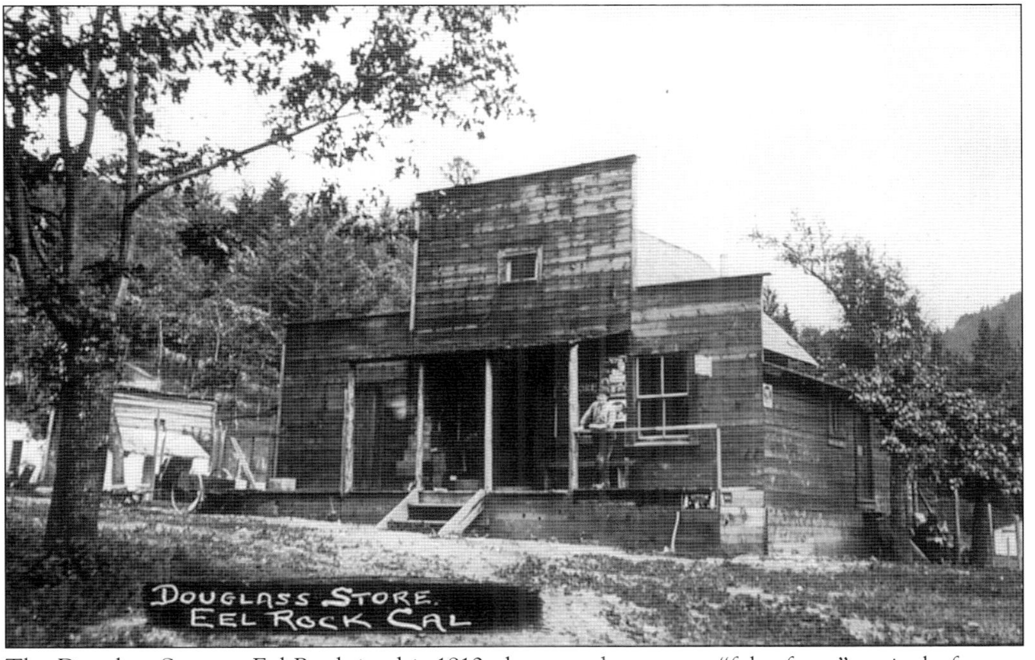

The Douglass Store at Eel Rock in this 1910 photograph, sports a "false front" typical of many early commercial buildings in small western towns. They were designed to provide a more impressive looking façade.

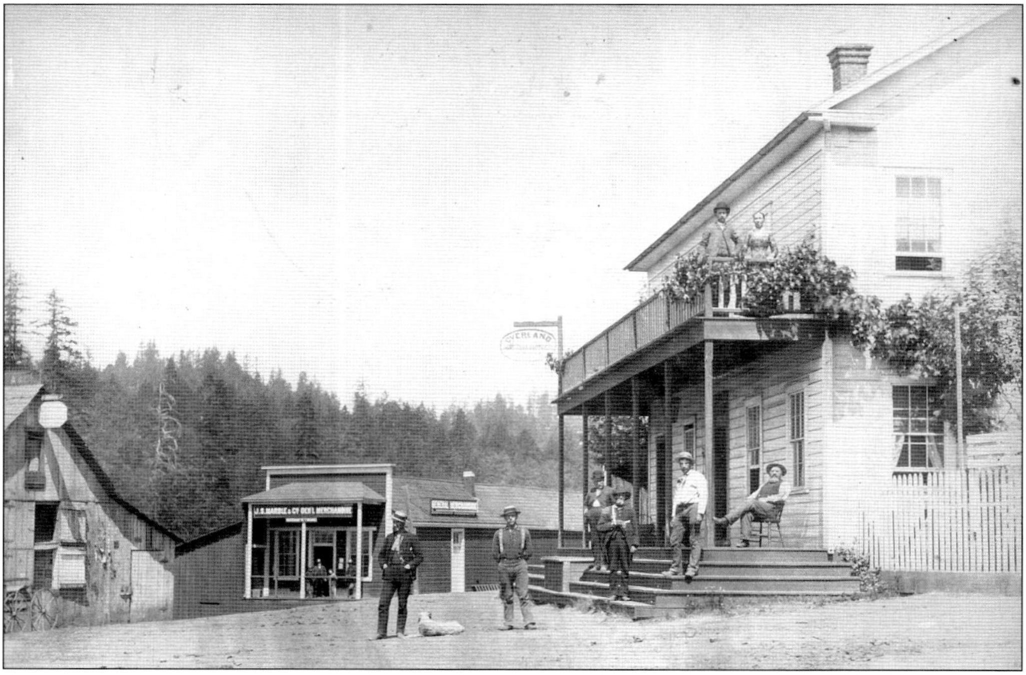

Blocksburg in the late 19th century was an important stop on the stage route into Humboldt County. Its hotels, stores, and telegraph office supplied the needs of travelers, and its streets occasionally saw the passage of mule trains. Much sheep and cattle raising took place in this mountainous area. Livestock continues to be important in the area today, although when the stage route gave way to railroads and highways, these communities declined or disappeared altogether.

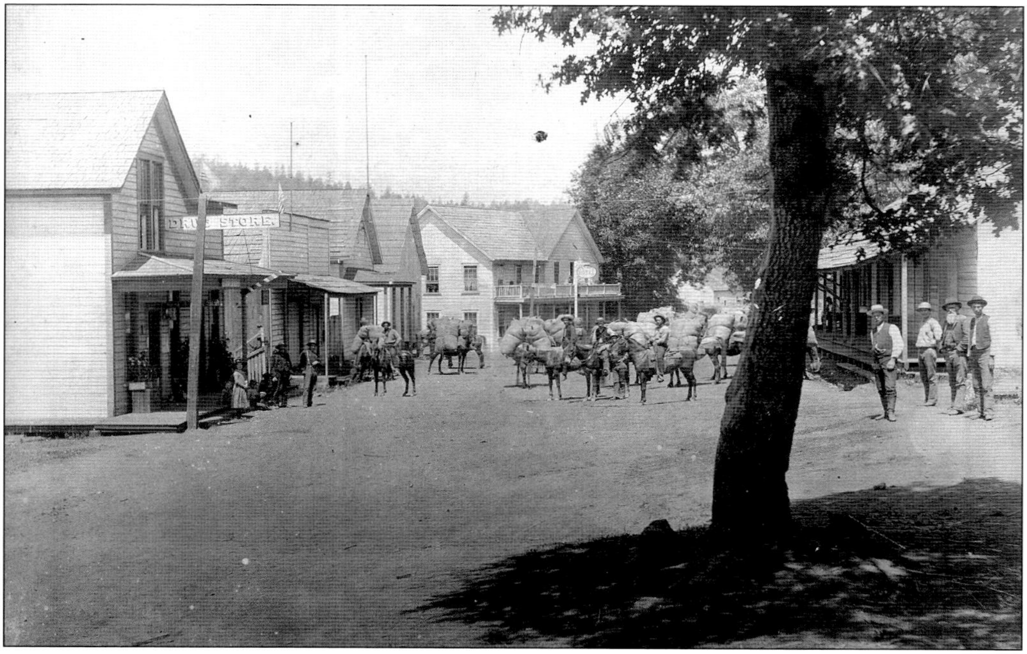

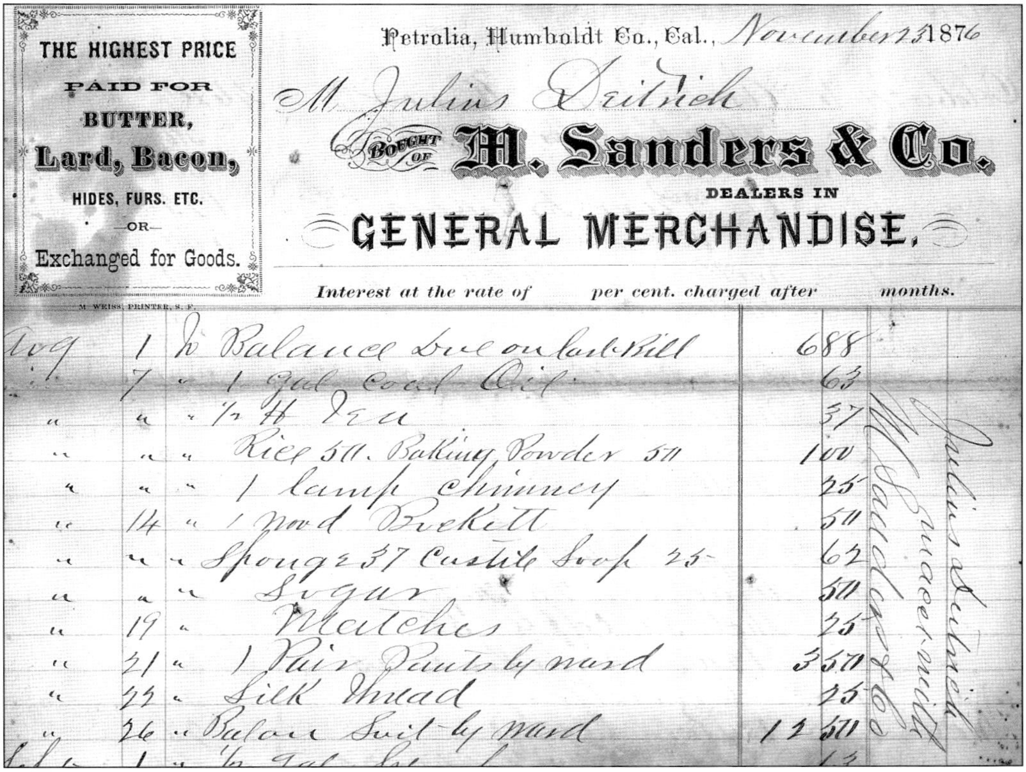

THE HIGHEST PRICE PAID FOR BUTTER, Lard, Bacon, HIDES, FURS. ETC. —OR— Exchanged for Goods.

Petrolia, Humboldt Co., Cal., November 23 1876

M Julius Deitrich

Bought of M. Sanders & Co.

DEALERS IN

GENERAL MERCHANDISE.

Interest at the rate of per cent. charged after months.

M. WEISS, PRINTER, S. F.

Aug	1	To Balance Due on last Bill	6 88
"	7	" 1 Gal Coal Oil	63
"	"	" 1/2 lb Tea	37
"	"	" Rice 50. Baking Powder 50	1 00
"	"	" 1 lamp chimney	25
"	14	" 1 Wood Bucket	50
"	"	" Sponge 37 Castile Soap 25	62
"	"	" Sugar	50
"	19	" Matches	25
"	21	" 1 Pair Pants by mail	3 50
"	22	" Silk Thread	25
"	26	" Balm Suit by mail	12 50

Merchants in rural Humboldt communities not only sold goods, they bought and traded products from farmers and hunters, as this receipt from 1876 Petrolia shows.

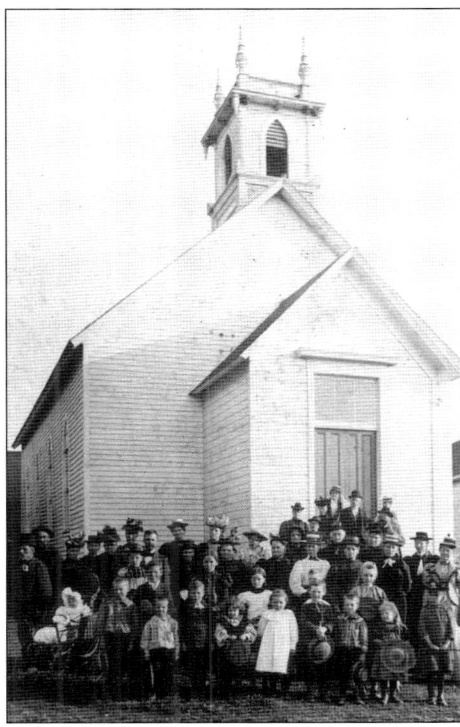

Humboldt's small towns served as important supply and social centers for outlying farms and residents of even smaller communities. Here the congregation of Rohnerville's Methodist Church gather for their photograph in the 1890s.

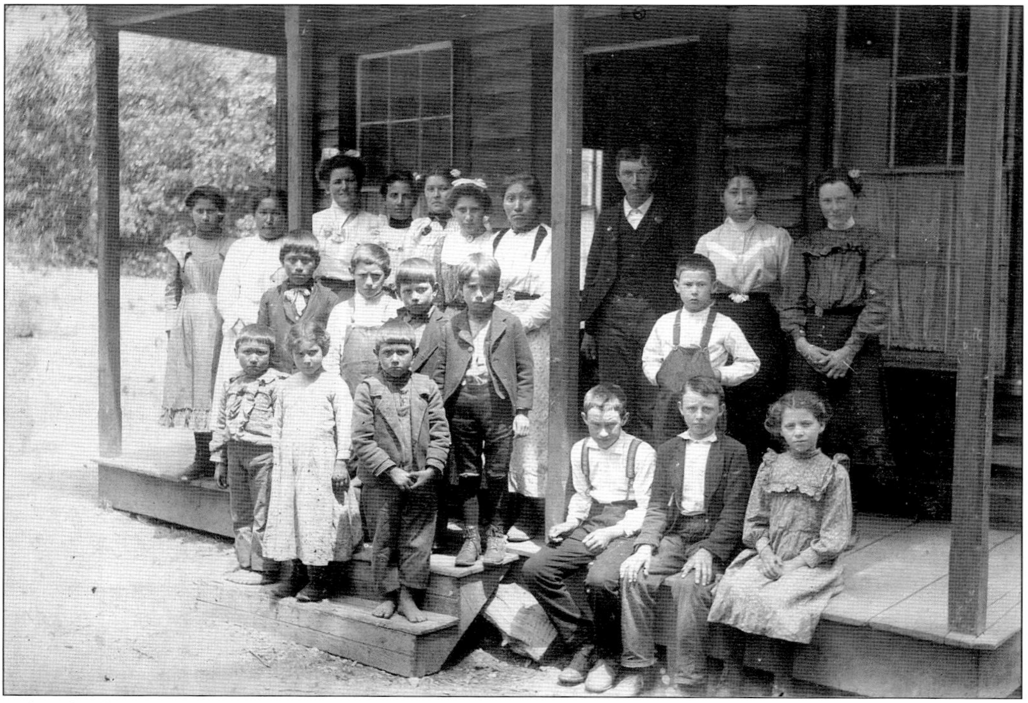

Schools also drew students from surrounding areas. At the China Flat one-room school near Willow Creek, E. Morris poses with her students (including several Native Americans) in 1903.

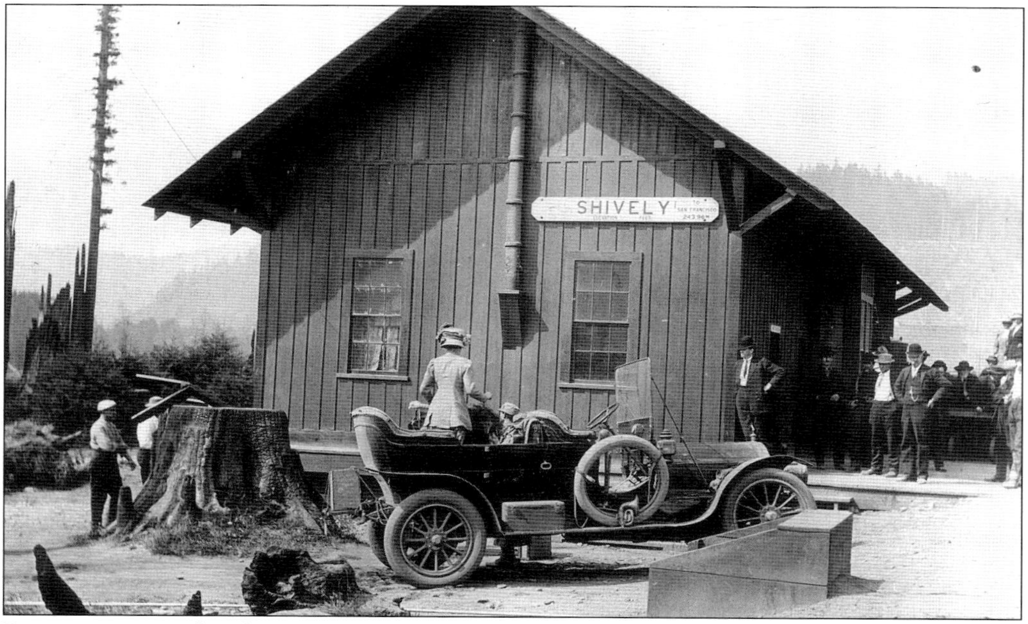

For many years, Shively was the railhead of the rail line south from Eureka. After 1914 when the Northwestern Pacific Railroad connected to San Francisco and beyond, its depot became a stop along the line. The lady waiting for the train is standing in a 1911 Pierce Arrow.

Six

Parting the Redwood Curtain

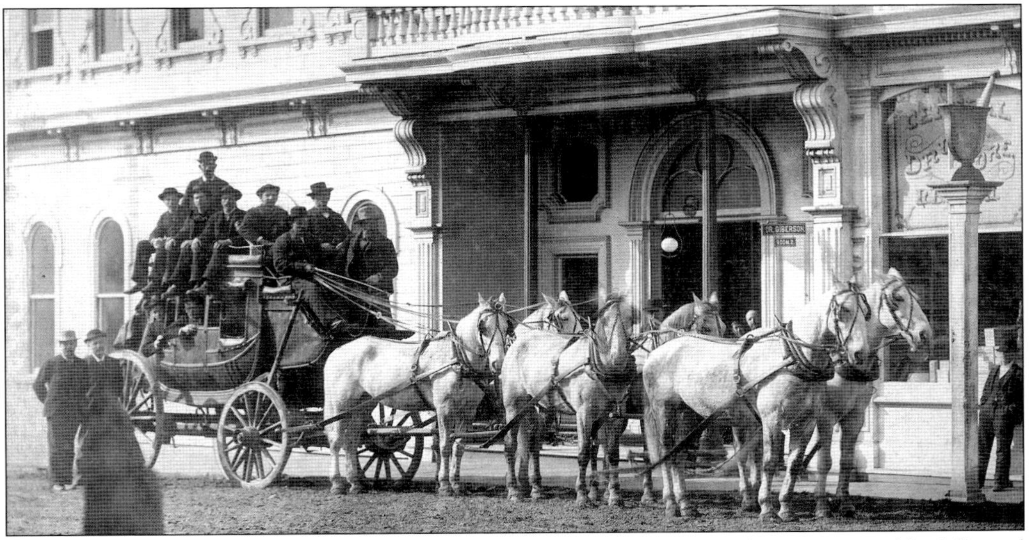

By land, Humboldt County was not easy to reach. Roads, which whenever possible followed the ridges, were rough, steep, and often made impassible by mud. The mountainous journey toward the coast from Willits via Blocksburg and Bridgeville could take over two days. Here, the Eureka/Hydesville stage waits in front of Eureka's Vance Hotel around 1875.

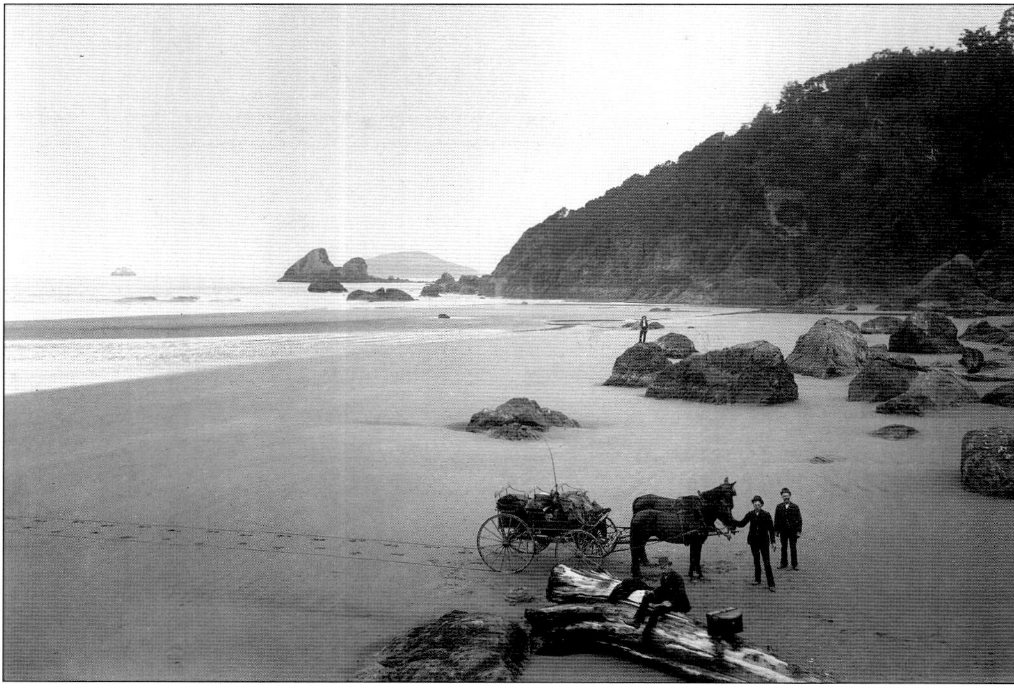

Excursions to the beach were popular with locals, such as this 1890s group on Moonstone Beach, at the mouth of Little River. However, in early years, the difficulty of reaching Humboldt's coast by land discouraged tourists from more distant locales.

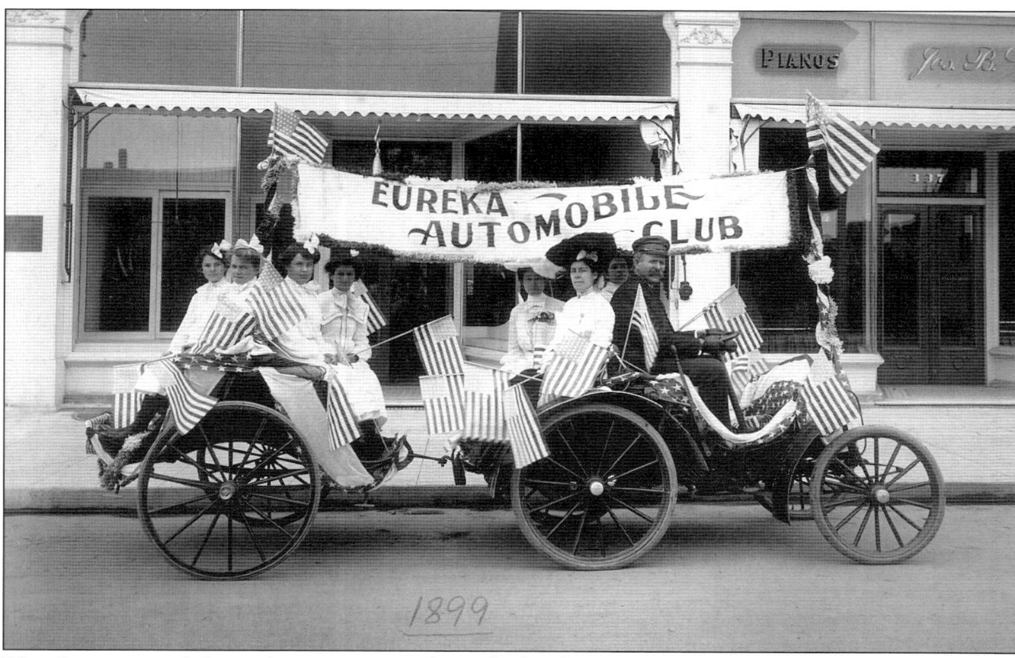

The first automobile in the county was brought by ship for shingle mill operator J.G. Lovern in 1899. Here that auto is ready for entry in the 1904 Fourth of July parade.

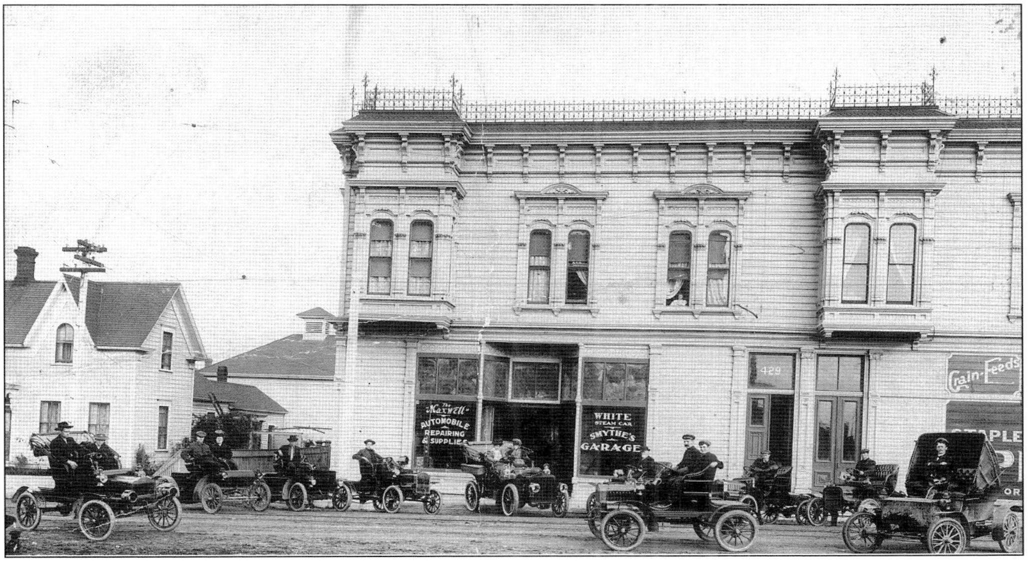

In 1904, other Humboldt automobiles gathered in front of a new type of business, an automobile repair shop at Fifth and J Streets in Eureka.

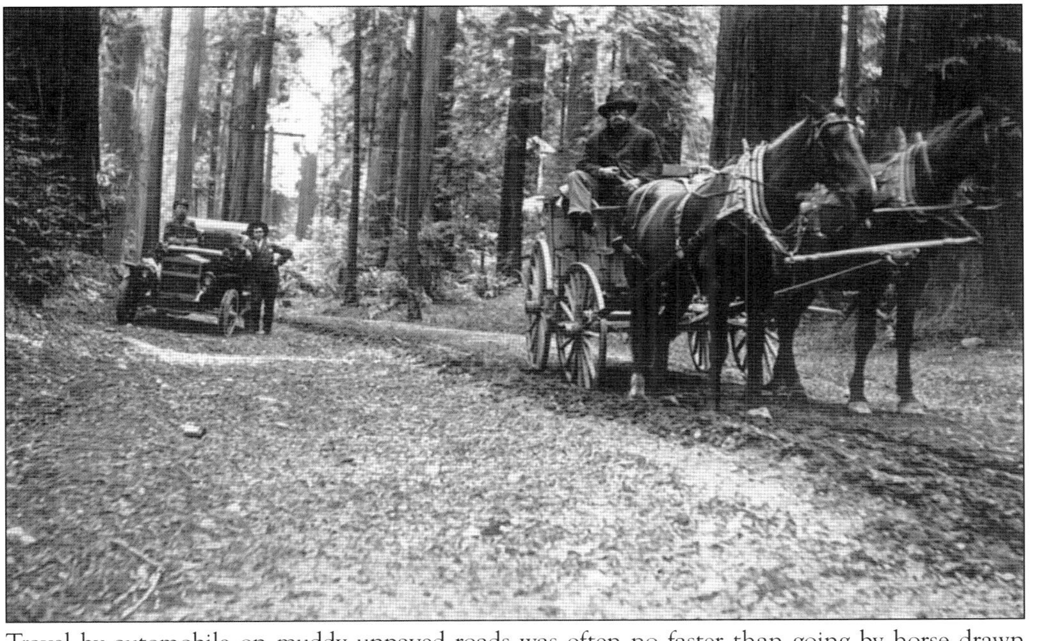

Travel by automobile on muddy unpaved roads was often no faster than going by horse drawn wagon. This photo was taken on the "overland" route between Dyerville and Englewood in 1910.

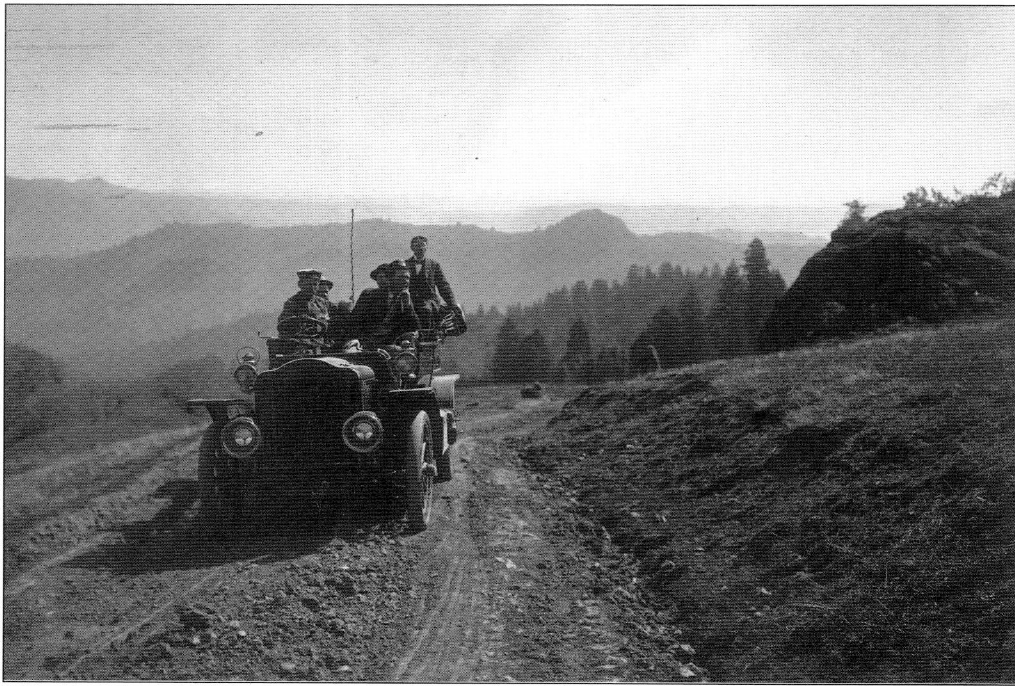

In wet weather, unpaved mountain roads were often impassable. When the weather was fine, crossing the mountains by auto was a challenging but exhilarating experience.

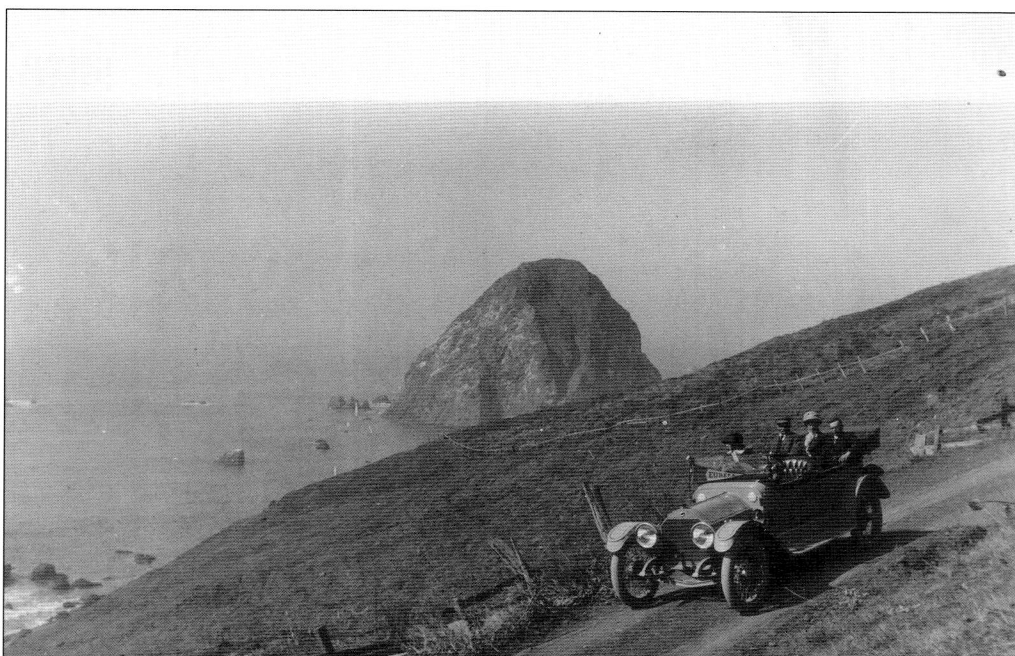

Excursions to the sea by auto could also be a challenge. This intrepid party has ventured over steep unpaved roads from Eureka to the Cape Mendocino area.

In 1914, Humboldt's relative isolation came to an end with the driving of the Golden Spike at Cain Rock in southern Humboldt County. This ceremony joined two sections of the Northwestern Pacific Railroad, connecting Eureka with San Francisco and beyond. This was the culmination of a herculean effort by the Southern Pacific and Santa Fe railroads

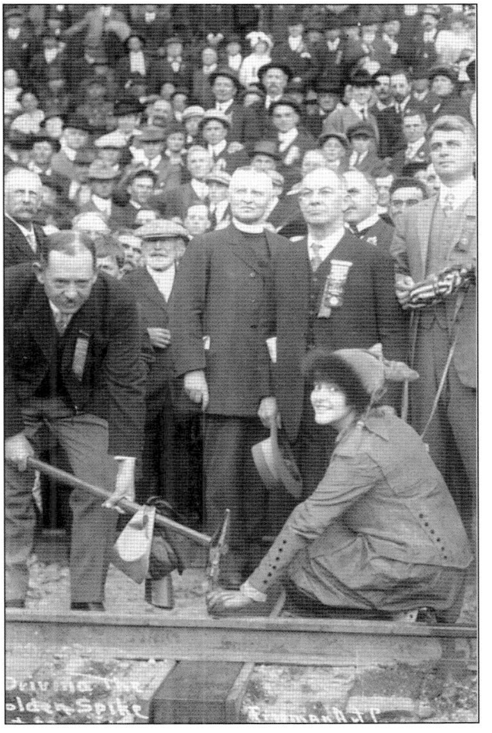

One of the region's first motion pictures recorded the passage of the first San Francisco/ Eureka train. The site of the linkage at Cain Rock was 205 miles from San Francisco and 78 miles from Eureka.

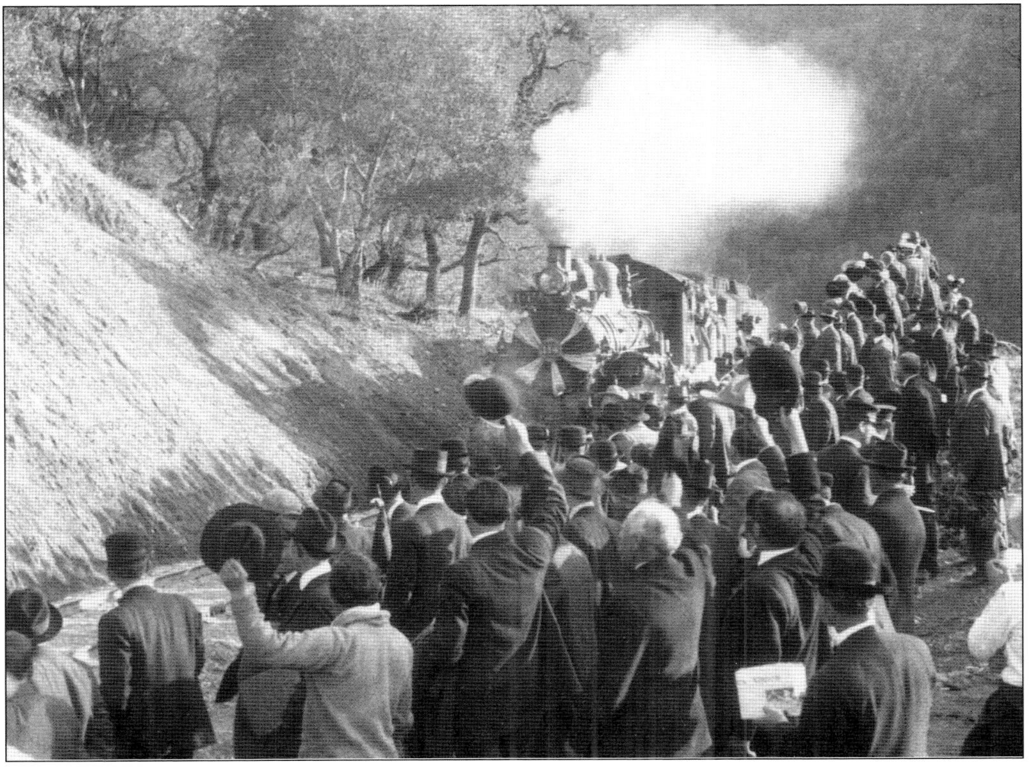

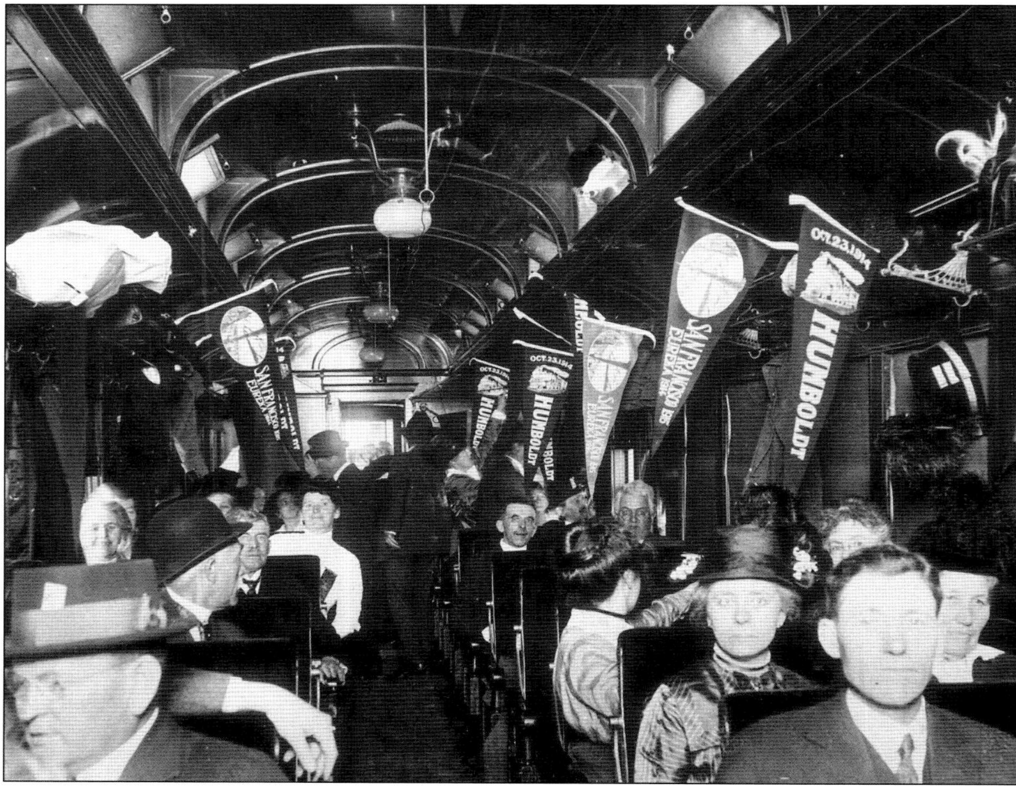

Excited passengers on that first train are shown already sporting their souvenir pennants.

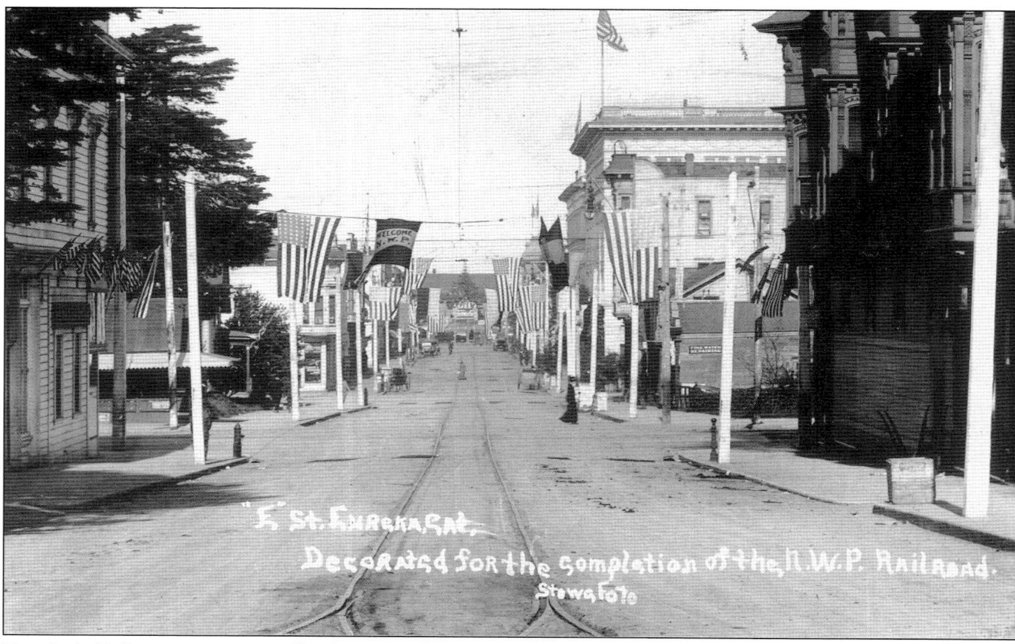

Eureka's E Street was grandly decorated to welcome the first Northwestern Pacific train.

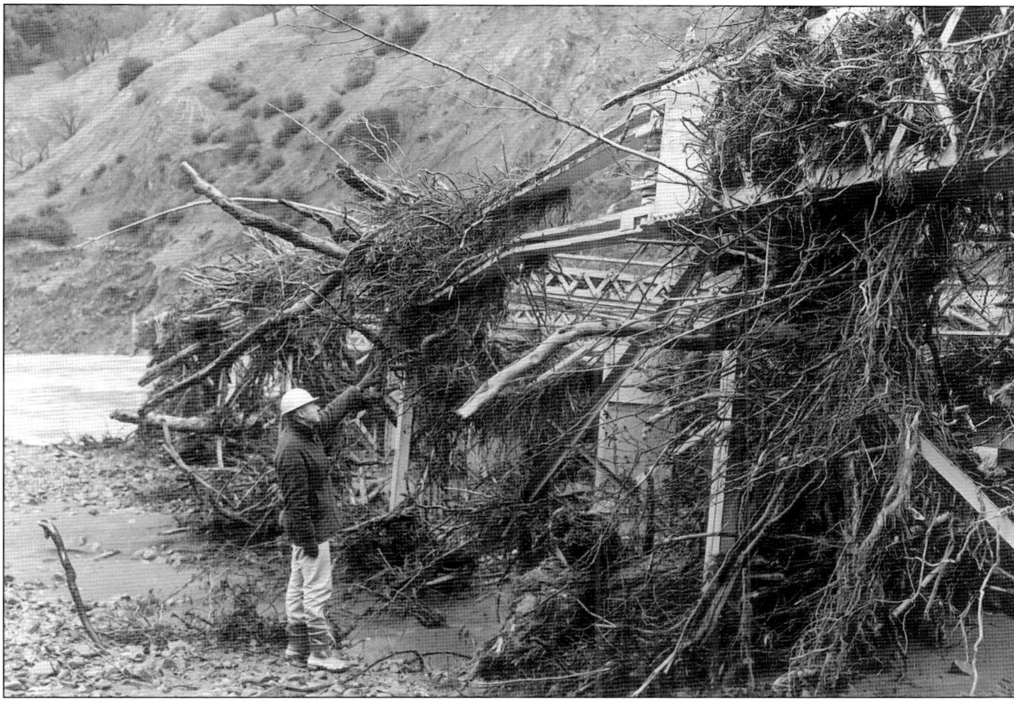

A major flood on the Eel river around Christmas 1964 destroyed over 100 miles of the N.W.P. track that had been laid down 50 years earlier.

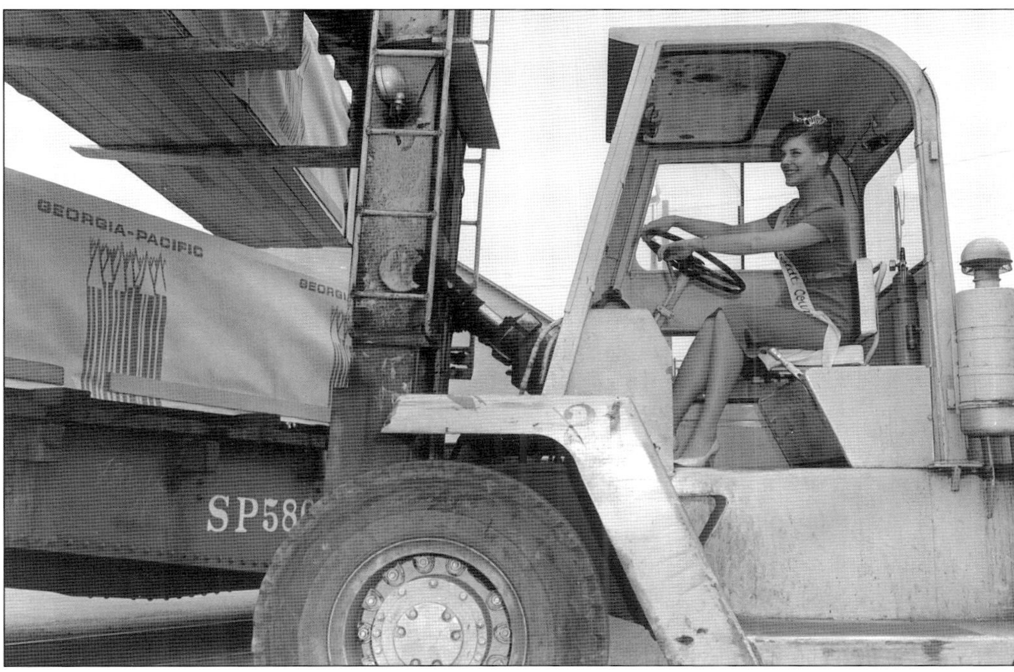

Rail and lumber companies united in a 117-day effort to restore the rail link. Again, beautiful girls helped publicize the event. Here Gail Wilcox, Miss Humboldt County, pitches in.

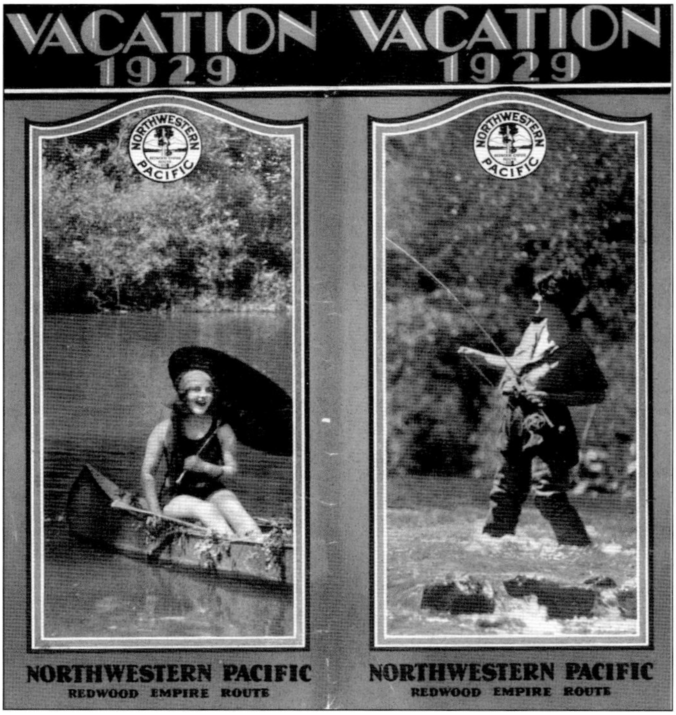

The railroads and Humboldt promoters made a big effort to draw tourists by rail as seen by this 1929 N.W.P. brochure touting Humboldt's riverside recreation. Trains would stop at major fishing holes along the Eel River to accommodate passengers.

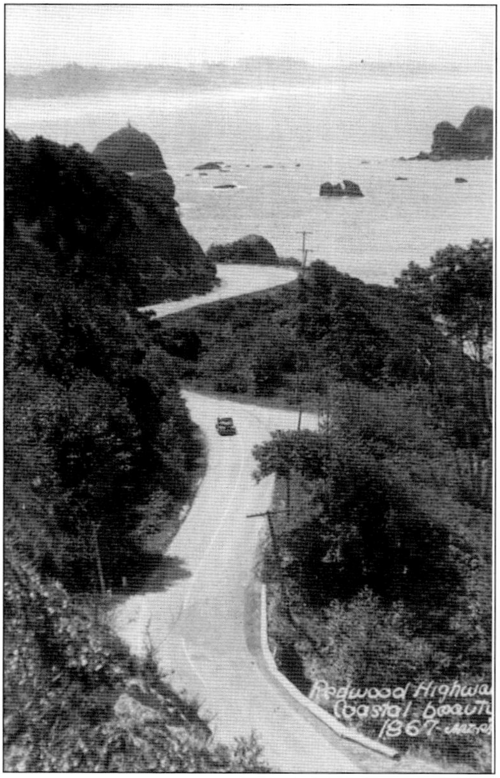

About the same time the rail connection was being made, roads into Humboldt were being paved, and by the 1920s the Redwood Highway (later U.S. 101) linked California's north coast with the rest of the state.

Auto tourism was also heavily promoted, and "roadside attractions" were developed including a number of drive-through trees.

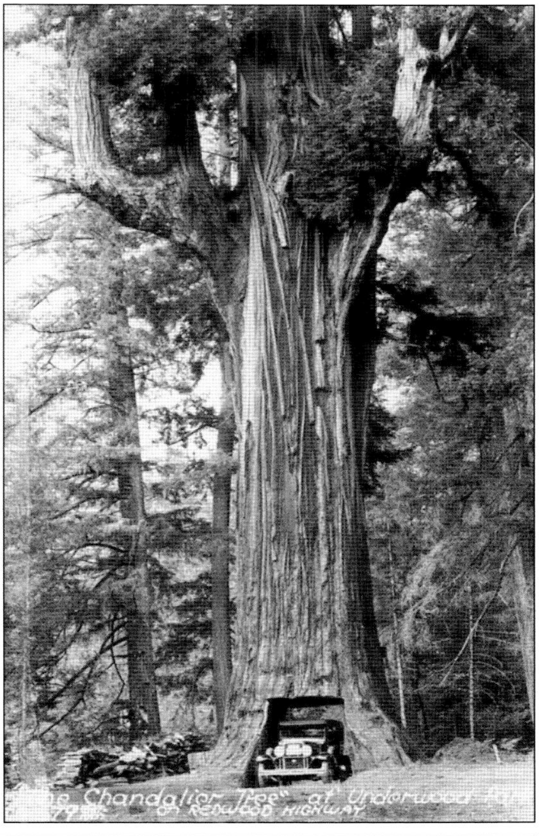

The Stump House, established just after 1900, was an early "attraction" and souvenir shop at Clark and Broadway in Eureka and remained in business until the early 1990s. It promoted itself as "manufacturer of Bark and Burhl novelties of all kinds. Headquarters of Indian Baskets and Humboldt Redwood views." The building had a wood and tarpaper framework covered with redwood bark and with huge redwood rounds at the ends.

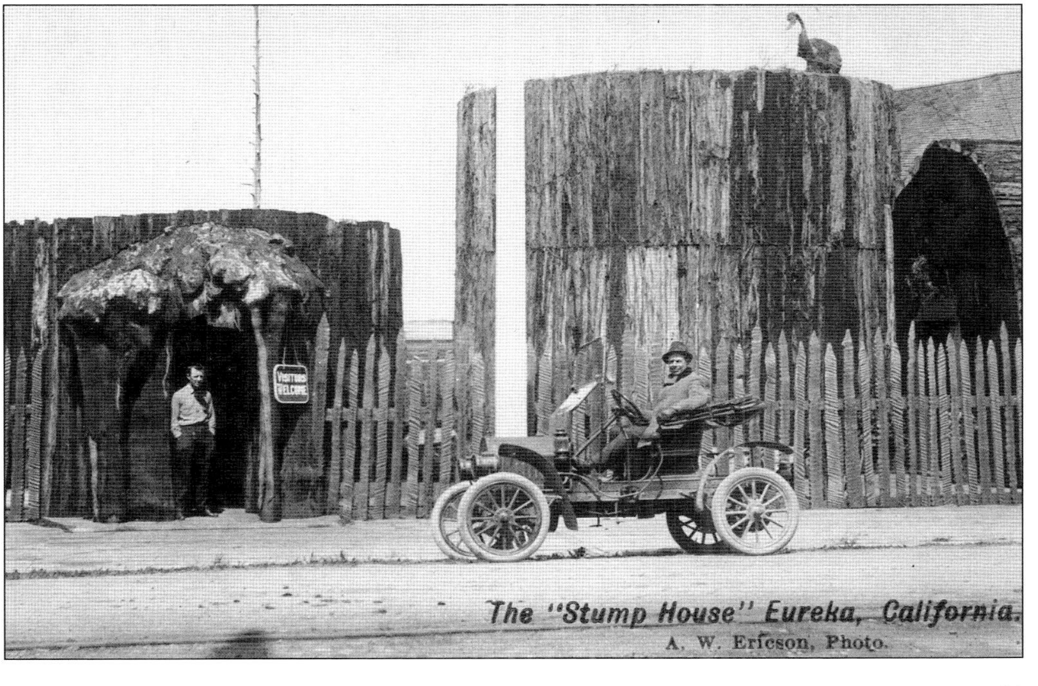

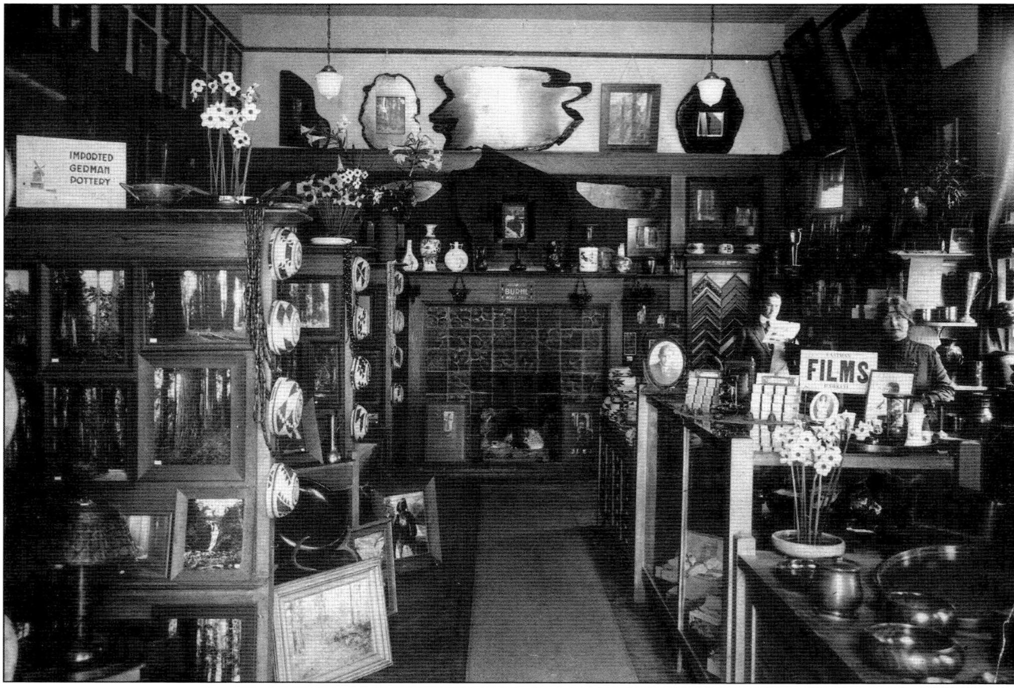

Another souvenir shop was the Freeman Art Company on F Street in Eureka. The showroom of this commercial photo studio, pictured here around 1915, also featured baskets and items carved from redwood.

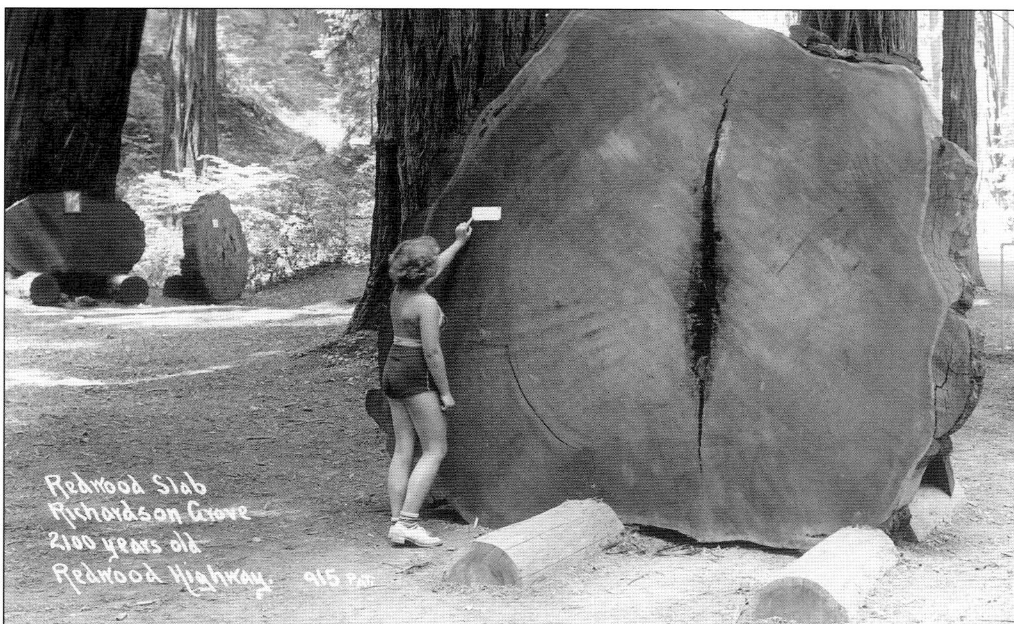

Pretty, often scantily dressed, girls have regularly been used to attract tourism, this 1930s postcard being a good example.

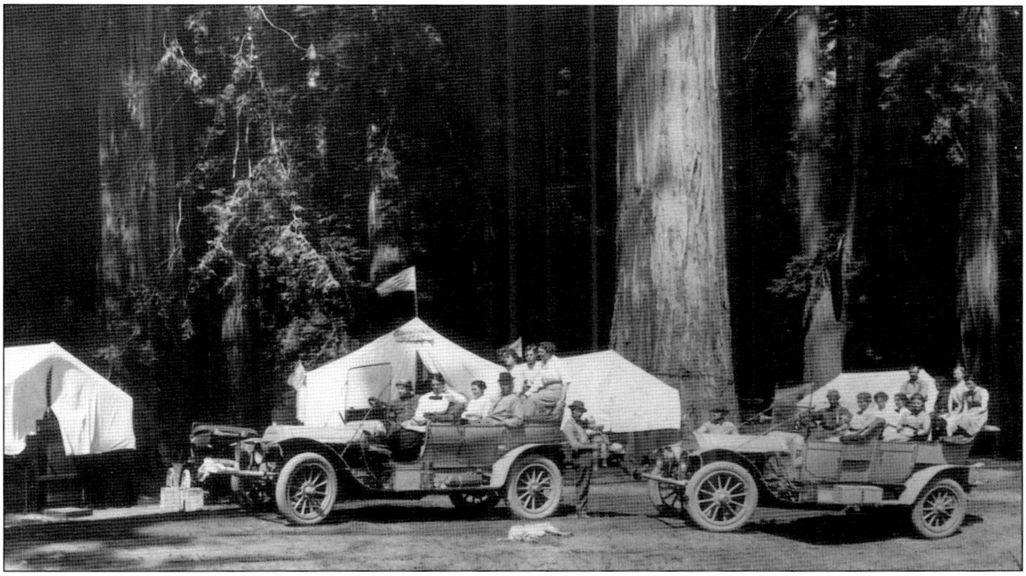

Initially the tourist appeal of hunting and fishing was most heavily promoted, although camping among the redwoods also attracted the adventurous tourist. This campground was on the South Fork of the Eel River near Dyerville.

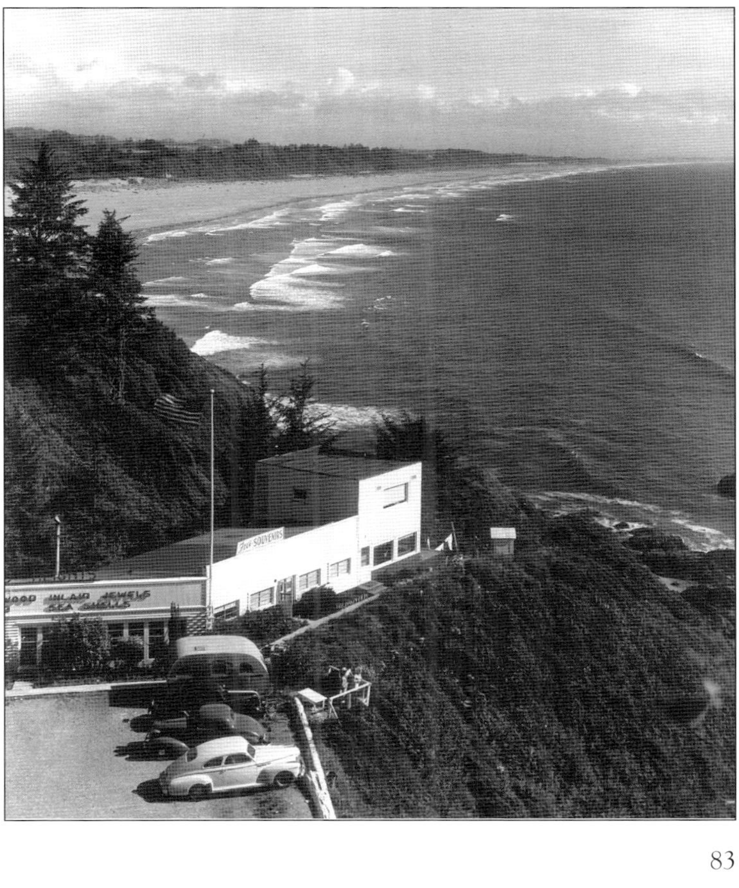

Businesses catering to automobile tourists contributed to the local economy. This 1930s photo was taken at Moonstone Beach overlooking uninterrupted miles of Clam Beach.

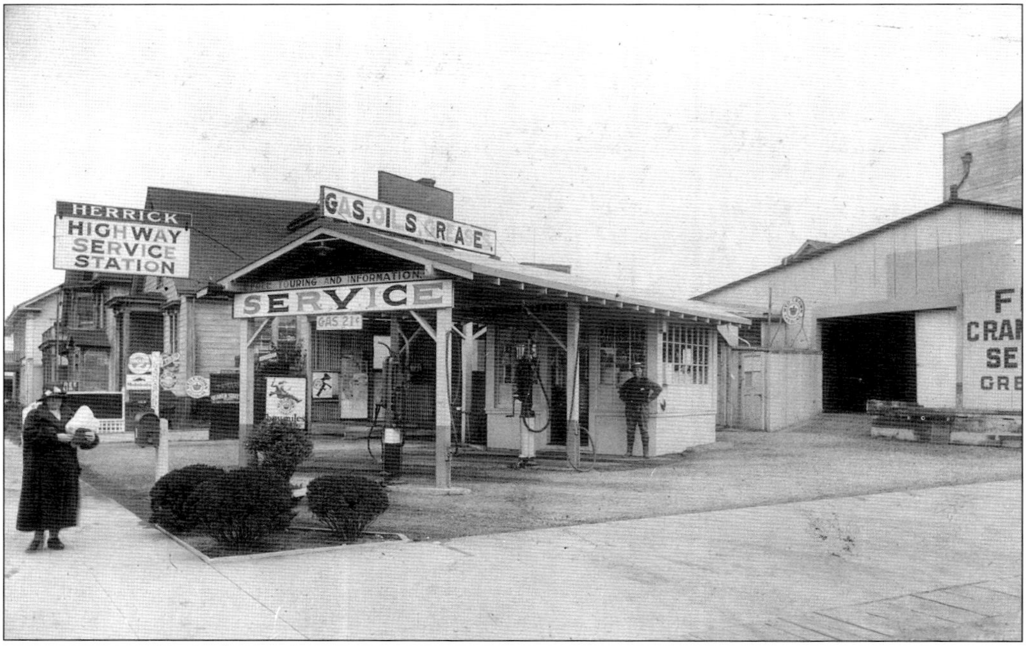

As tourists rolled along the Redwood Highway, auto-oriented businesses sprang up. In the 1930s, Herrick's Service Station was at B and Fifth Streets (Fifth was the highway as it ran through Eureka).

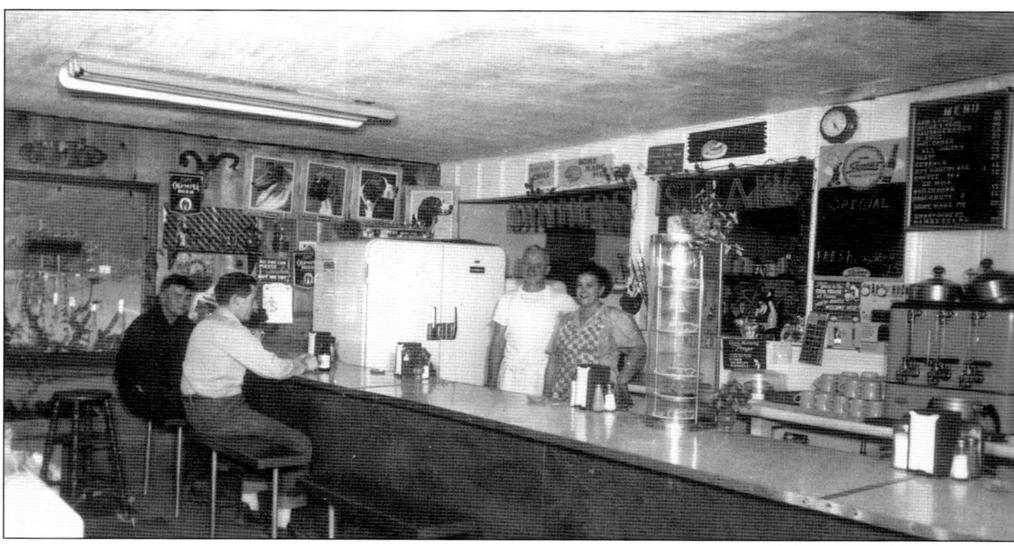

Cafes and diners were other businesses that flourished along the highway. During the 1940s and 1950s, the Fern Café at Stone Lagoon was a popular stop.

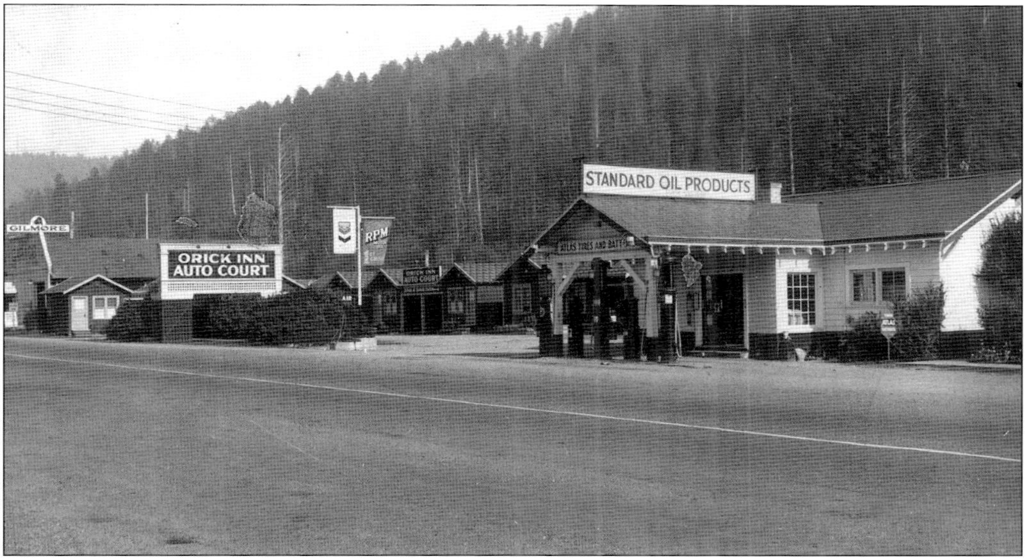

Auto courts, the predecessor of the motel, offered travelers individual cabins. Orick, located on Highway 101, still relies heavily on the tourist trade, particularly on the sale of "chainsaw art" and other redwood souvenirs.

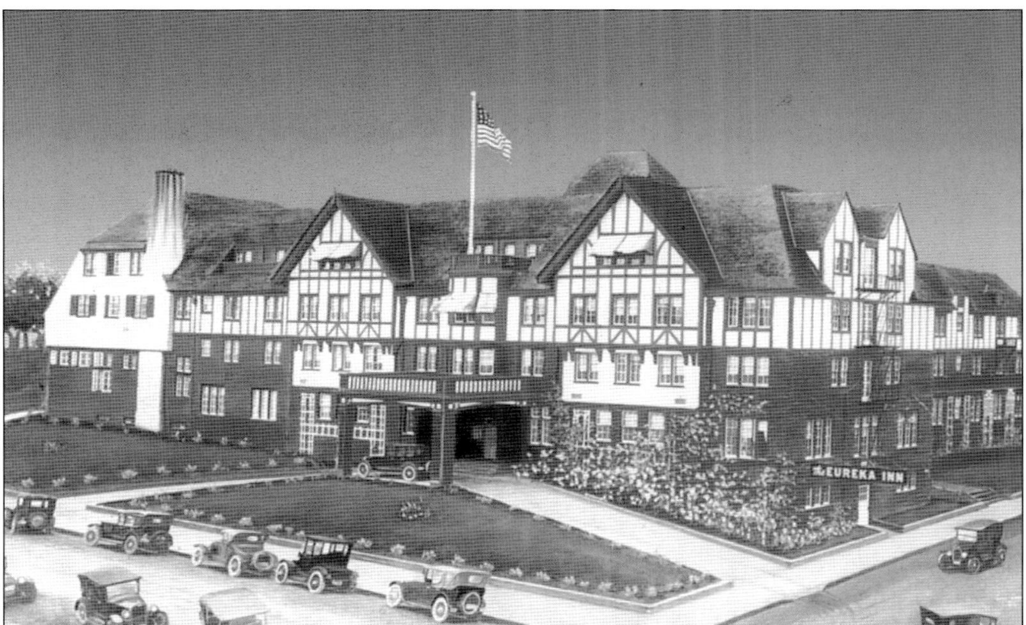

The Tudor style Eureka Inn was built in 1922 to accommodate the increasing number of auto tourists, particularly from the San Francisco Bay area. It has more board footage of redwood than any other building in the world.

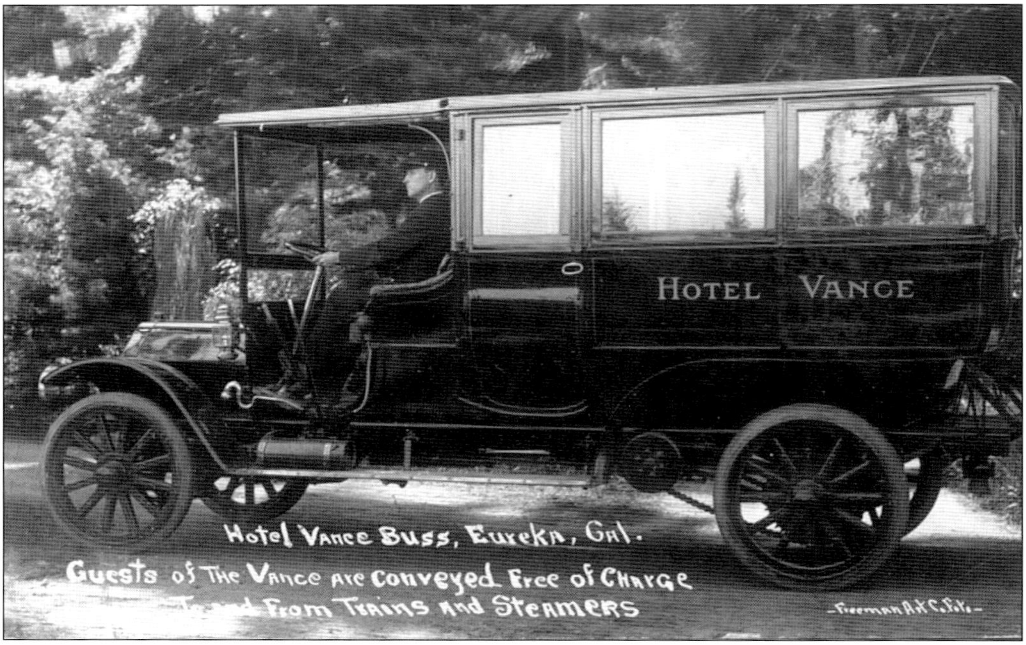

Eureka's older grand hotel, the Vance, catered to tourists coming on train or steamer by providing transportation to the hotel.

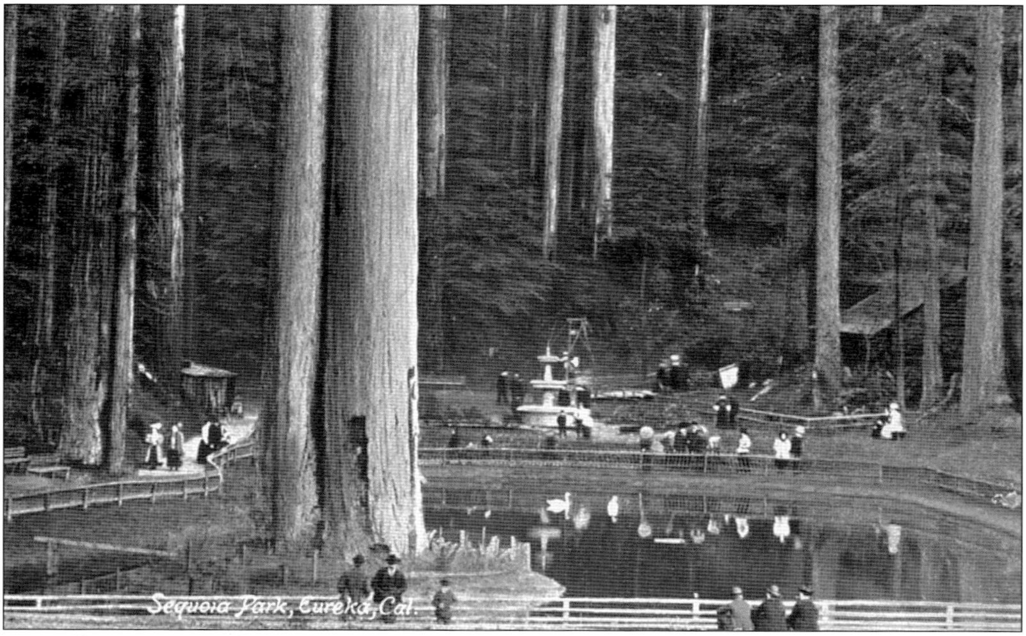

A Eureka tourist attraction that was developed prior to the rail and highway links was Sequoia Park. Built beyond what was then the southern edge of town, it preserved large numbers of old growth and second growth redwood that today stand in the heart of the growing city. In the early 20th century, the park's paths, fountains, and picnic facilities were an attraction for convention groups that took trolleys there from downtown hotels.

Some farsighted people realized that the redwood's natural beauty and economic value as a tourist attraction could rival their worth as lumber. Tourist promoters and early environmentalists formed the Save the Redwoods League in 1918. Gradually it bought up parcels of forestland and dedicated them to public use.

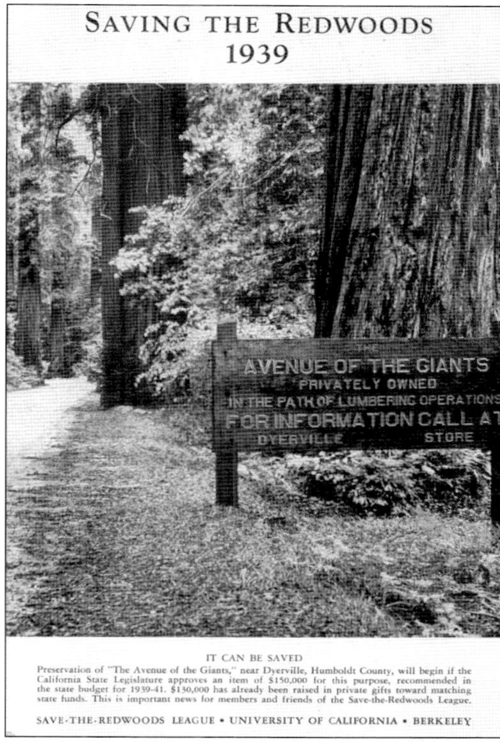

Local, state, and federal parks were established to protect major tracts of redwoods. The Ladybird Johnson Grove was dedicated in 1969. Seen at the ceremony are Rev. Billy Graham, Governor Ronald Reagan, Congressman Don Clausen, Interior Secretary Walter Hickle, President Richard Nixon, First Lady Pat Nixon, and former president Lyndon Johnson.

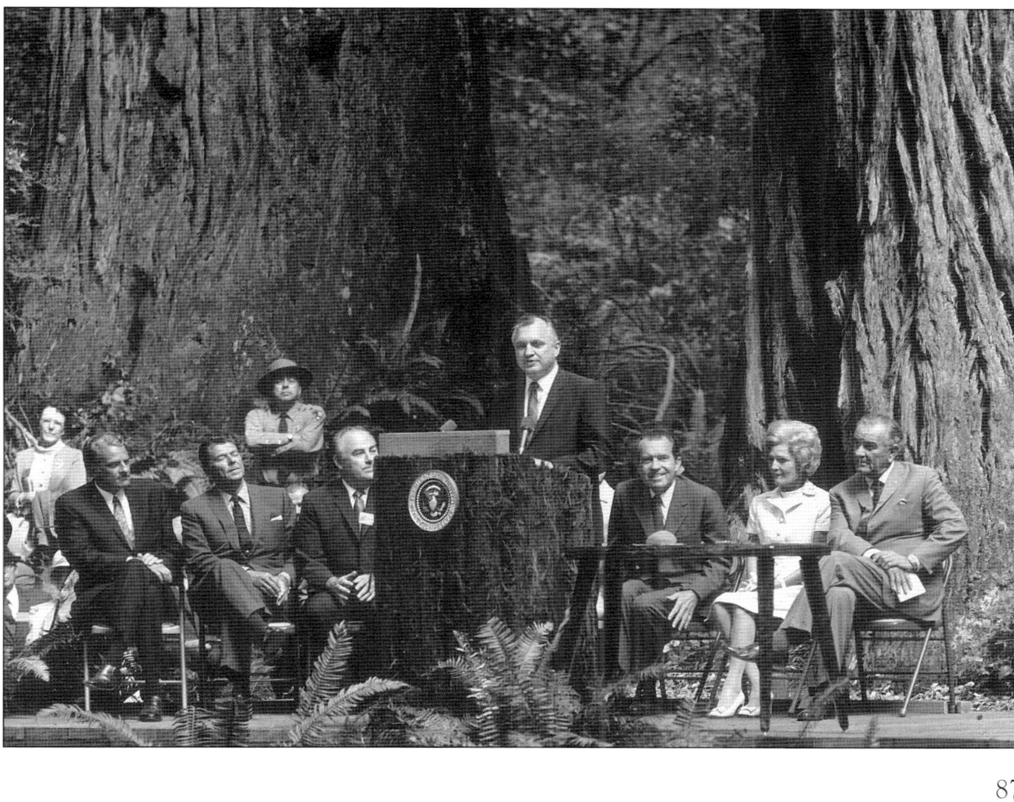

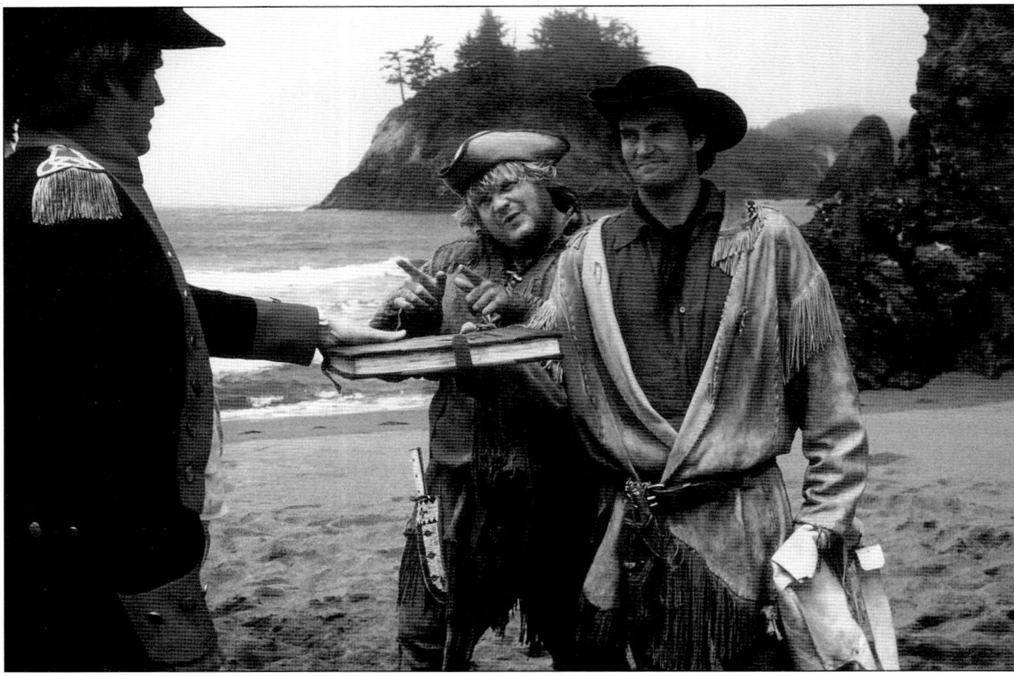

Once access was easier, Humboldt's scenery and architecture attracted film makers from the silent era to the present. Ferndale's Victorian streetscapes have often appeared on film while area redwoods have seen Jurassic dinosaurs and Star Wars battles. Here Chris Farley and Matthew Perry are *Almost Heroes* on Trinidad Beach in the 1998 film. (Photo courtesy of the Humboldt County Film Commission.)

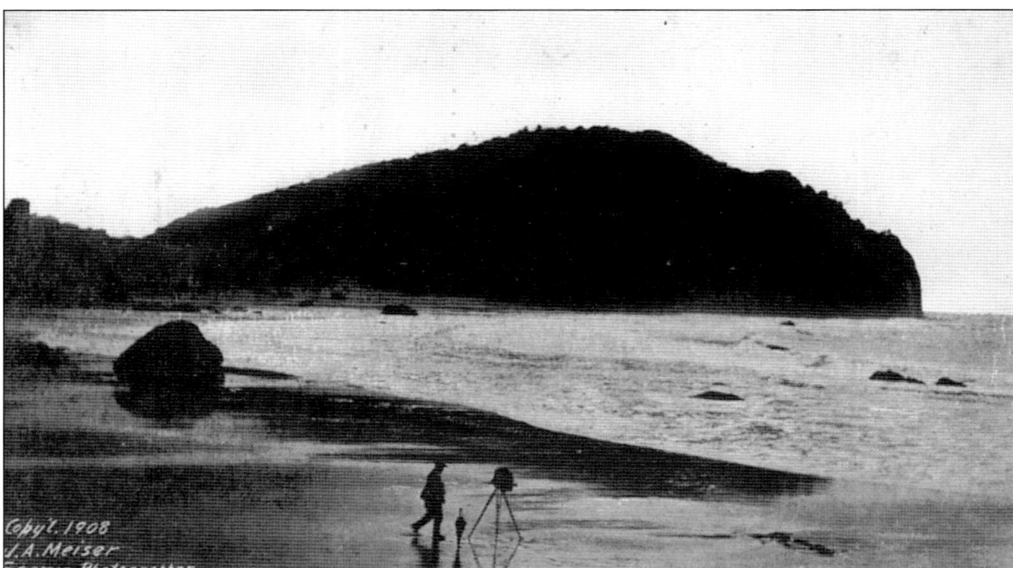

Ninety years earlier, the same beach was the subject for Eureka photographer J.A. Meiser, one of many photographers and painters attracted by the area's natural beauty. Here Meiser's camera is pointed north toward the same view captured by later filmmakers.

Seven

Doing Business in Humboldt

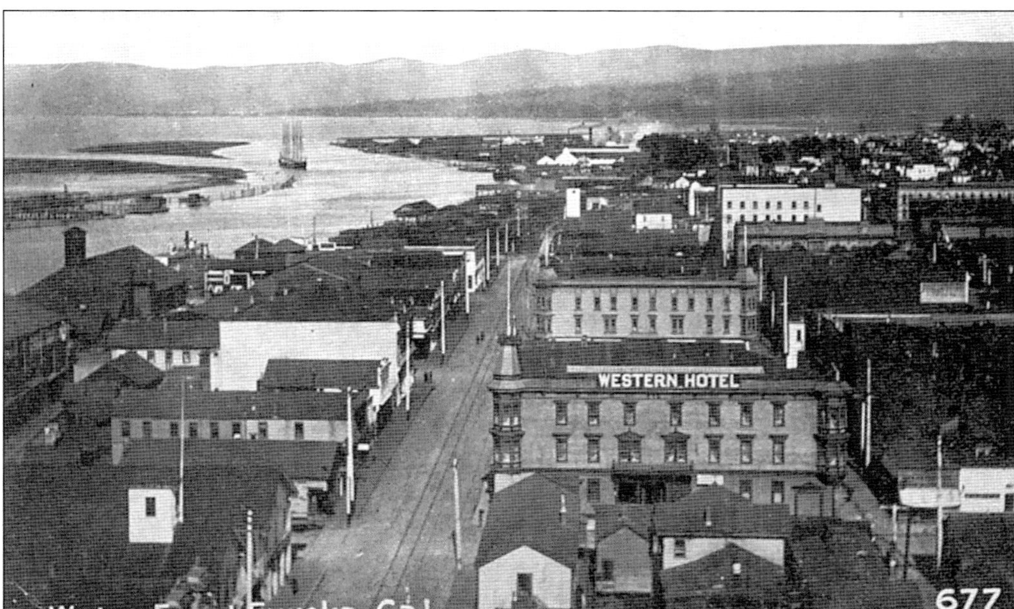

This early-20th-century photograph taken from a power plant at C and First Streets shows Eureka's "Old Town," the north portion of Humboldt Bay and the Arcata hills beyond.

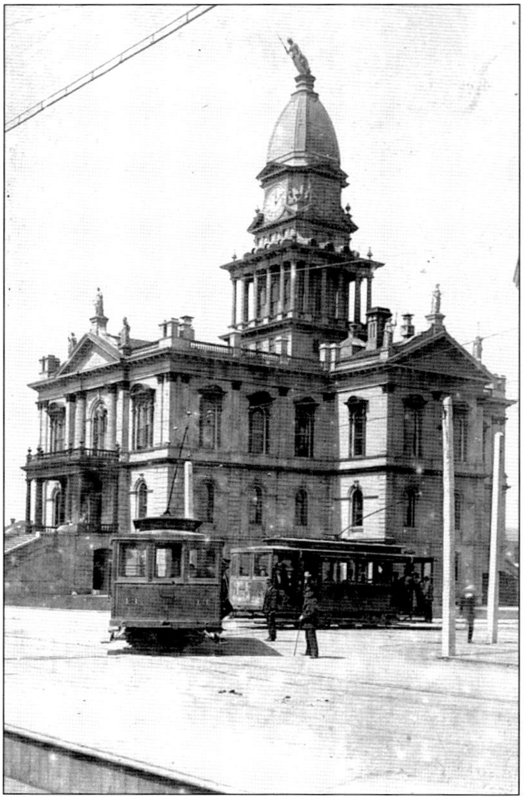

This, the second Humboldt County Courthouse, was completed in 1889. The tilted statue on top is the most dramatic evidence of damage from the 1906 earthquake that devastated San Francisco and also caused heavy damage in Ferndale. After subsequent earthquake damage, the central tower was dismantled. The whole building had to be demolished several years after a 1954 quake. Humboldt County is one of the most seismically active areas in the country. Minor earthquakes occur frequently and occasional tsunamis are reported.

Eureka's early-20th-century City Hall at Third and G Streets also suffered from earthquake damage, as well as the expanding space needs of a growing city, and its site is now the location of a city parking lot. At the time of this photograph the city offices and police court were upstairs, and the city jail and fire station were located on the lower level of the building. The double doors seen on the right are the fire station entrance.

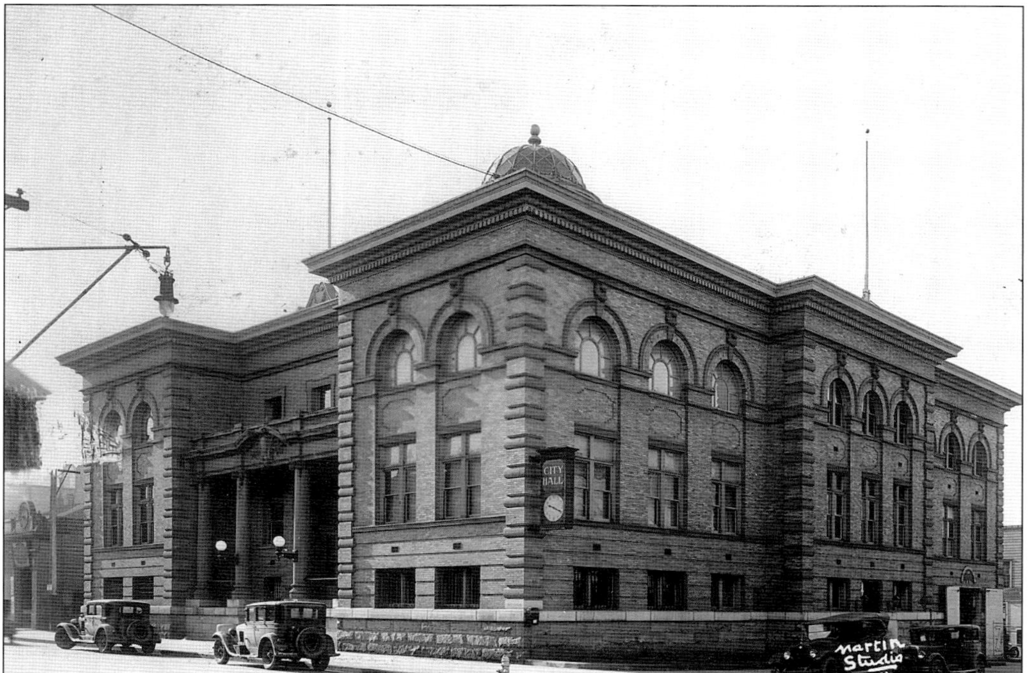

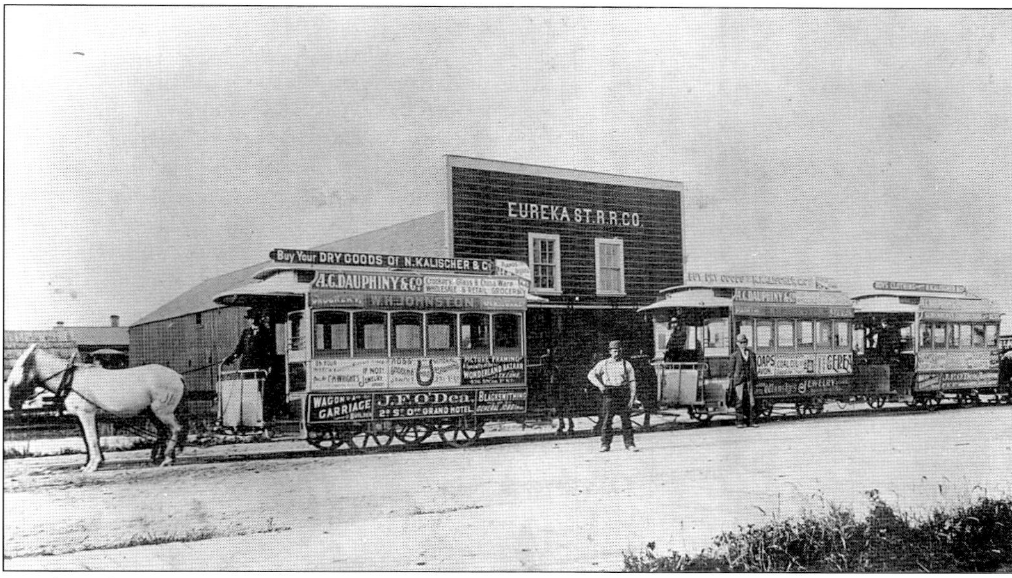

Eureka's first street-car system, run by the Eureka Street Rail Road Co., was composed of horse-drawn rail cars. Festooned with local ads, the cars assemble in front of the company office on First Street.

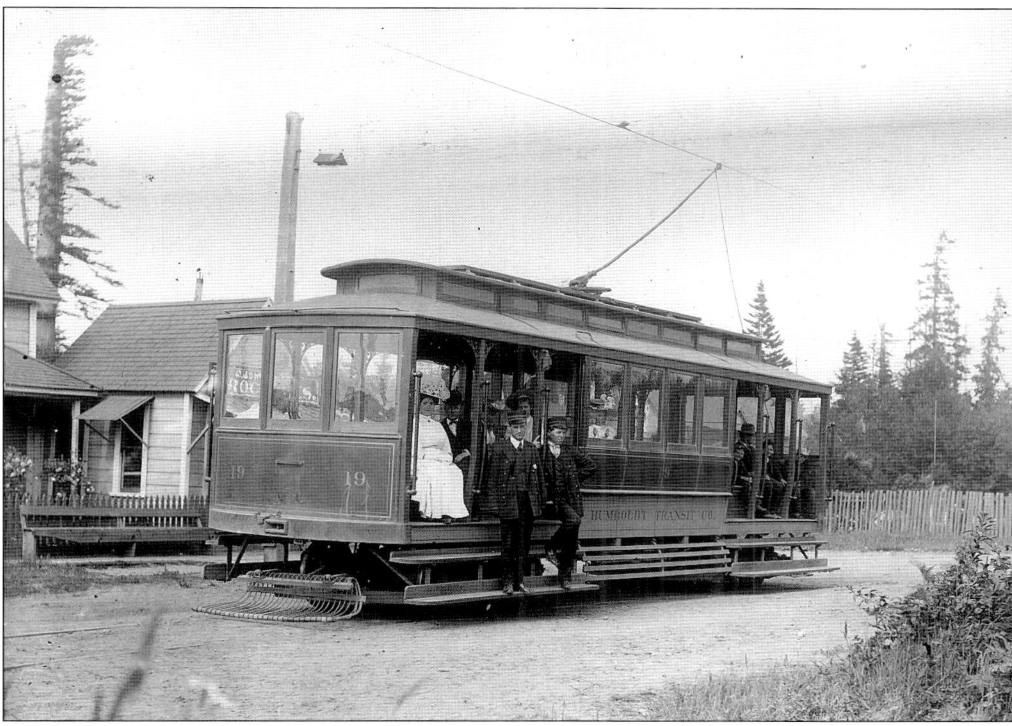

Electric trolley cars operated by the Humboldt Transit Company plied Eureka streets from the 1890s until 1940. This photograph was taken around 1906 at the corner of W and Harris Streets on the line serving Sequoia Park.

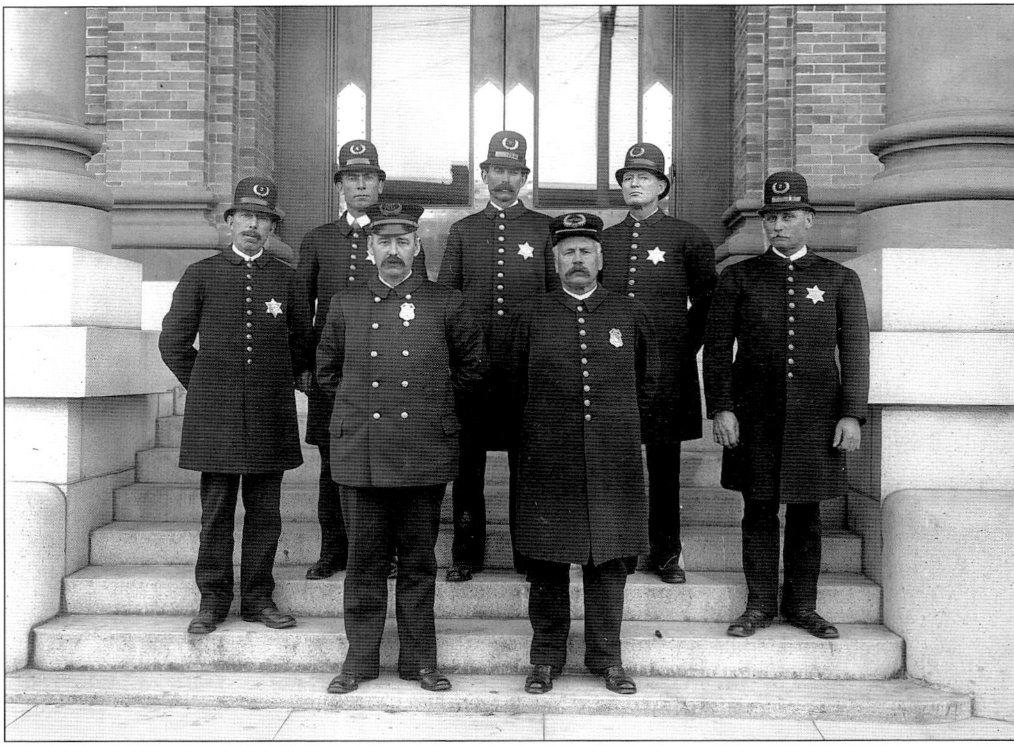

Eureka's early 20th century police force poses on the steps of City Hall.

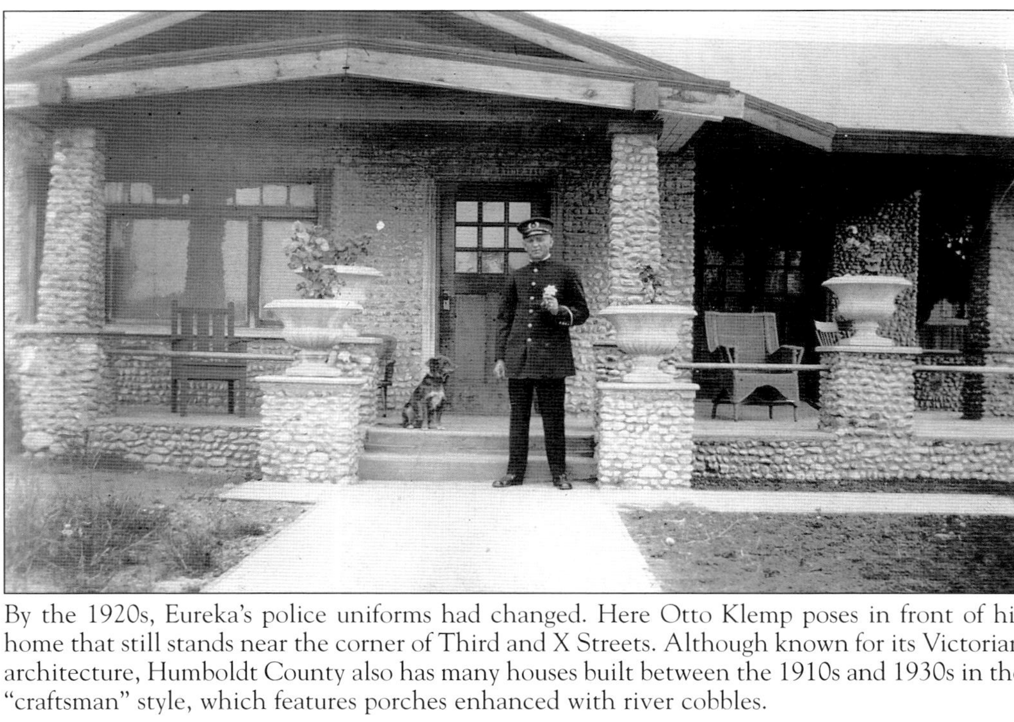

By the 1920s, Eureka's police uniforms had changed. Here Otto Klemp poses in front of his home that still stands near the corner of Third and X Streets. Although known for its Victorian architecture, Humboldt County also has many houses built between the 1910s and 1930s in the "craftsman" style, which features porches enhanced with river cobbles.

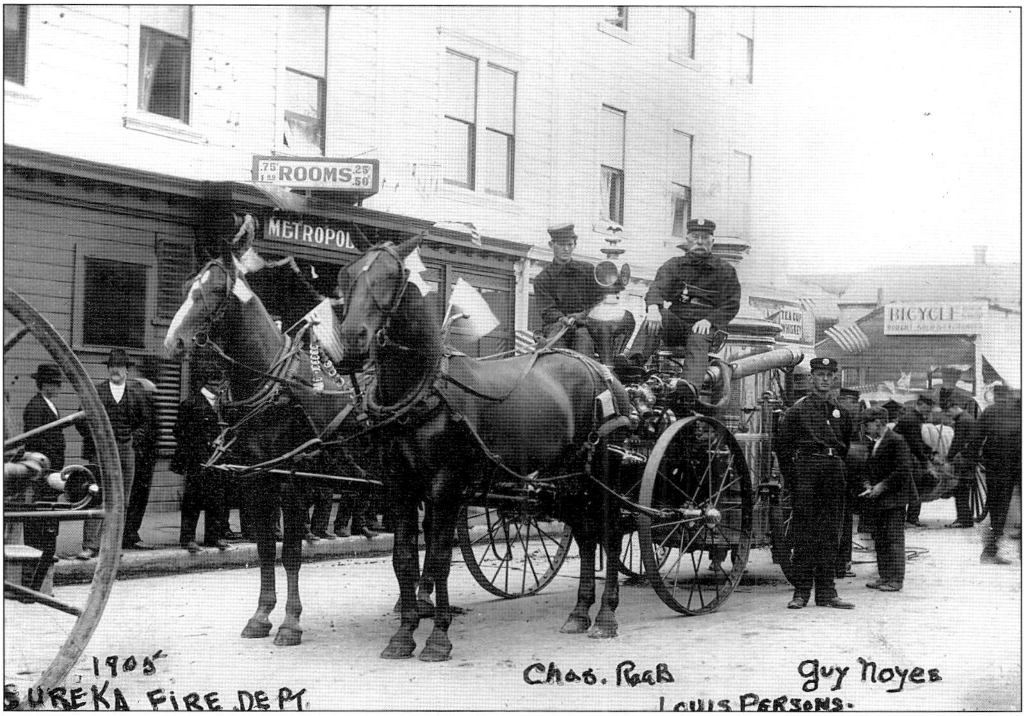

Eureka's fire fighters proudly pose in 1905 with one of their steam-pumpers. This photograph was taken at the corner of Second and D Streets.

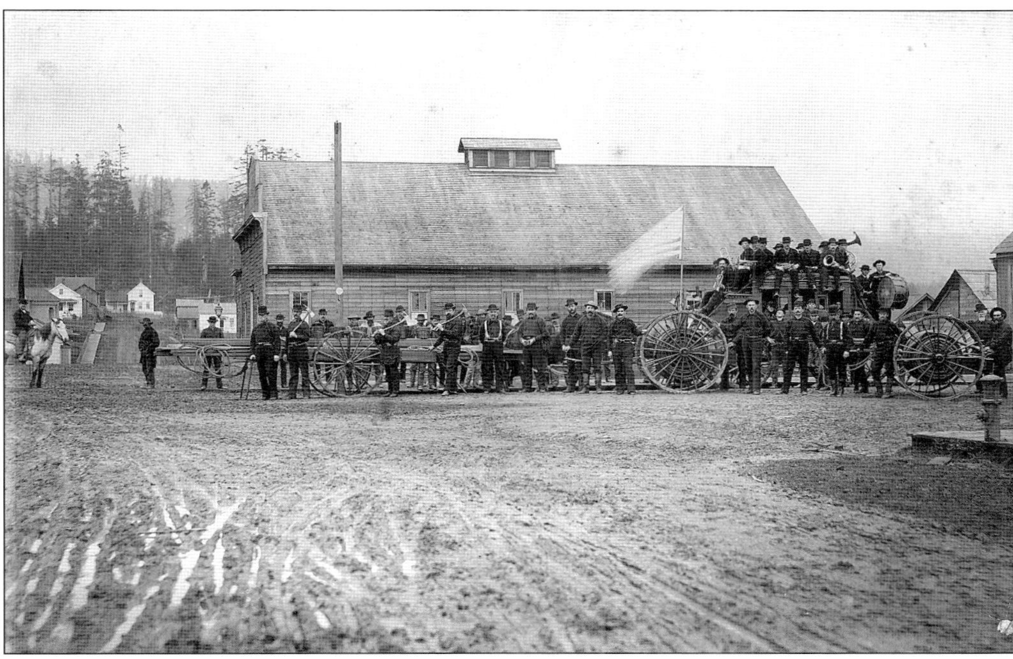

Arcata's Volunteer Fire Department waits in readiness with two hose carts and a hook and ladder in the early 1880s.

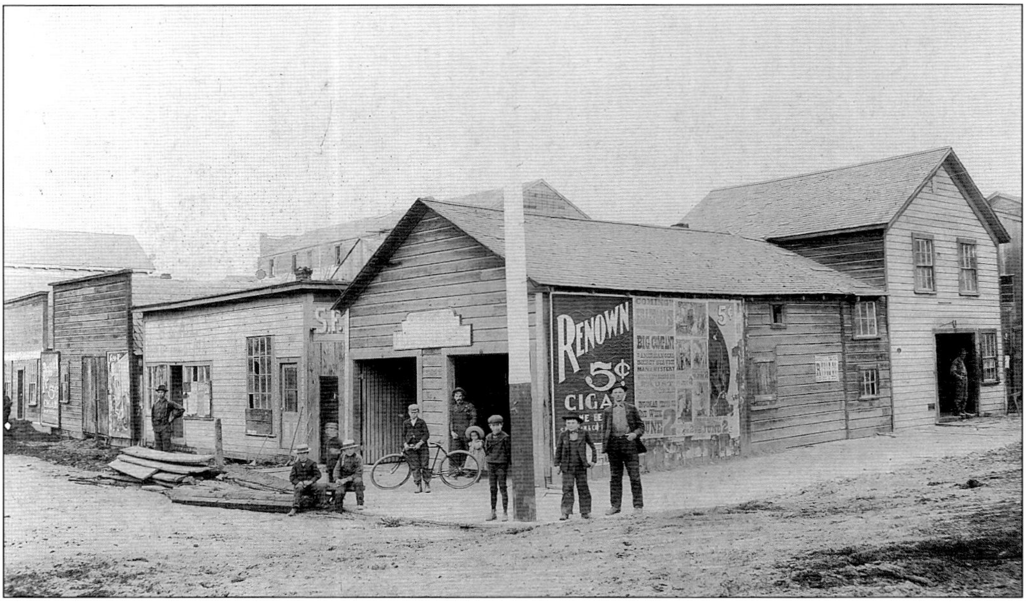

Eureka's streets in the late 19th century were unpaved, and the waterfront town generally had a rough frontier look.

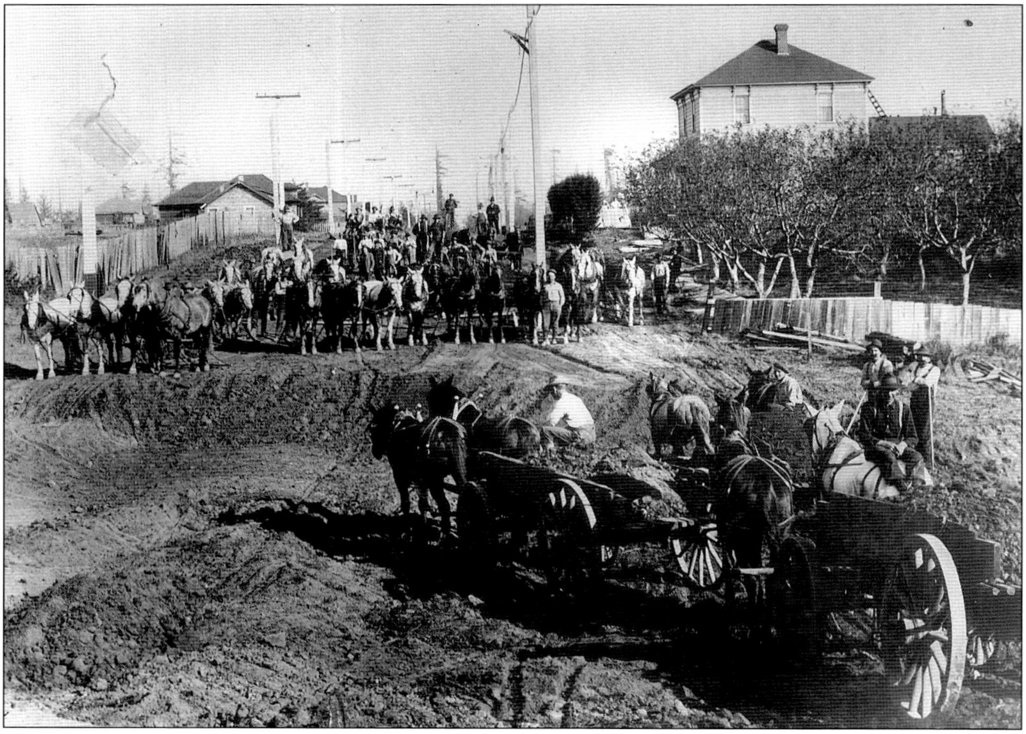

As Eureka expanded south from the waterfront, new streets had to be graded and eventually paved. Here street crews are dumping and spreading fill at the corner of P and Harris Streets. The photograph looks east.

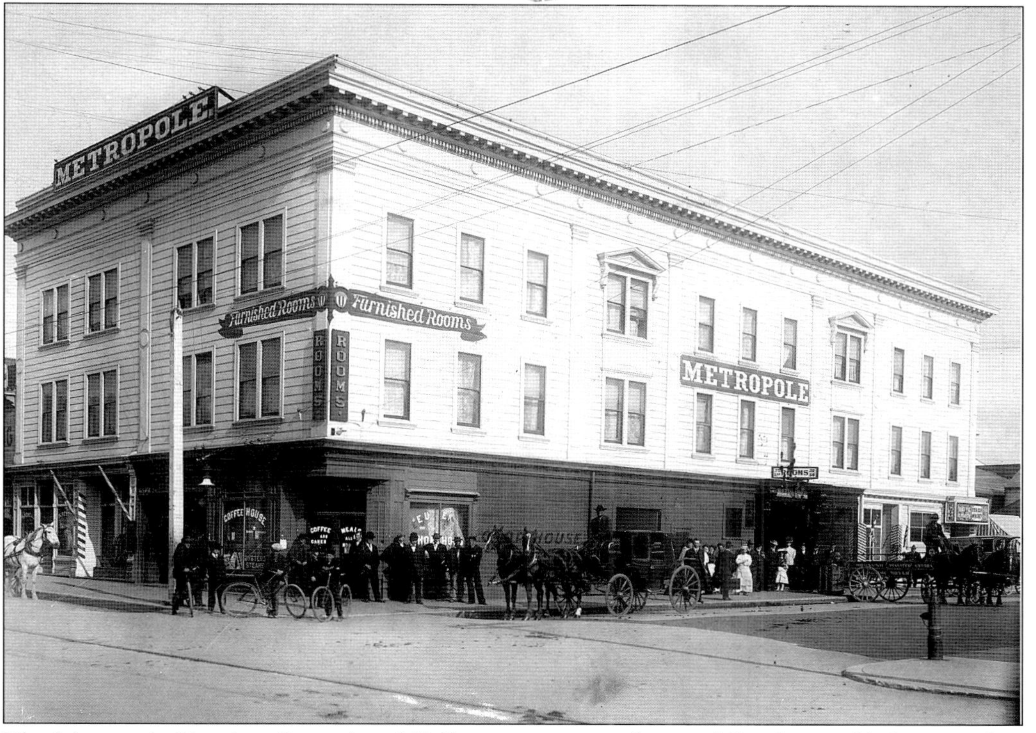

The Metropole Hotel at Second and D Streets was one of several Eureka establishments that catered to travelers and transient workers. It was revamped into apartments in the 1970s, and its exterior looks much the same today.

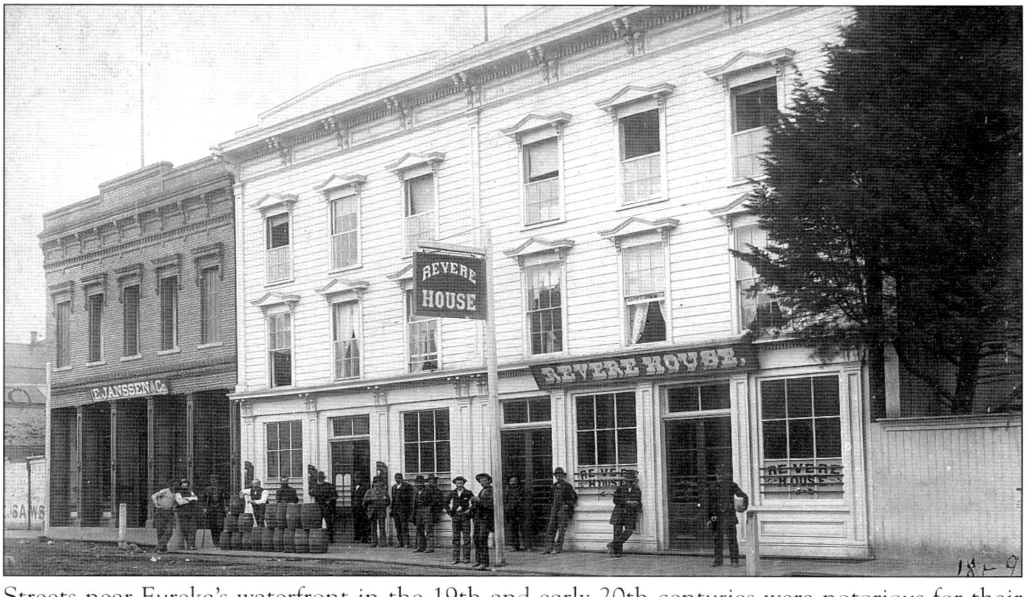

Streets near Eureka's waterfront in the 19th and early 20th centuries were notorious for their many saloons and brothels. Patrons of the more respected Revere House on First Street between F and E pose among beer and wine kegs in the 1890s.

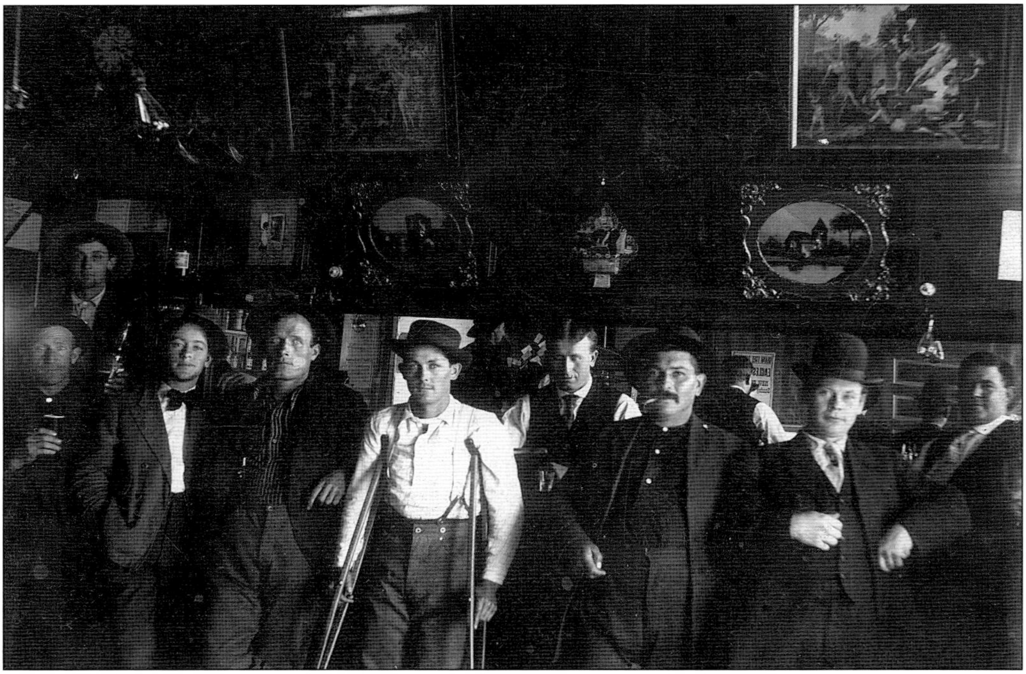

Customers at this turn-of-the century Eureka saloon are identified as Bob Ruseau, Bill Brandt, Amos McKinney (called Candy Kid), Bill Underwood, Charles Goodwin, Tony Kness (bartender), Job Montgomery, John Swanson, and Tom (?). Note the opulent examples of "saloon art."

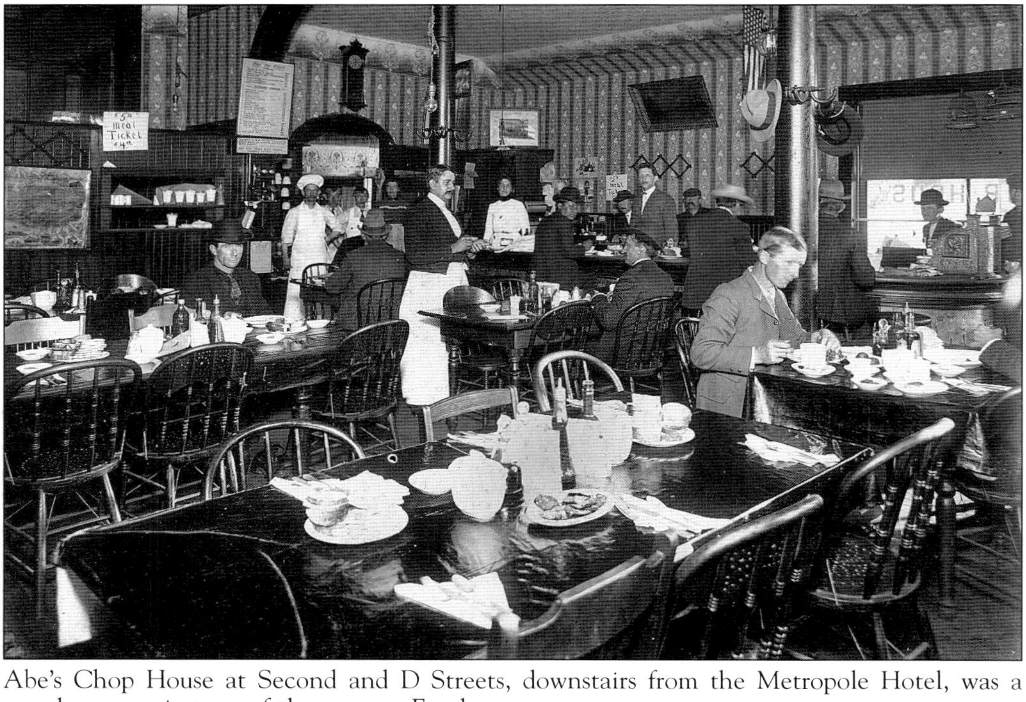

Abe's Chop House at Second and D Streets, downstairs from the Metropole Hotel, was a popular eatery in turn-of-the-century Eureka.

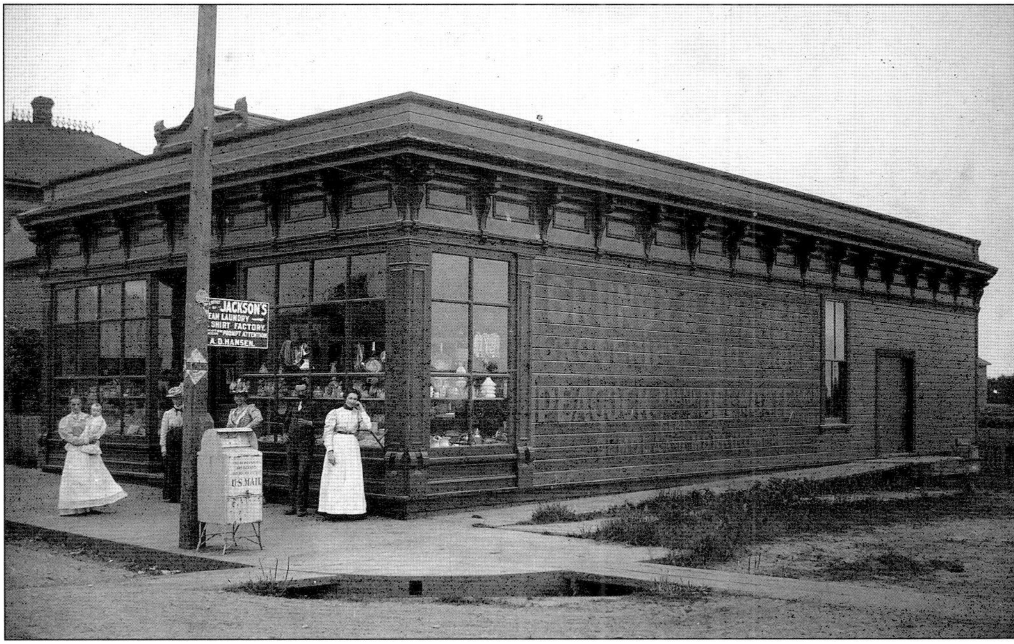

Mel Grundt's grocery store on Myrtle Avenue served the expanding eastern portion of Eureka around the turn of the century. A mailbox also marks the neighborhood significance of this corner.

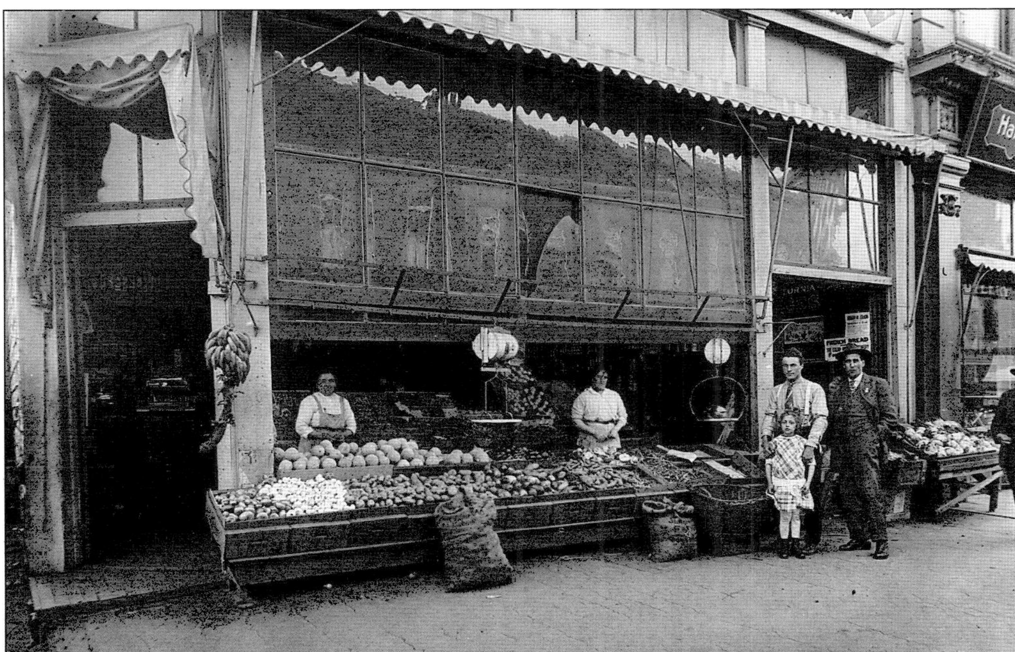

Italians were among the nationalities that contributed to Humboldt's commercial activity. The Diamond Fruit Company on Eureka's F Street between Fourth and Fifth had a typical open front. The four people on the left in this 1910 photo are identified as Mrs. Frigosa, Mrs. Teresa Rosaia, Mr. Rosaia, and their daughter.

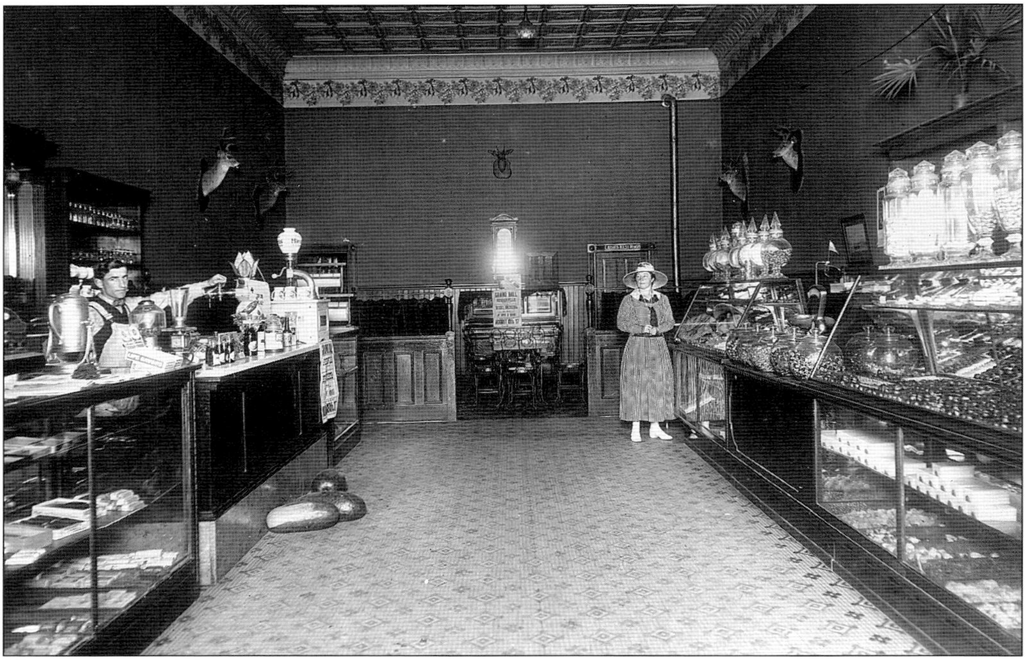

Under its high pressed-tin ceiling, the Mills Candy Store in Ferndale around 1915 sold watermelon as well as candy and also boasted a small soda fountain.

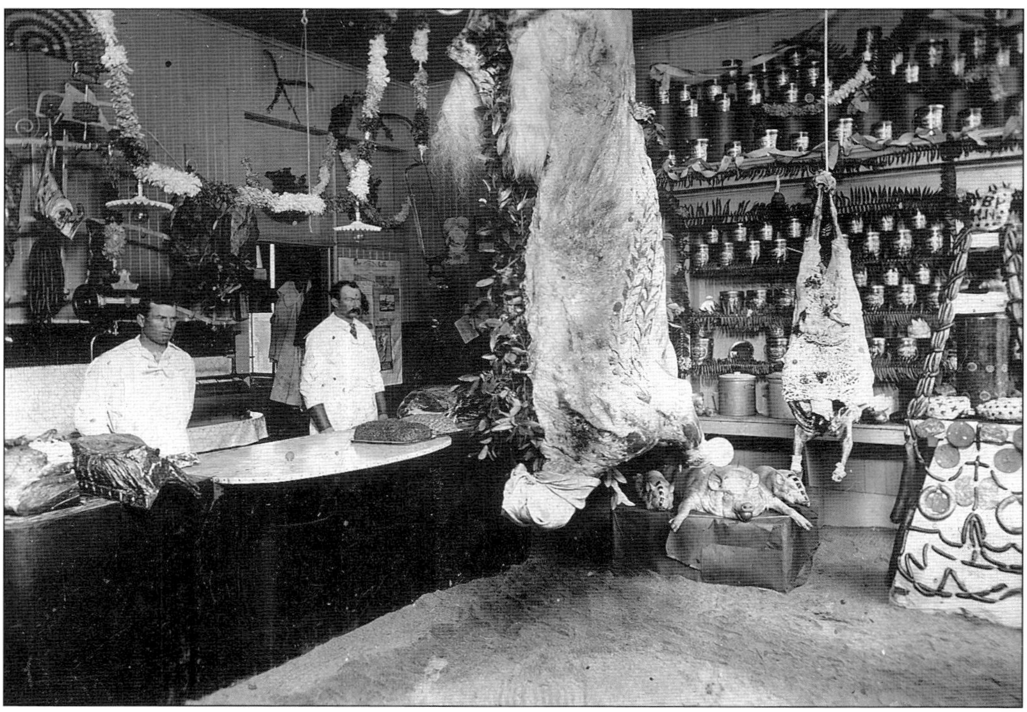

The Fortuna Meat Market offered canned lard, whole carcasses, and decoratively displayed sausages.

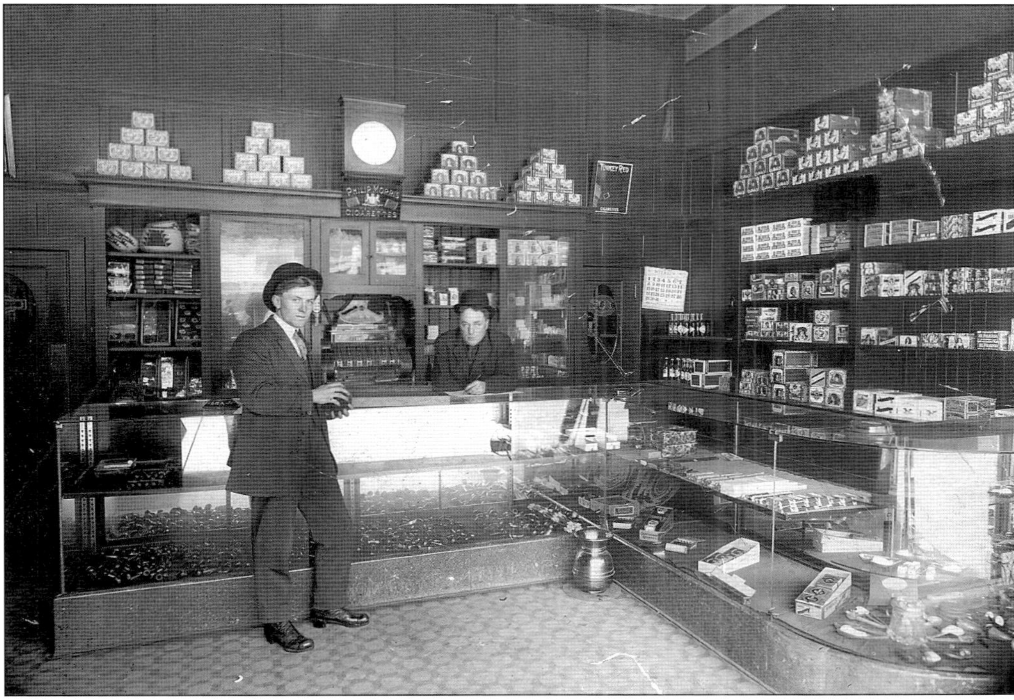

A spittoon was important to the early-20th-century customers of McDonough's Cigar Store in Eureka.

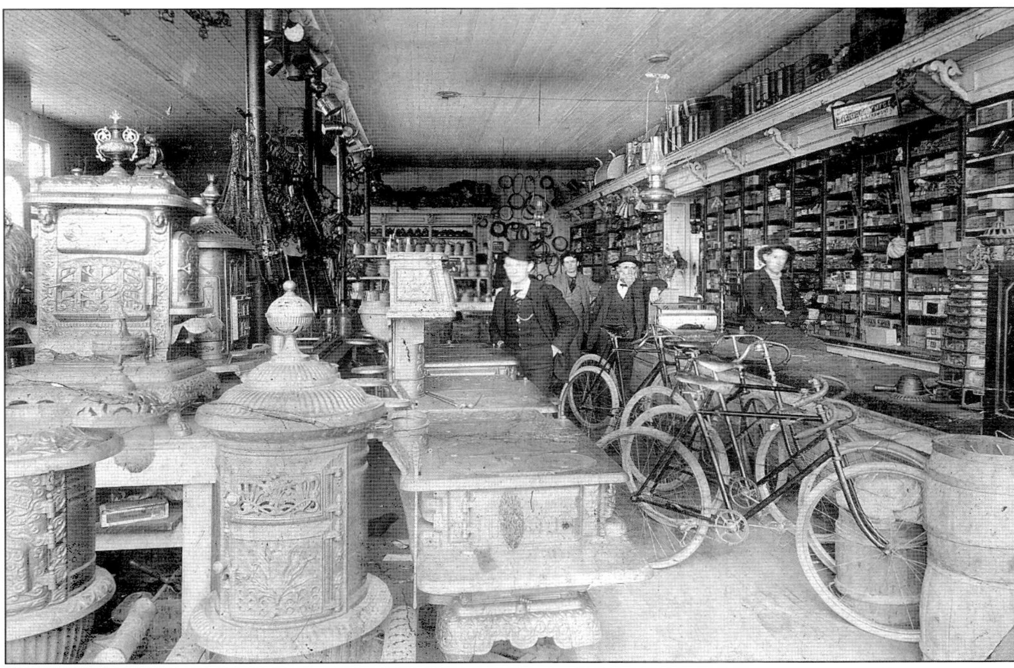

This early-20th-century Eureka hardware store used every available space to sell everything from coffee pots and nails to stoves and bicycles.

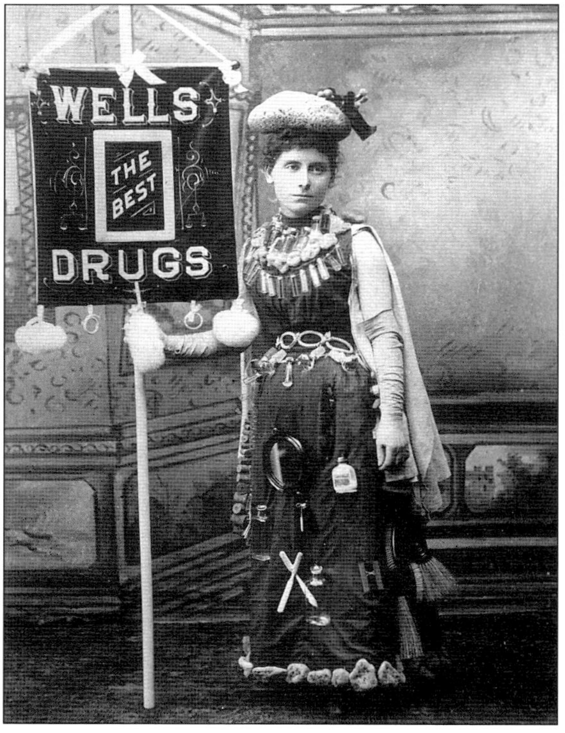

In the late 19th century, Wells Drug Store on F Street in Eureka used this unique way to advertise its merchandise.

Around 1915, Miss Mary Prosser tries a hat on a customer in her millenary shop at 428 F Street in Eureka.

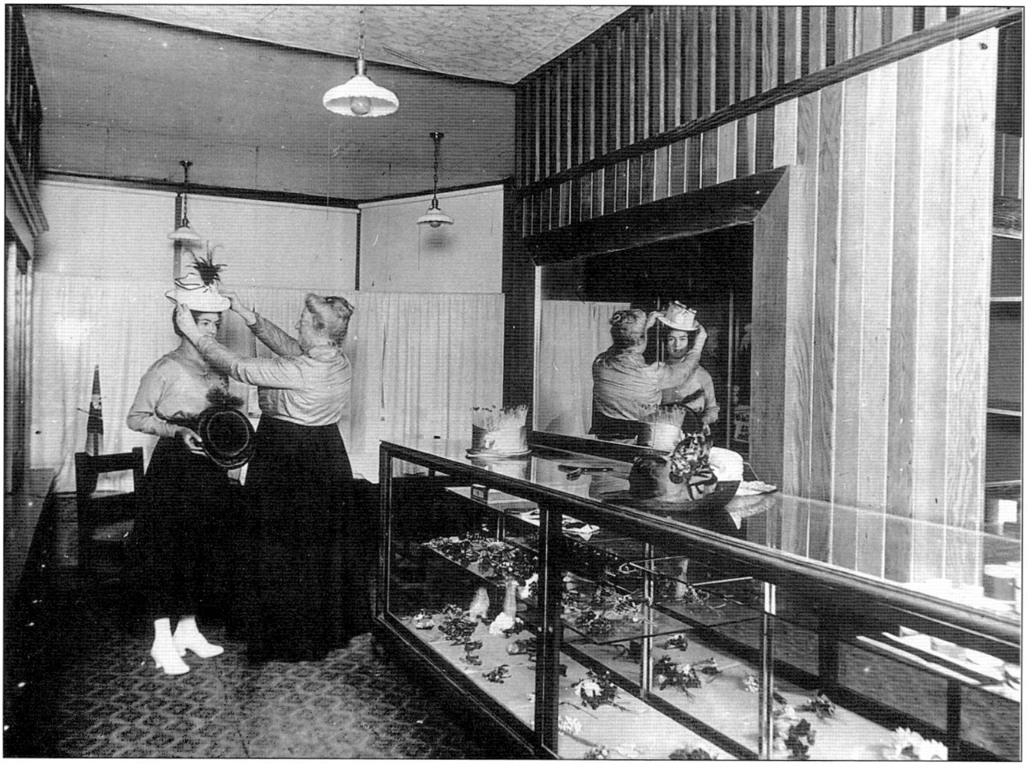

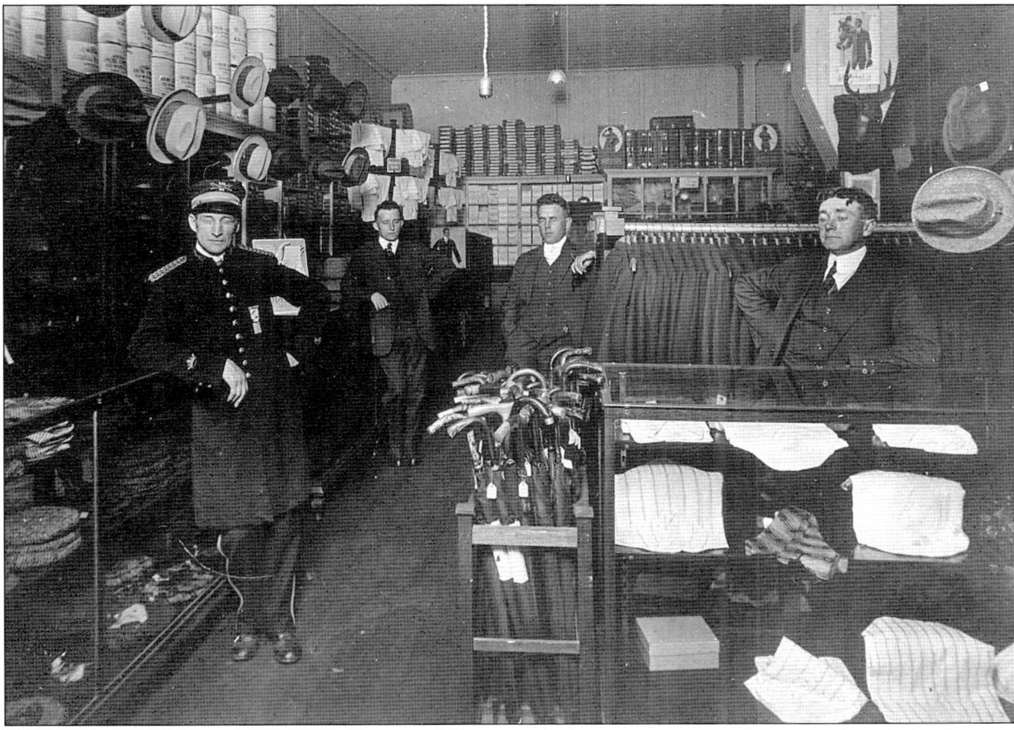

During a 1916 convention of Oddfellows in Eureka, a conventioneer visits the A.A. Canepa Clothing store. The employees are identified as Mr. Rutledge, Lawrence Canepa, and Archie Canepa.

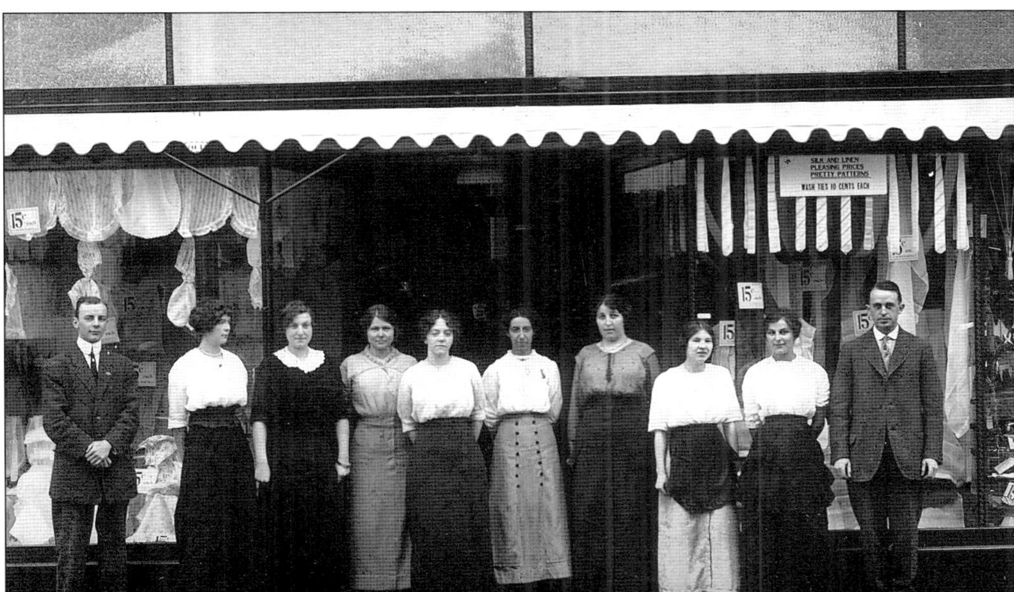

Employees in front of Eureka's new Woolworth's store at F and Third Streets pose for its grand opening.

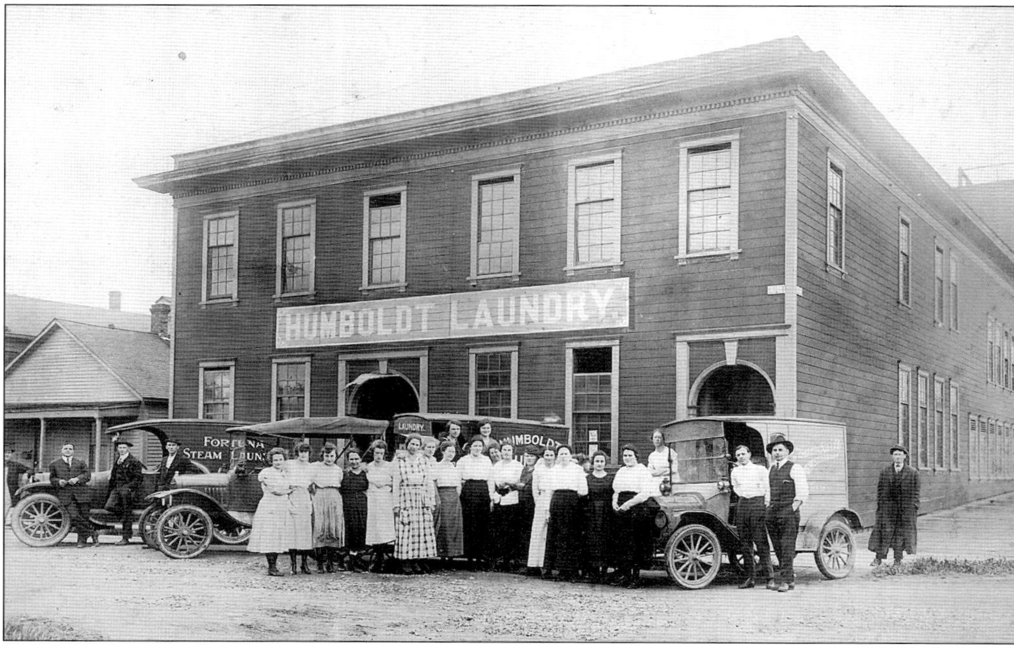

Fortuna's Humboldt Laundry employees are photographed with their delivery fleet around 1910.

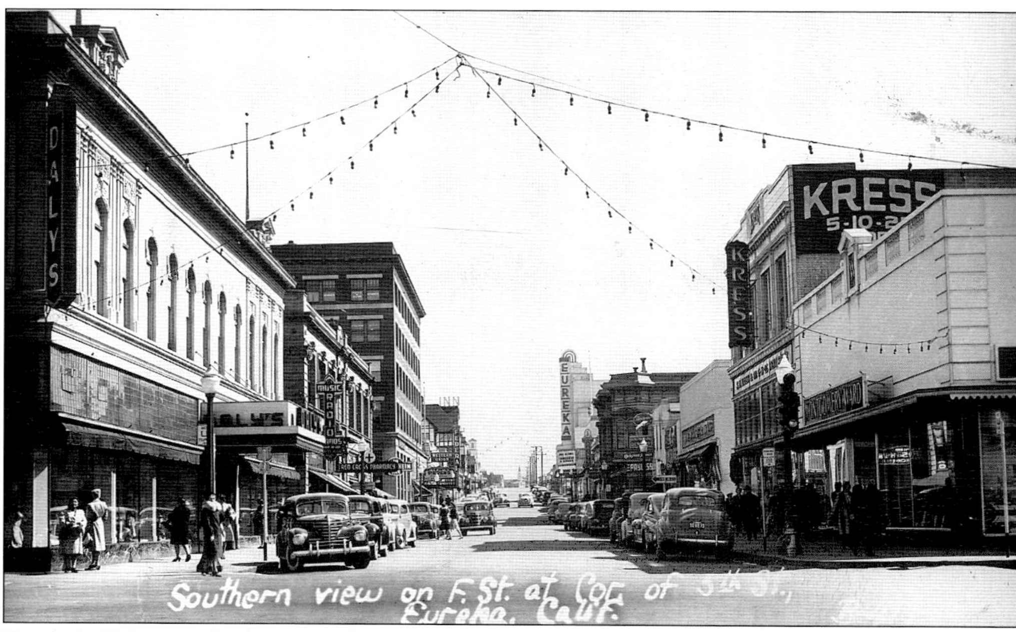

Eureka's F Street, looking south from Fourth Street, is strung with lights for a Christmas shopping season in the early 1940s.

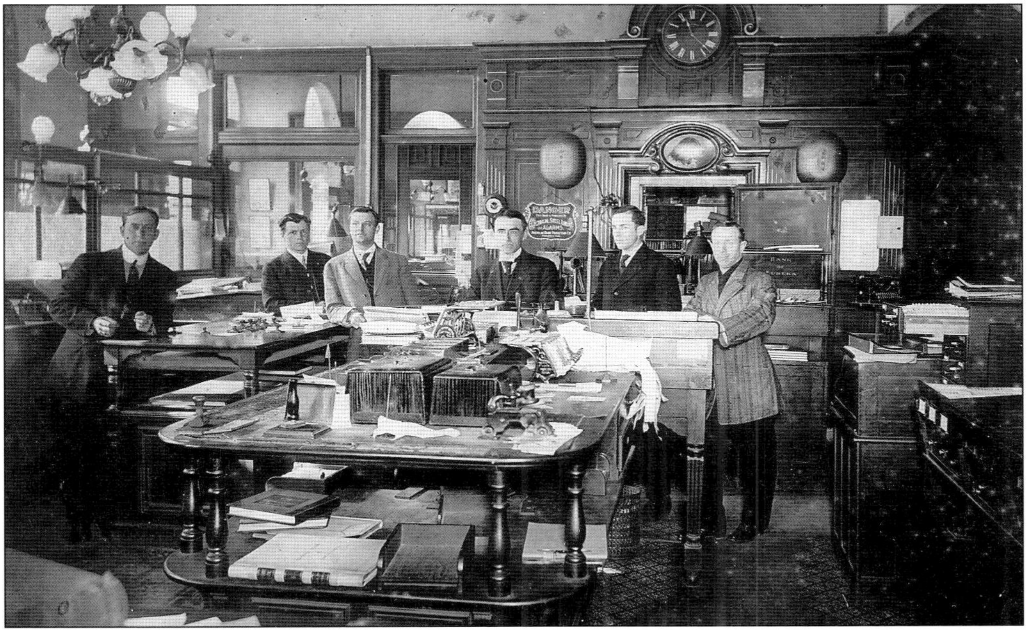

The staff of the Bank of Eureka poses around 1910 as they contemplated construction of their new, grander building on the same site.

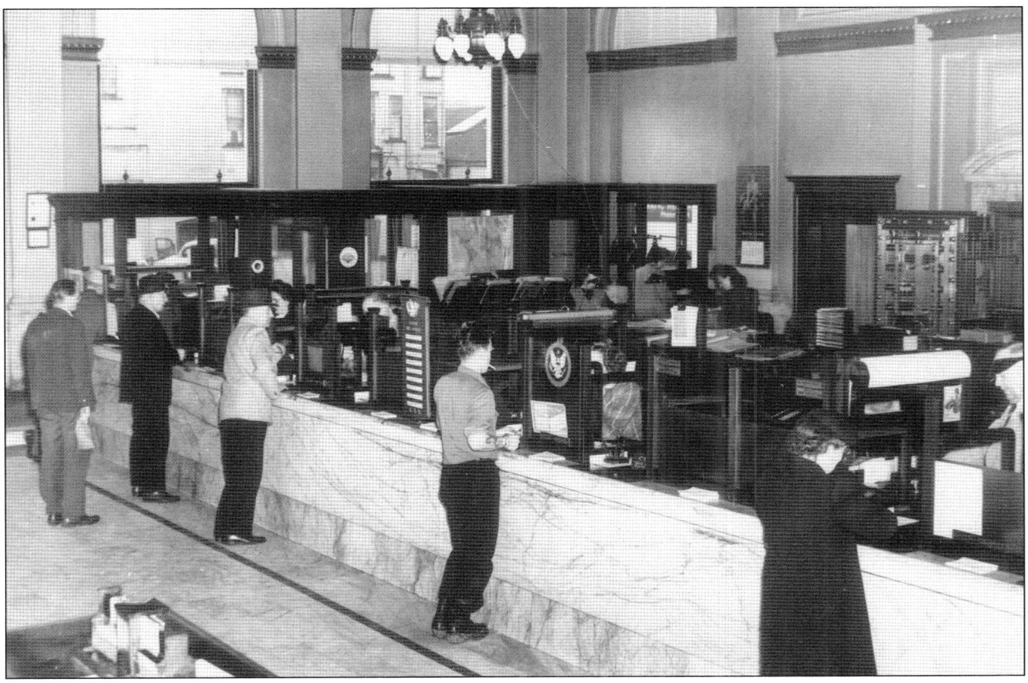

In 1912, the Bank of Eureka moved across Third Street from a temporary location back to 240 E Street. Designed by San Francisco architect Albert Pissis, the new structure was built of granite and marble and was faced with glazed terra cotta tiles that were packed and shipped in from the Sacramento area with great care. This photo was taken in the 1940s.

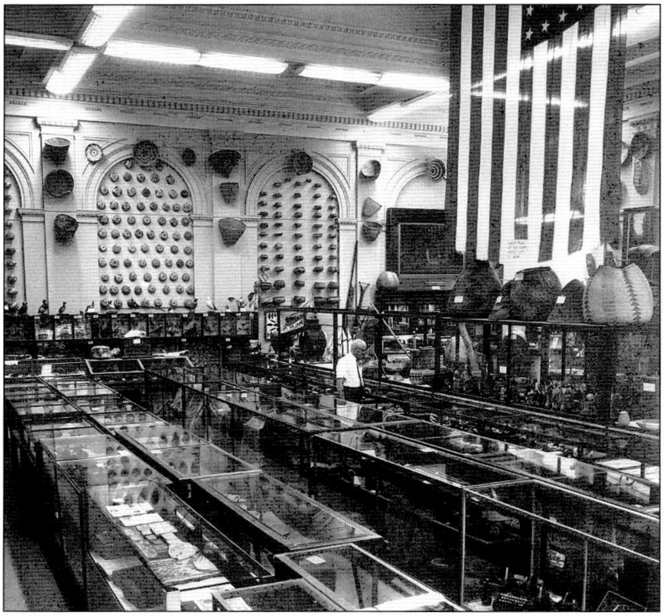

In 1960, retired Eureka school teacher Cecile Clarke purchased the former bank building for her museum which for years had been housed at Eureka High School. Since then, the collection has grown, and in 1979 an annex was added to house the extensive Native American collection. Changing exhibits in the main hall are now designed according to more contemporary museum standards.

This 1890 studio photograph shows the staff of what was then Eureka's leading newspaper, *The Humboldt Daily Standard*.

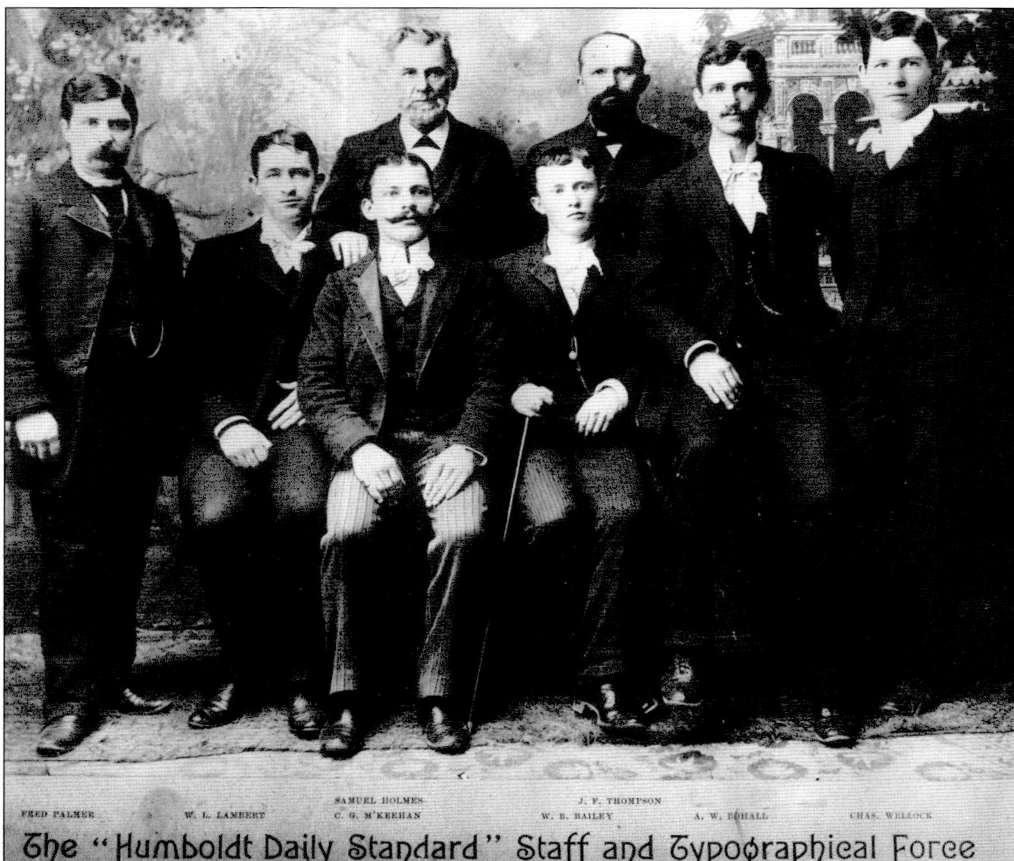

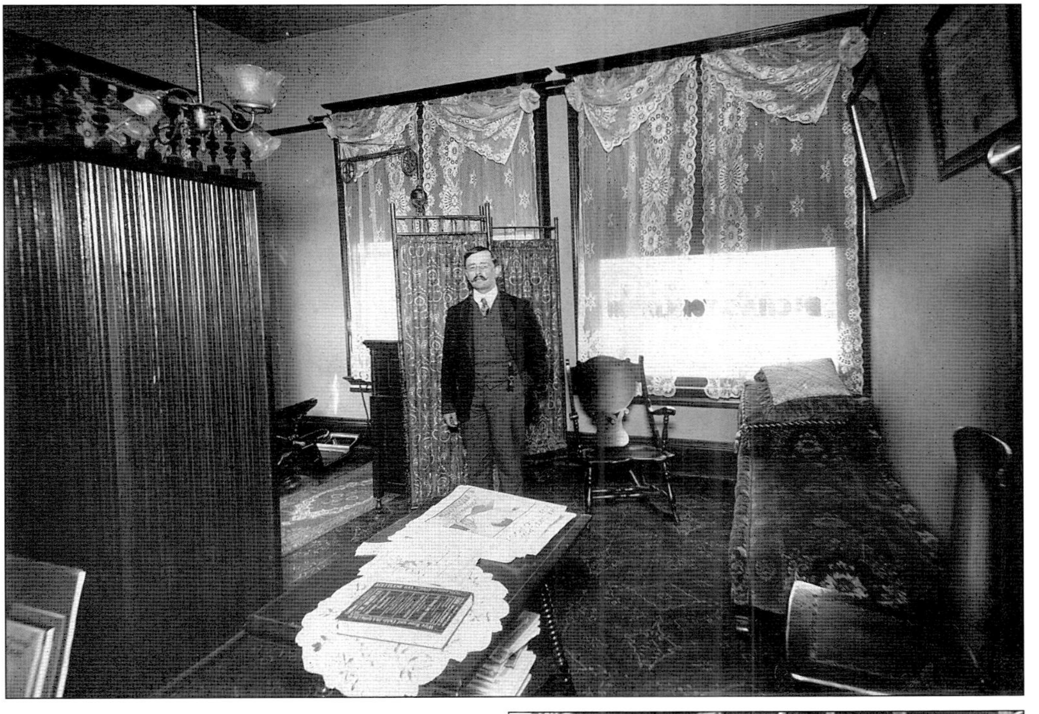

Dr. Charles Tomlinson's dental office at Fourth and E Streets in Eureka included a "fainting couch" in the waiting room. Note the chandeliers that were both gas and electric.

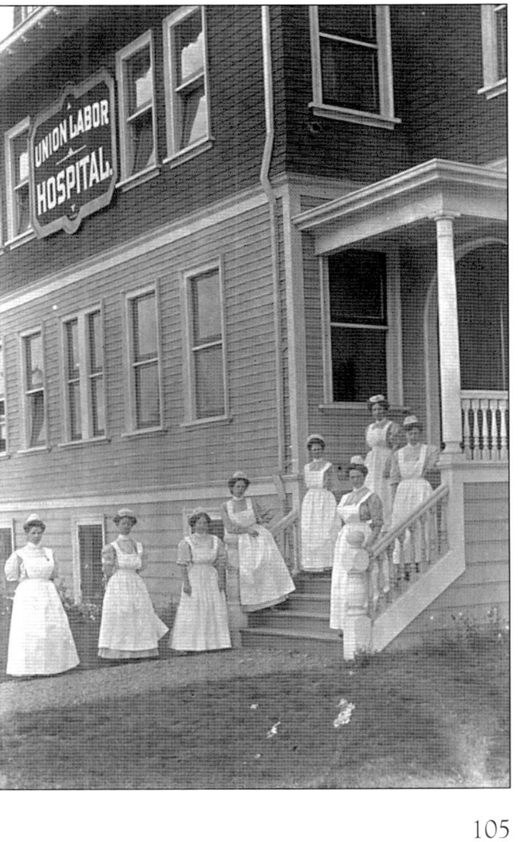

Eureka's Union Labor Hospital was founded in 1906 to serve loggers and mill workers who bought insurance to cover illness or accidents in businesses they frequented. The hospital went on to become General Hospital, which was taken over by St. Joseph's Hospital in 2000. This original building is now a county office complex.

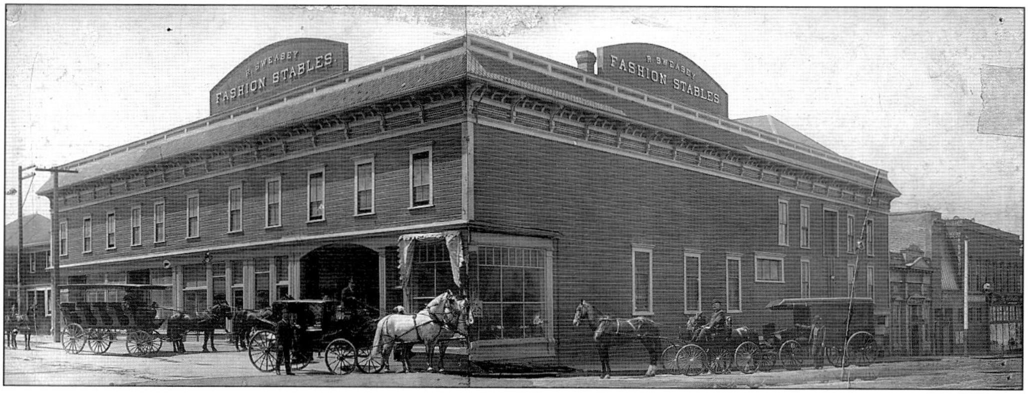

The Sweasey Fashion Stable at the corner of Fourth and G Streets was a grand establishment in turn-of-the-century Eureka.

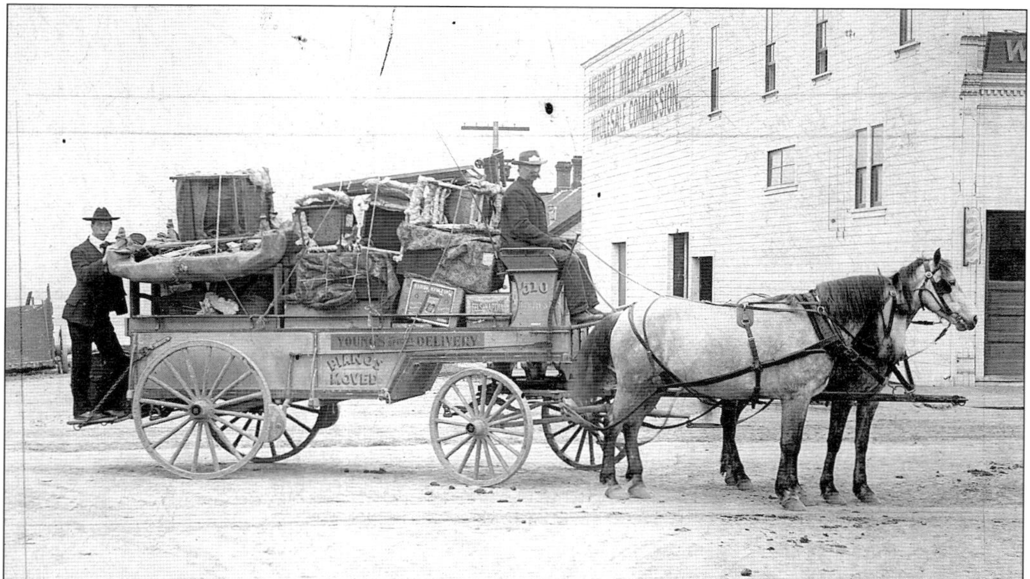

Young's Special Delivery of Eureka claimed it could move pianos and everything else. J.H. Young is riding in the back and the driver is Jim Yates.

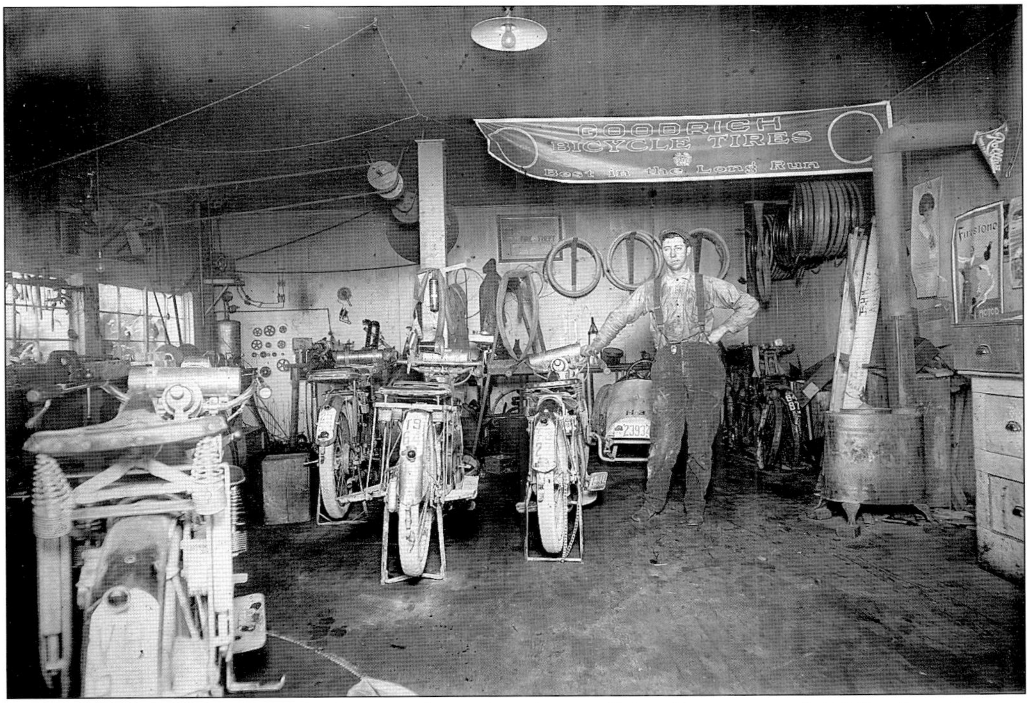

B.H. Moore was photographed at work in the Arcata Bike Shop around 1915 when he was particularly busy with motorcycles.

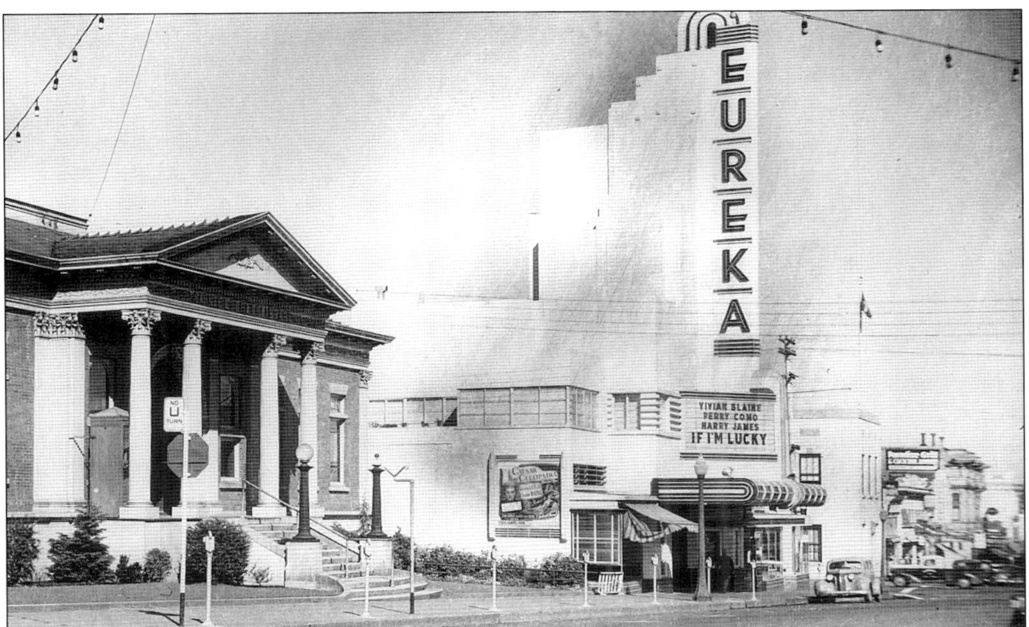

The Eureka Theater, a fine example of "streamline moderne" architecture, opened in 1939 on F Street next to the Carnegie Library. The library building is now an art museum and the theater is renovated as a community performing arts center.

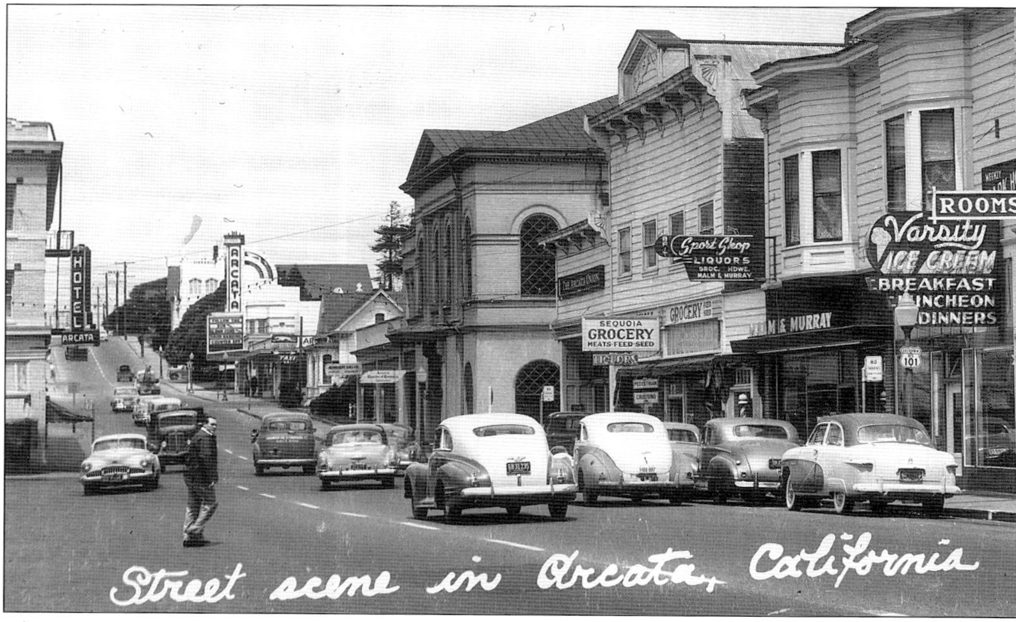

The Arcata Theater, another "streamline moderne" movie theater, is shown in this 1940s Arcata street scene. The streetscape looks much the same today except that the building with the arched windows, the Arcata City Hall, which was built on the corner of Ninth and G Streets in 1896, was demolished in 1971.

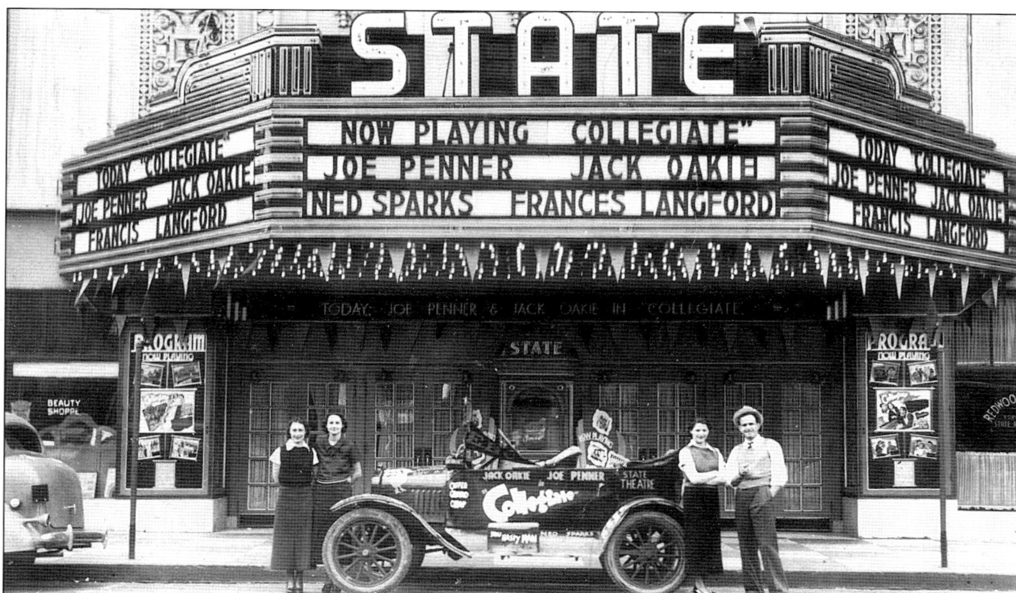

This 1930s photo shows that the State Theater on G Street in Eureka, like many theaters of the times, put on special attention-getting promotions for its films. Also designed for vaudeville shows, it was Eureka's premier "movie palace." Built in 1920, the State's interior later suffered from fire and was renovated to become part of the large Daly's Department Store. At the time of this printing, the entire complex stands vacant.

Eight

Humboldt Images

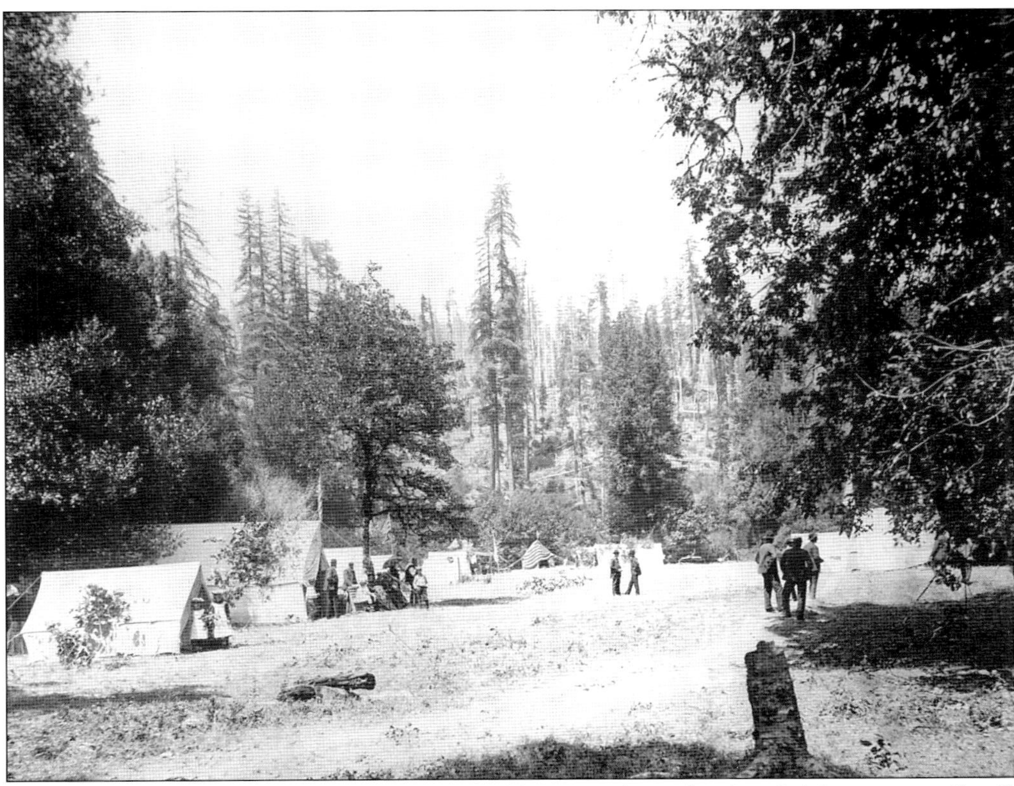

Although Humboldt County was well removed from Civil War battles, California was officially a Union state, and many war veterans settled here. This G.A.R. (Grand Army of the Republic) encampment for veterans was held on the North Fork of the Mad River in July of 1891.

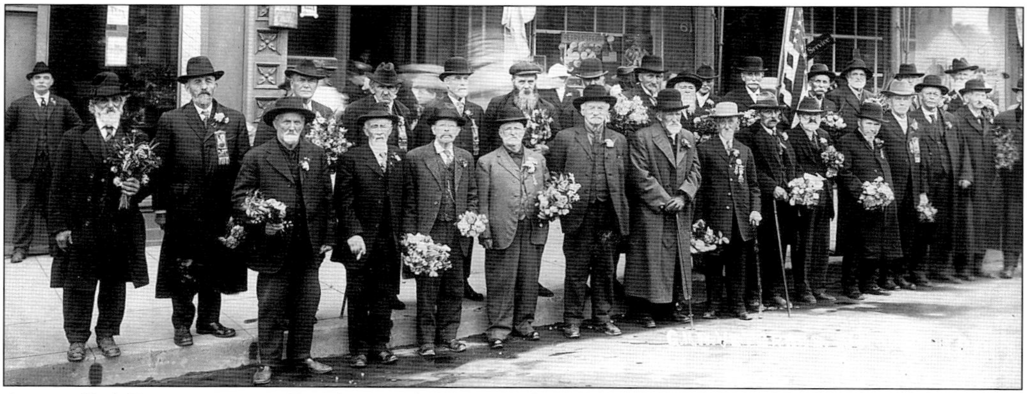

Aging G.A.R. veterans in Eureka mark Memorial Day, 1918.

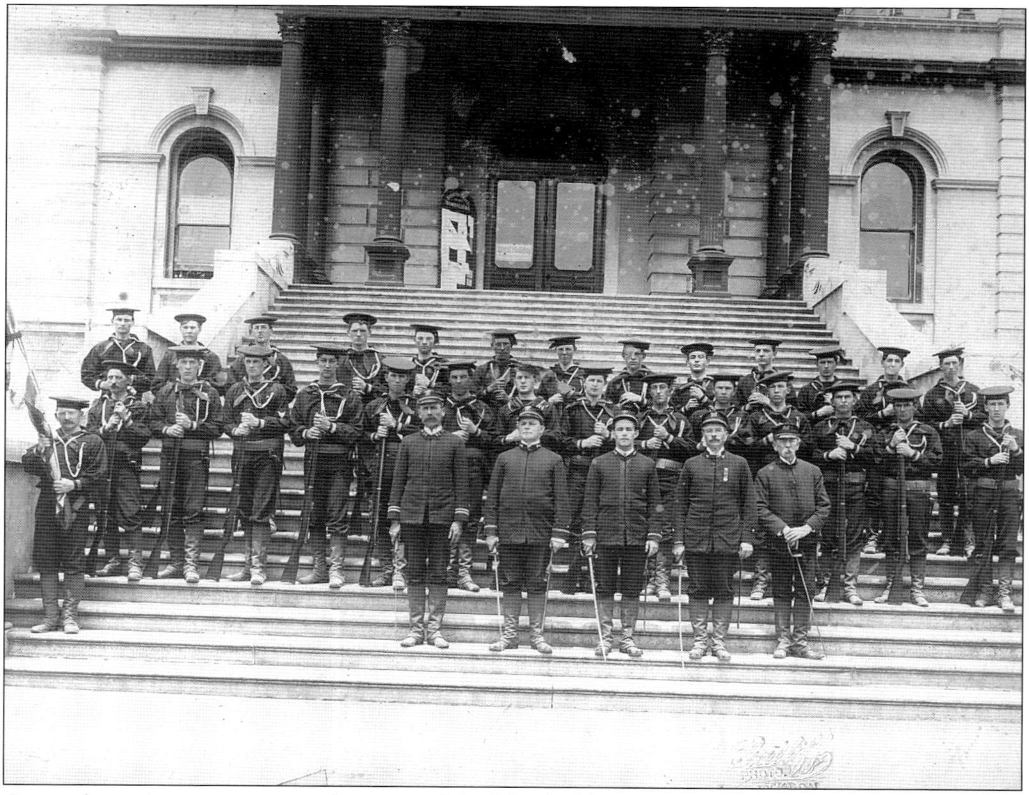

A naval contingent poses on the steps of the Humboldt County Courthouse around 1906.

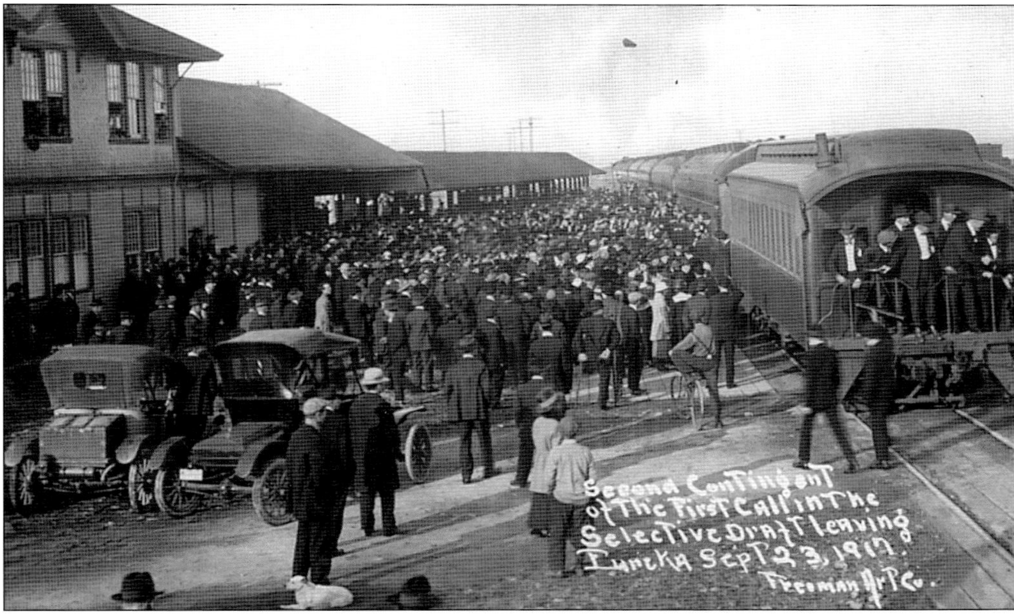

On Sept. 23, 1917, the Eureka depot was crowded with families and well wishers as the second contingent of the first selective service call departs for service in the First World War.

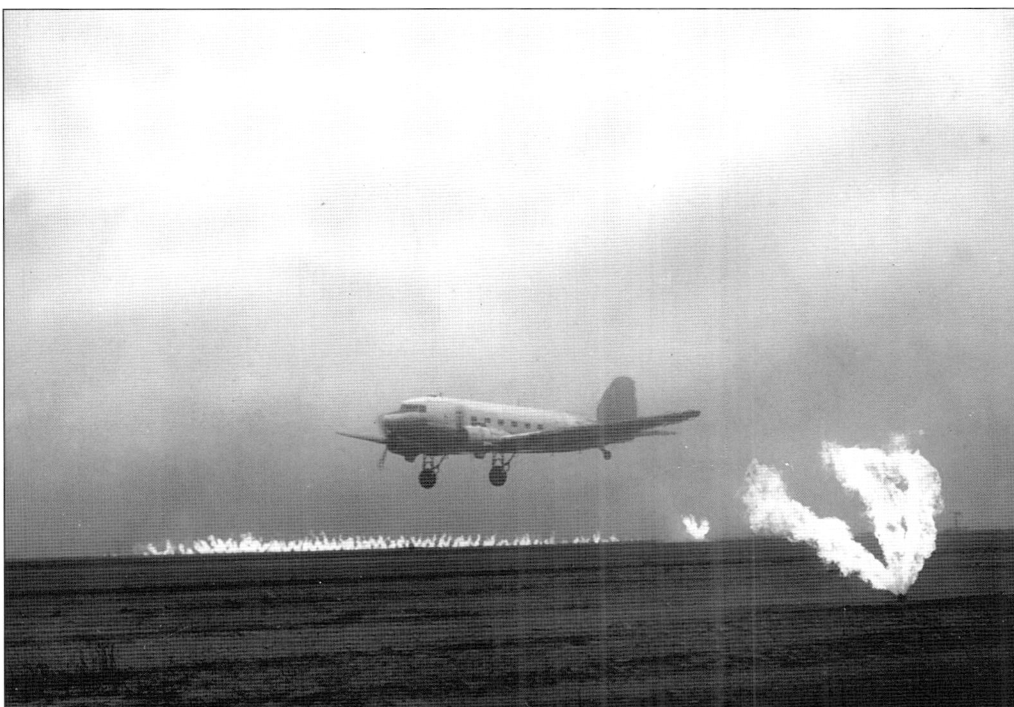

During the Second World War, the Eureka/Arcata airport was used for training U.S. military pilots to land and take off in fog. Gas flares were used as an experiment to improve visibility. The particularly long airstrip built at that time is still in use today for commercial flights.

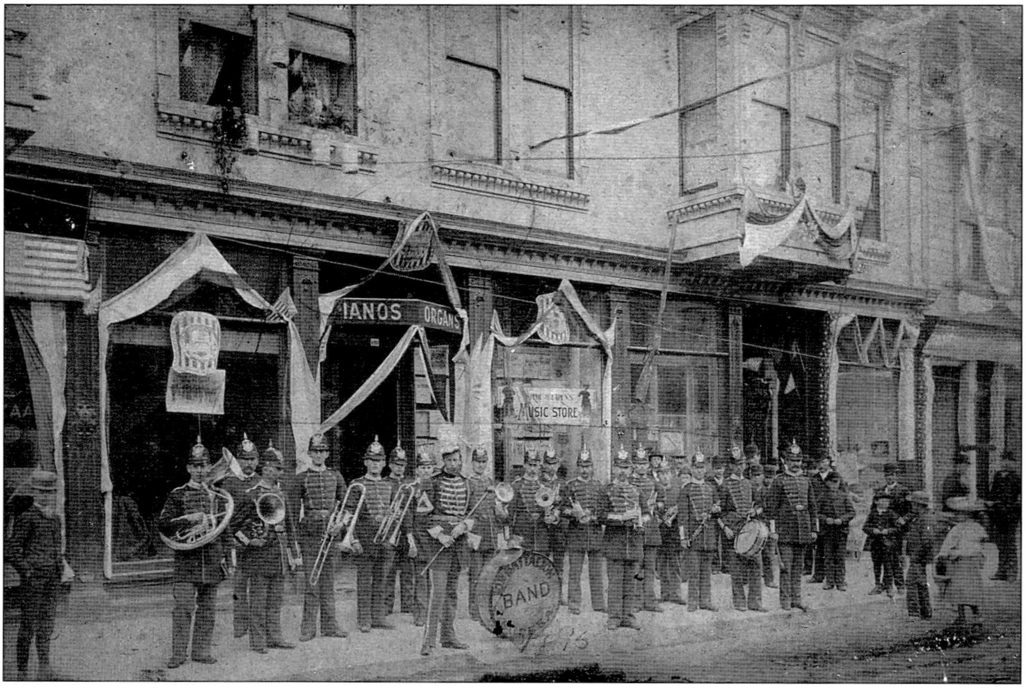

The 10th Battalion Band assembles for 1895's Fourth of July celebrations in front of a Third Street music store in Eureka.

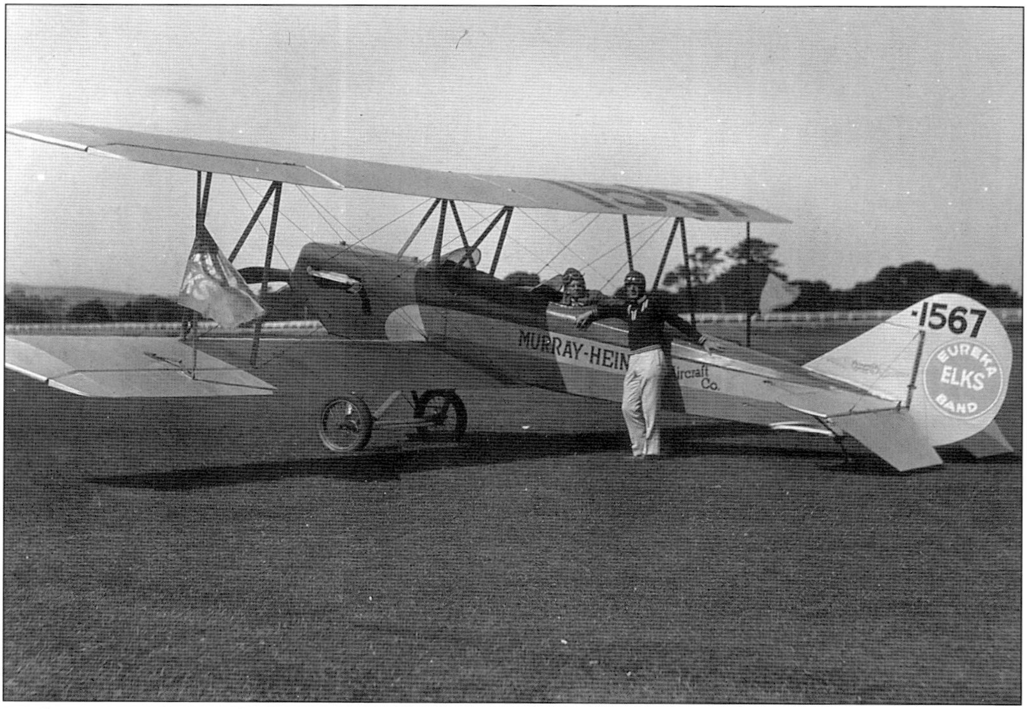

In the next century, the Eureka Elks Club Band had its own airplane.

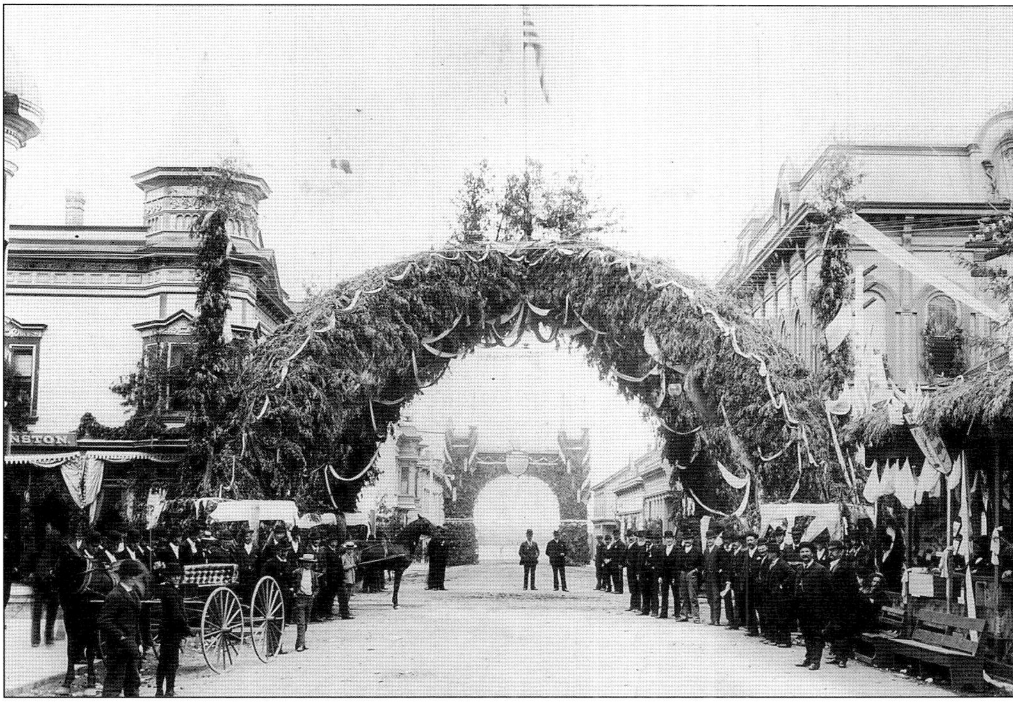

In redwood country, public celebrations often involved decorating with evergreen garlands and boughs. Here, people gather at Second and F Streets for the July 18, 1895 Sequoia Carnival.

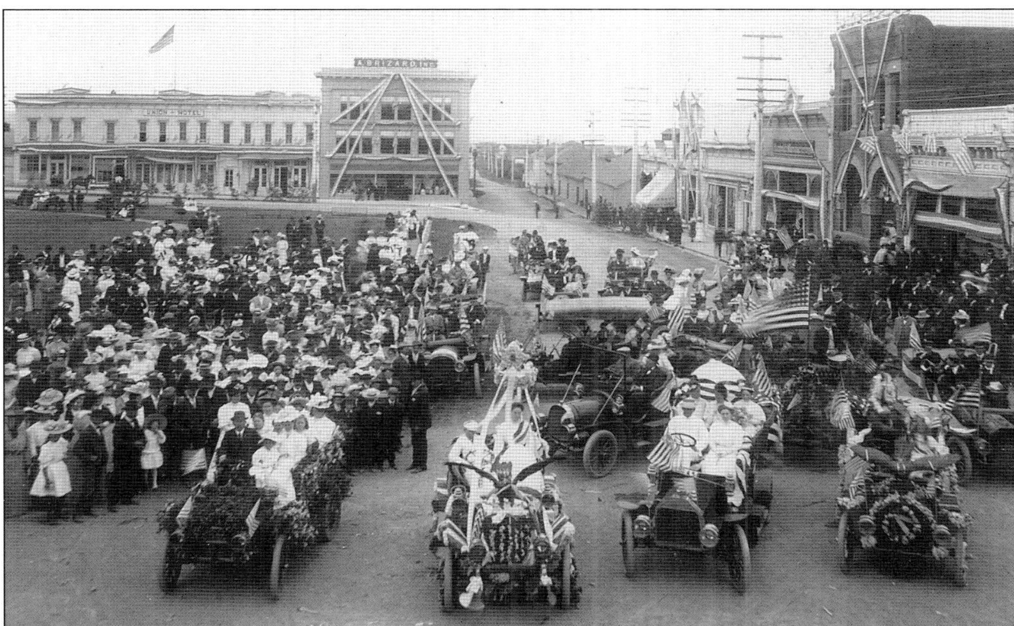

As Arcata readied itself for the 1908 Fourth of July celebrations, evergreens and flags festooned the plaza and the town's new automobiles. The Brizard store, important since Arcata's early days, was still a going concern, and the building remains a fixture of today's plaza.

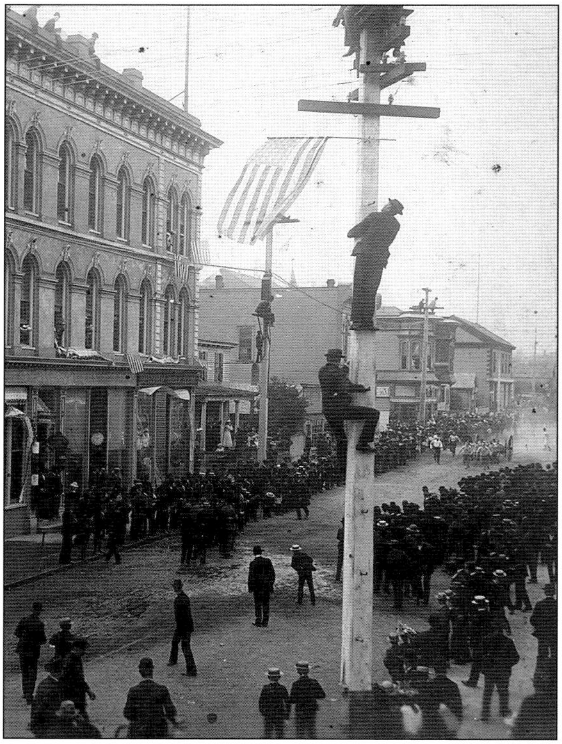

The annual Eureka volunteer fire department "hose cart race" drove some spectators on G Street up utility poles for a better view. Rival teams pulled the carts and competed to lay out and connect hoses that "threw water" in the shortest period of time.

For their "General Grant Days" celebrations, Eurekans dressed up in old-time clothes and men grew or applied beards and mustaches. Here employees of the Bank of Eureka pose during a 1930s celebration.

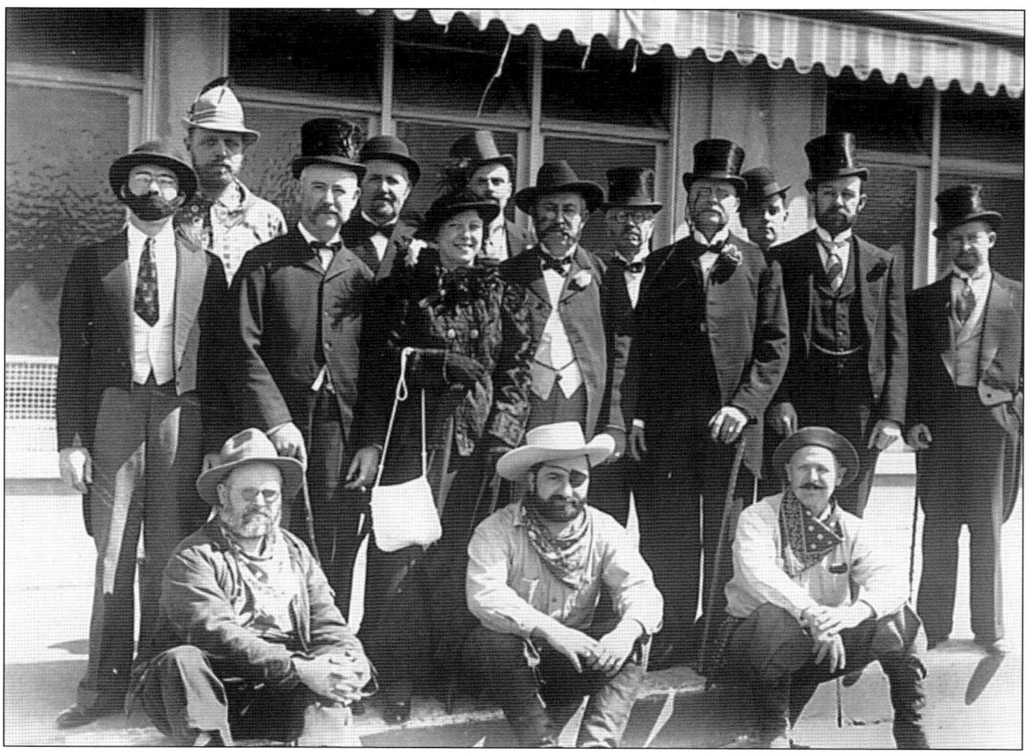

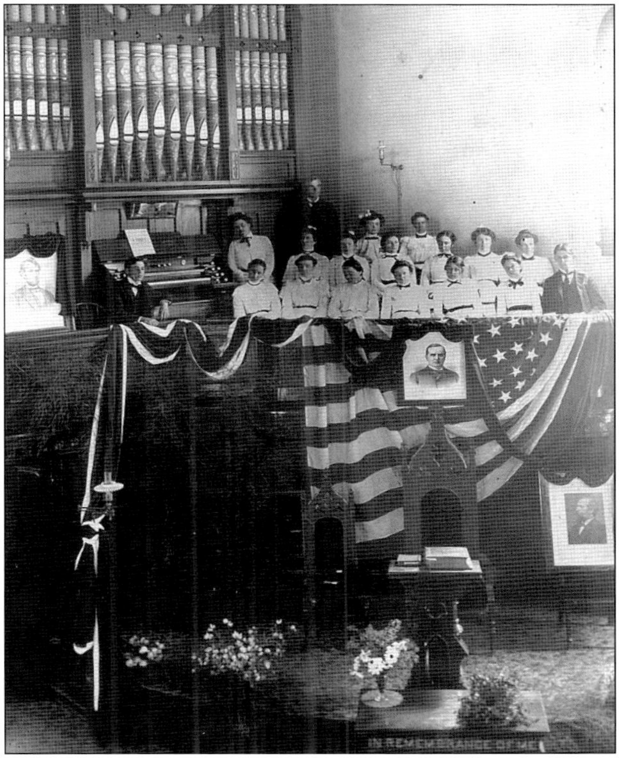

The memorial service for assassinated president William McKinley, who had been shot at an exposition in Buffalo, New York, drew a large crowd into Eureka's Congregational church on September 19, 1901.

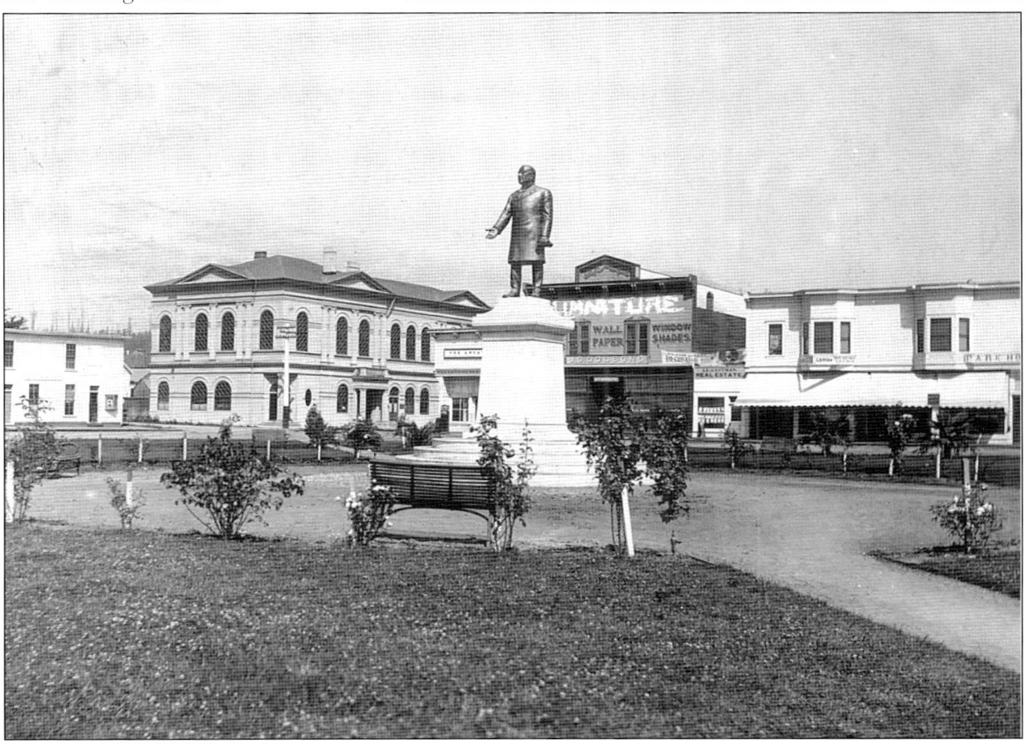

In the rush of public sentiment over McKinley's death, a bronze statue of the assassinated president was erected in the center of Arcata's plaza which has long served as a community gathering place. The statue was nearing completion in a San Francisco foundry when the 1906 earthquake hit. Dedicated workers pulled it from the foundry before the building burned.

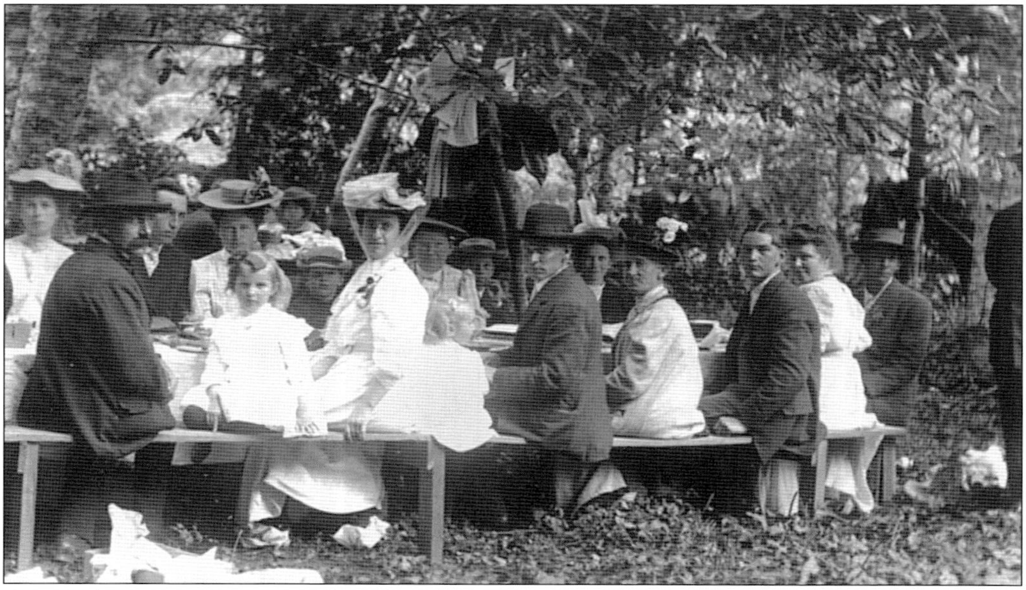

A special summer event in early 20th century in McKinleyville (the town was originally named after local businessman Isaac Minor) was the annual picnic for farming families. This photo was taken June 18, 1908.

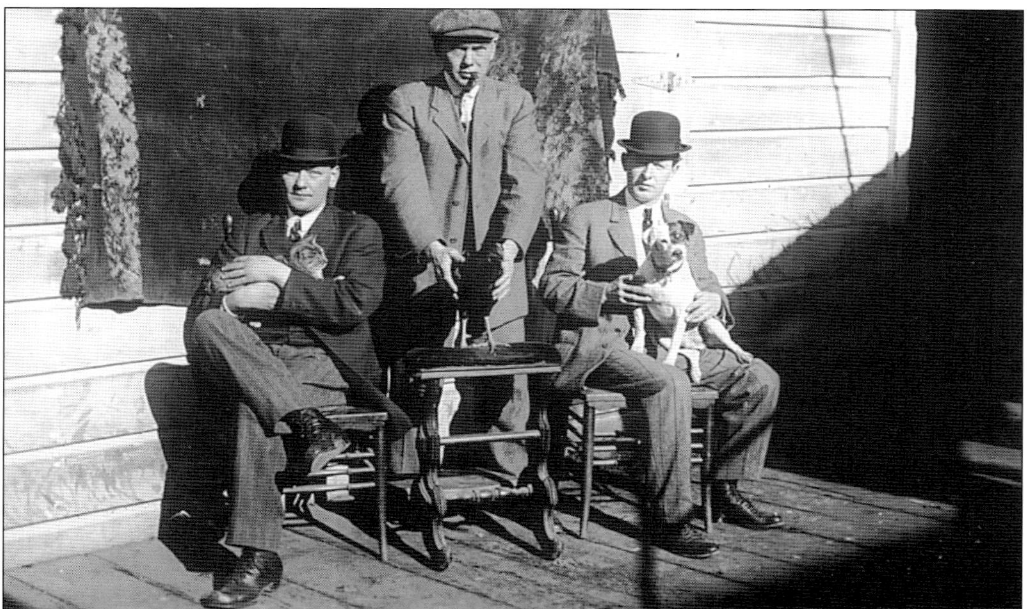

This photograph from around 1910 is identified only as "Little Willie and Family." But whether Little Willie is the cat, rooster, dog, or one of the gentlemen is not known.

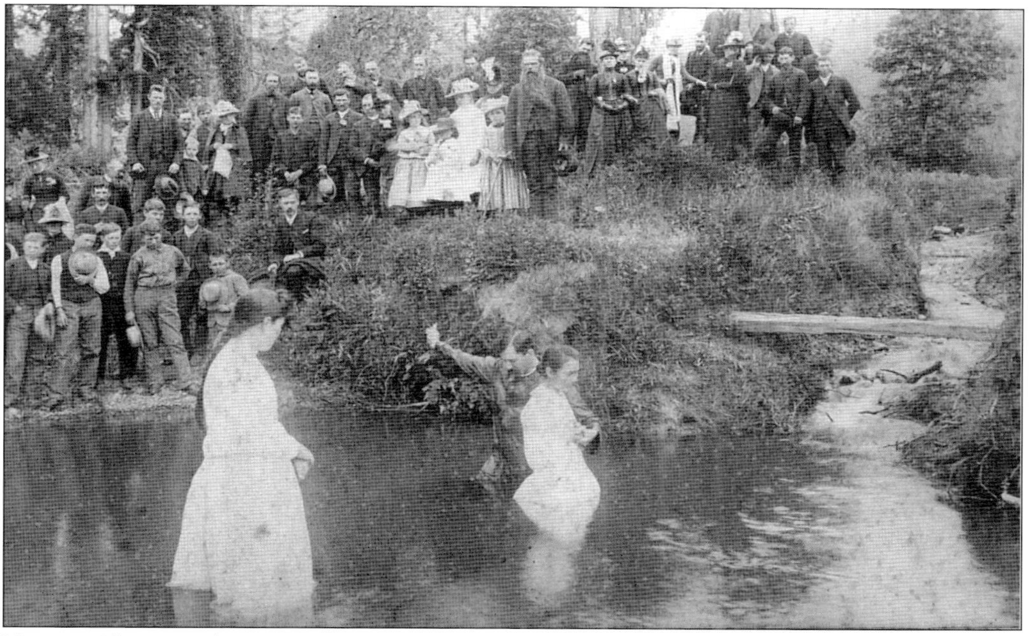

Various Christian denominations established themselves in Humboldt county, and the area's many rivers saw a number of baptisms. This service, probably in the 1890s, took place in the Mad River near Blue Lake.

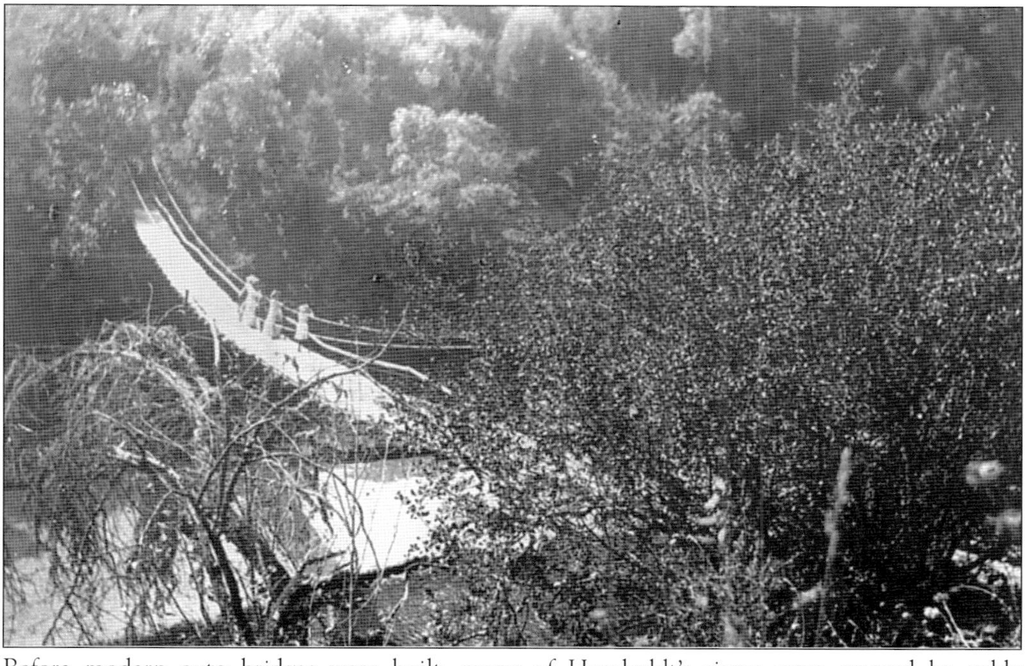

Before modern auto bridges were built, many of Humboldt's rivers were crossed by cable suspension bridges which even into the 20th century were regularly used by mule trains as well as pedestrians. This photo was taken near China Flat (modern Willow Creek) on the Trinity River around 1909.

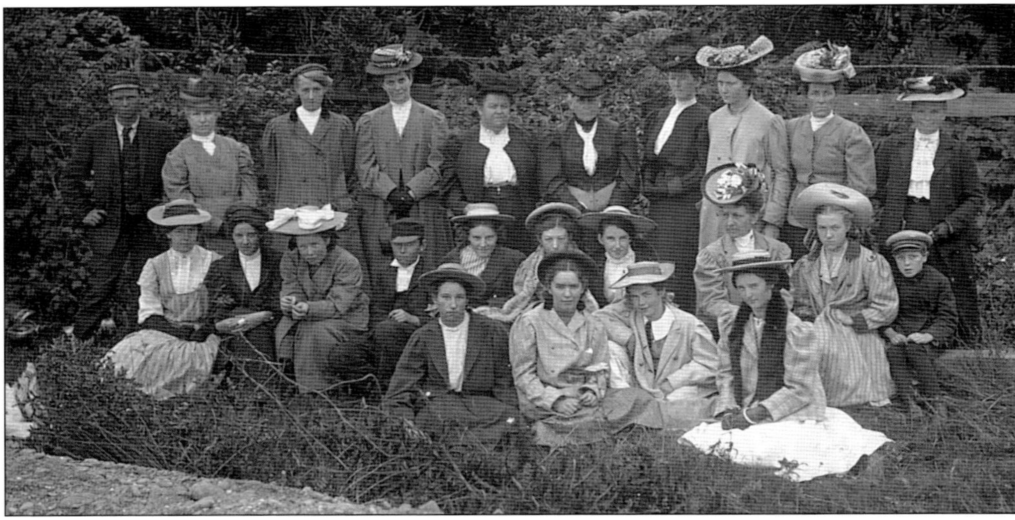

Around the turn of the last century, these young men and women gathered for a huckleberry picking party at the north end of Humboldt Bay.

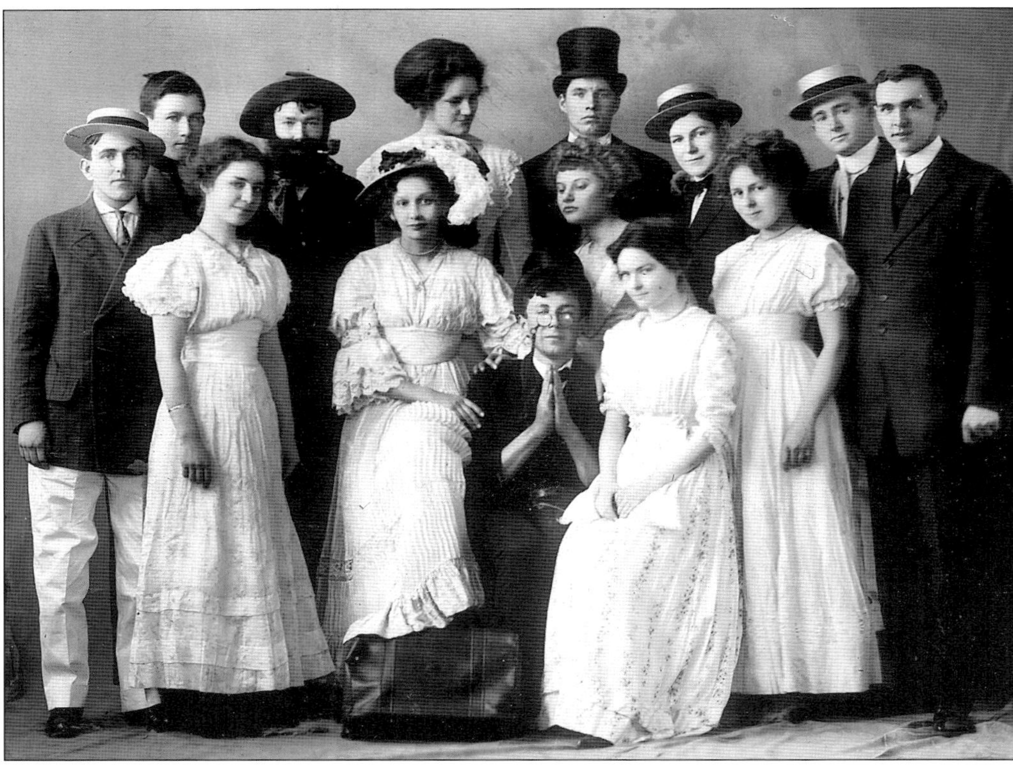

In Humboldt County towns large enough for high schools, school sporting and artistic activities were major community events. In this photo taken around 1910, the cast of a Eureka High School play assembles on the stage of the town's Ingomar Theater. This theater was built by William Carson and between 1892 and 1912 was considered the finest in the city. Though much altered, the theater space is still used by community theater groups for auditions and rehearsals.

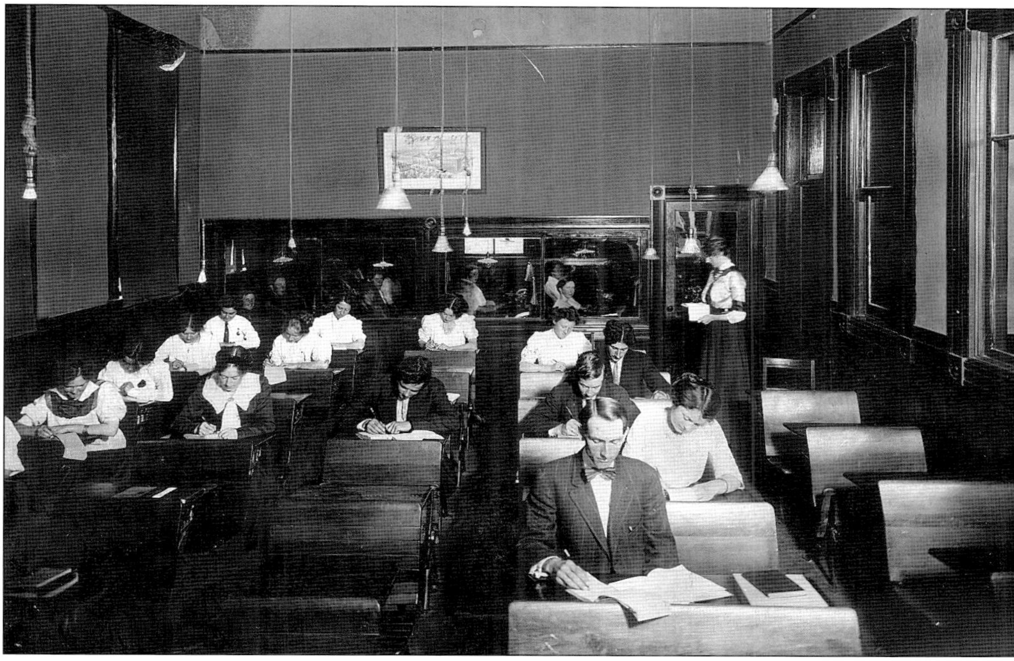

For those planning a business career, Humboldt County's principal school was the Eureka Business College. In this photo taken around 1910, students in front work on shorthand while those in the back room practice on typewriters. The building is still standing at Second and E Streets in Eureka.

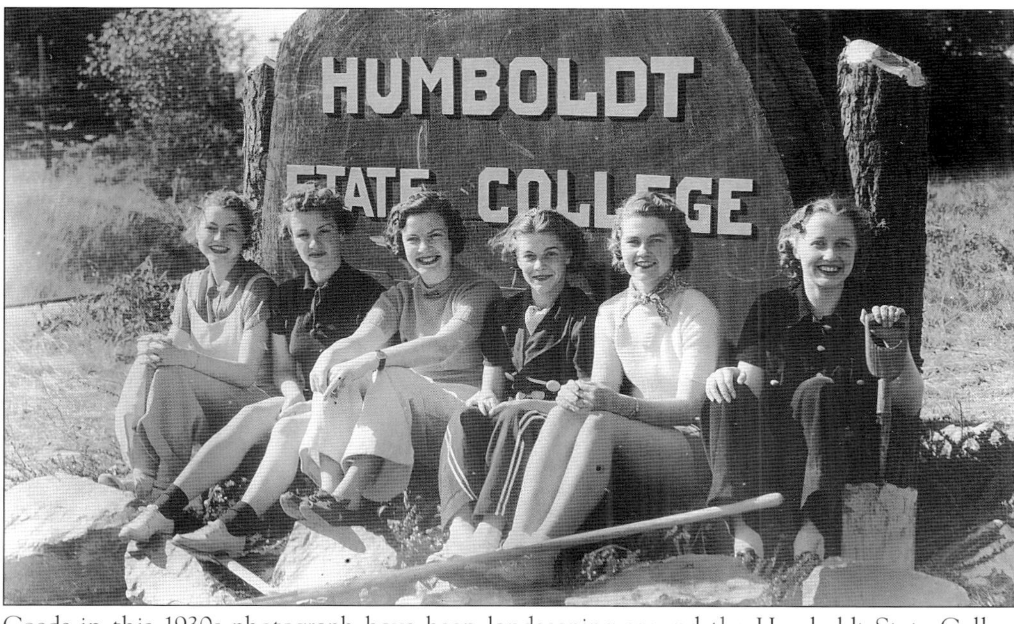

Coeds in this 1930s photograph have been landscaping around the Humboldt State College entry sign. The Arcata institution started in 1914 as a Normal School or teacher's college and now has become Humboldt State University. Its presence in Arcata gives the community a special "college town" character.

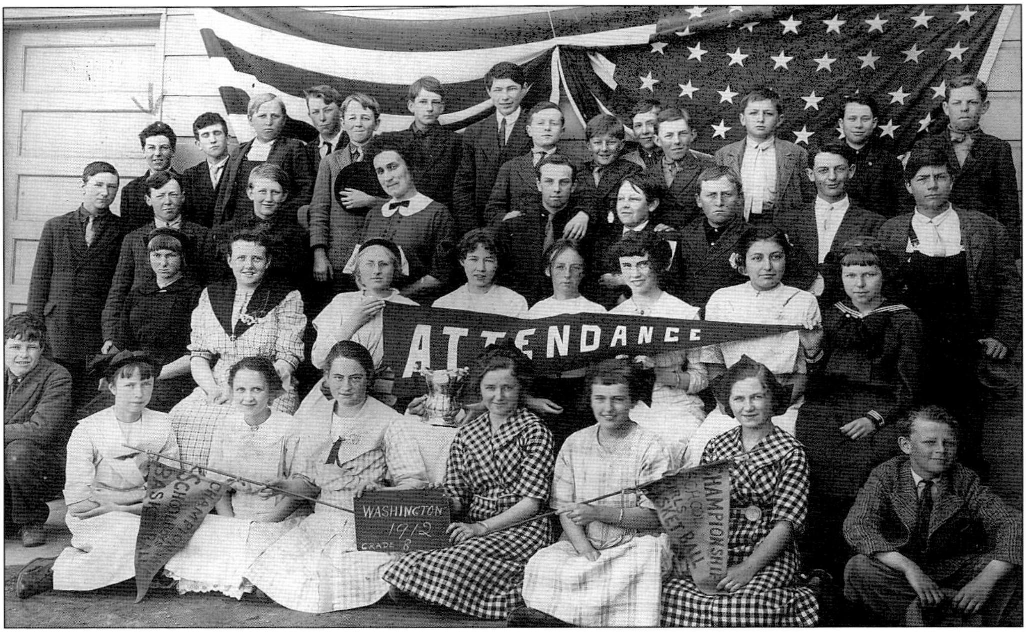

Every school had its yearly school pictures. Here the 1912 eighth grade at Eureka's Washington School poses with their banners for attendance and for the boys' and girls' basketball championships. The school building on California Street is now a senior center.

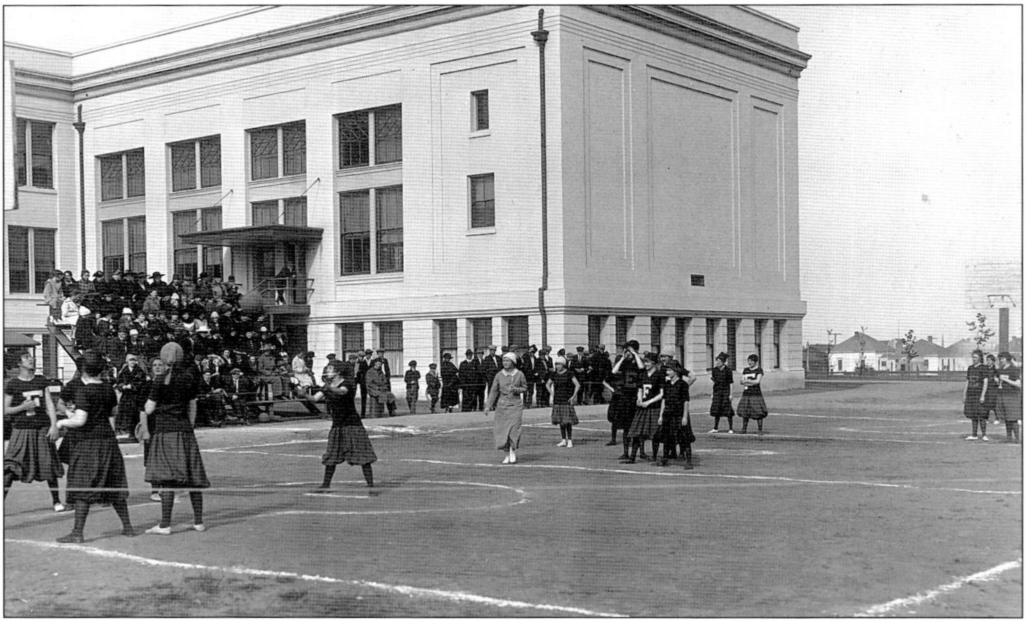

The girls' basketball teams of Eureka and possibly Fortuna high schools compete at Eureka High around 1920 when girl athletes still wore wide bloomers.

In the early 1920s Humboldt girl athletes graduated from bloomers to shorts. Here Eureka High's Elta Cartwright competes in a track meet around 1925. After the Olympic trials in 1928, Elta was called "the fastest woman in America" and became part of the U.S. Olympic Team at the Amsterdam games.

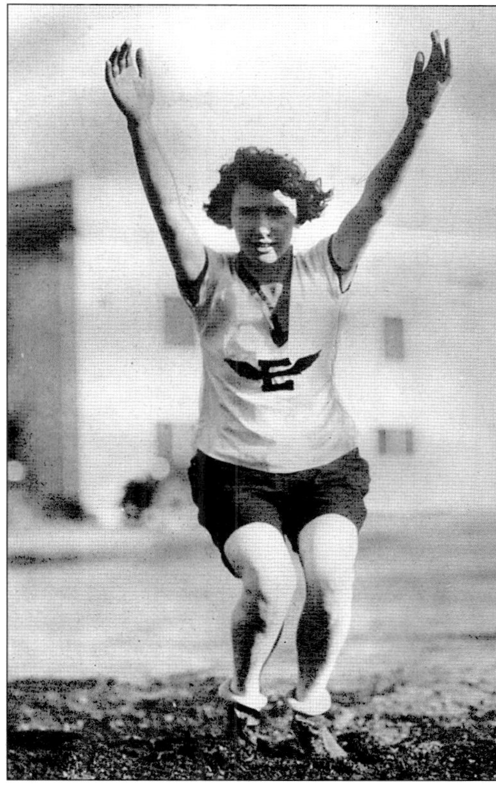

The Fortuna baseball team gathers with its official mascot at its home field in this early-20th-century photo.

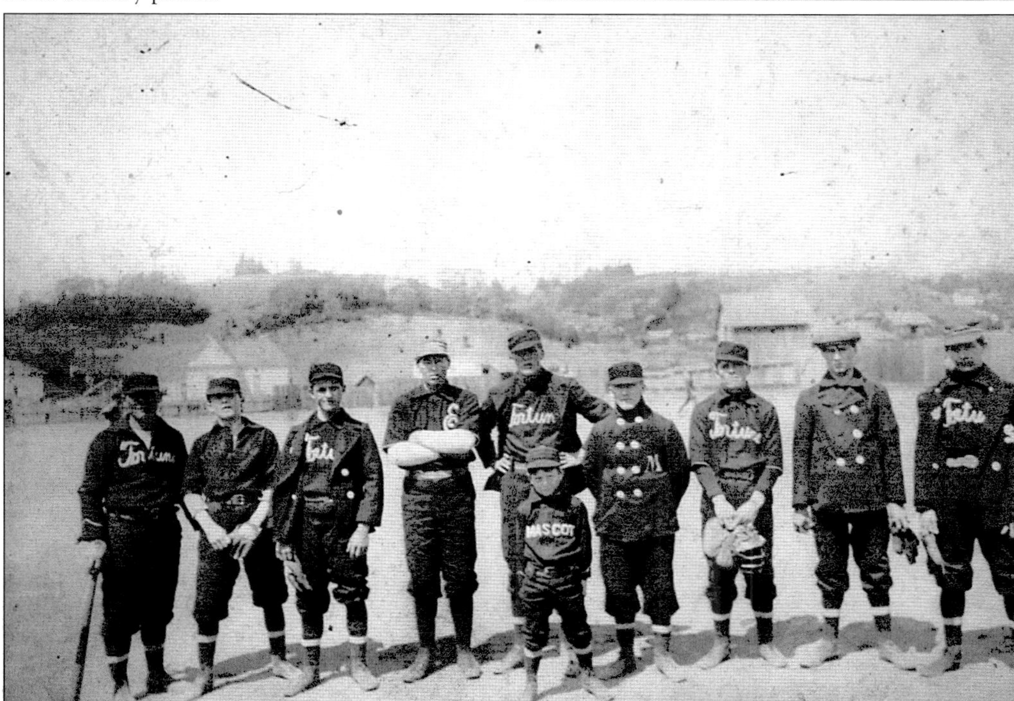

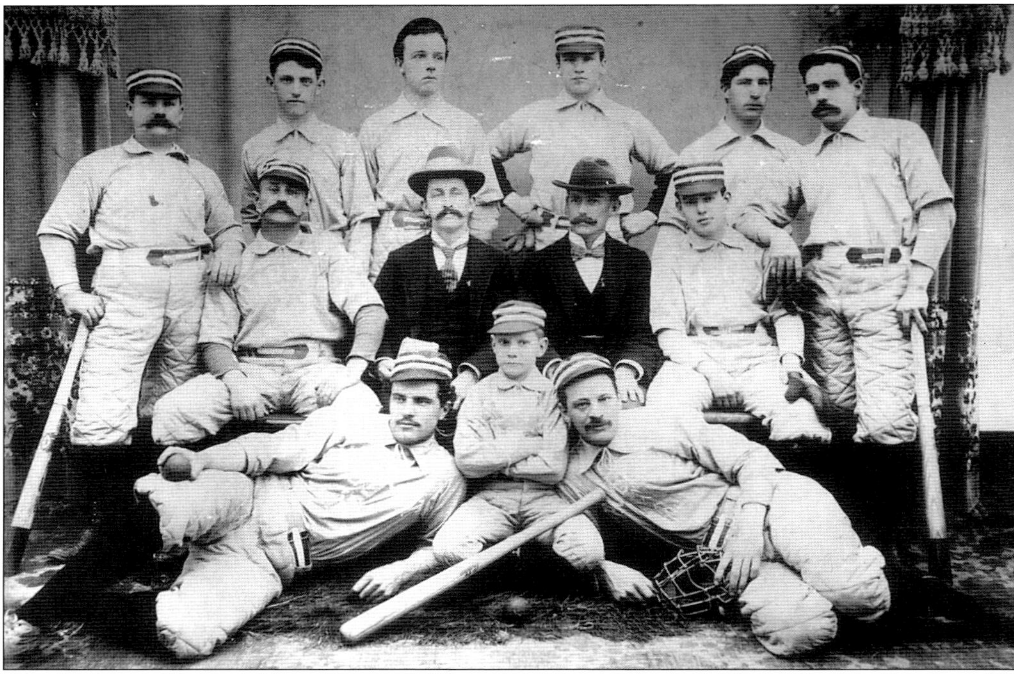

The Humboldt Baseball Club of 1898 , also with a young mascot, poses in a photography studio.

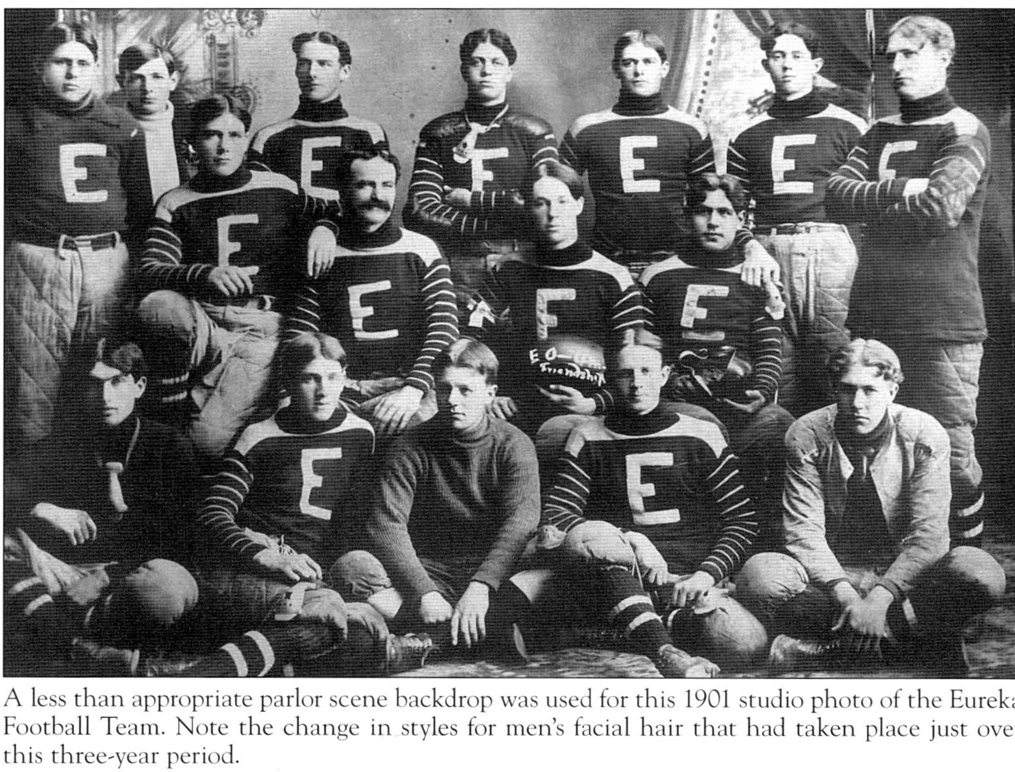

A less than appropriate parlor scene backdrop was used for this 1901 studio photo of the Eureka Football Team. Note the change in styles for men's facial hair that had taken place just over this three-year period.

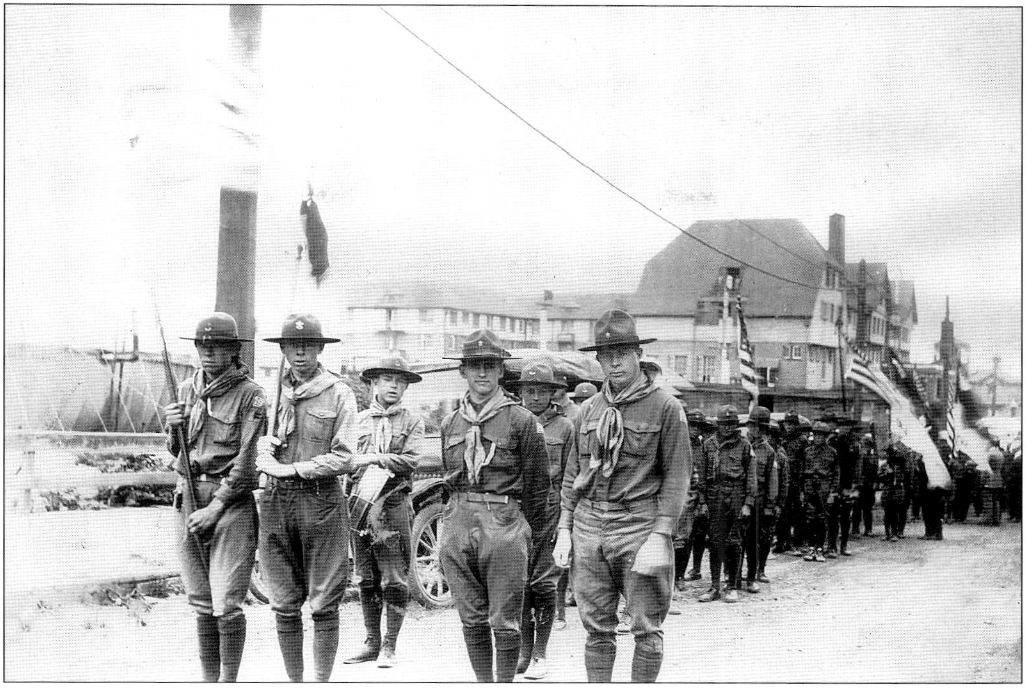

Organized under the Redwood Council of the Boy Scouts of America, these Humboldt County scouts march past the Eureka Inn in the Fourth of July parade of 1925.

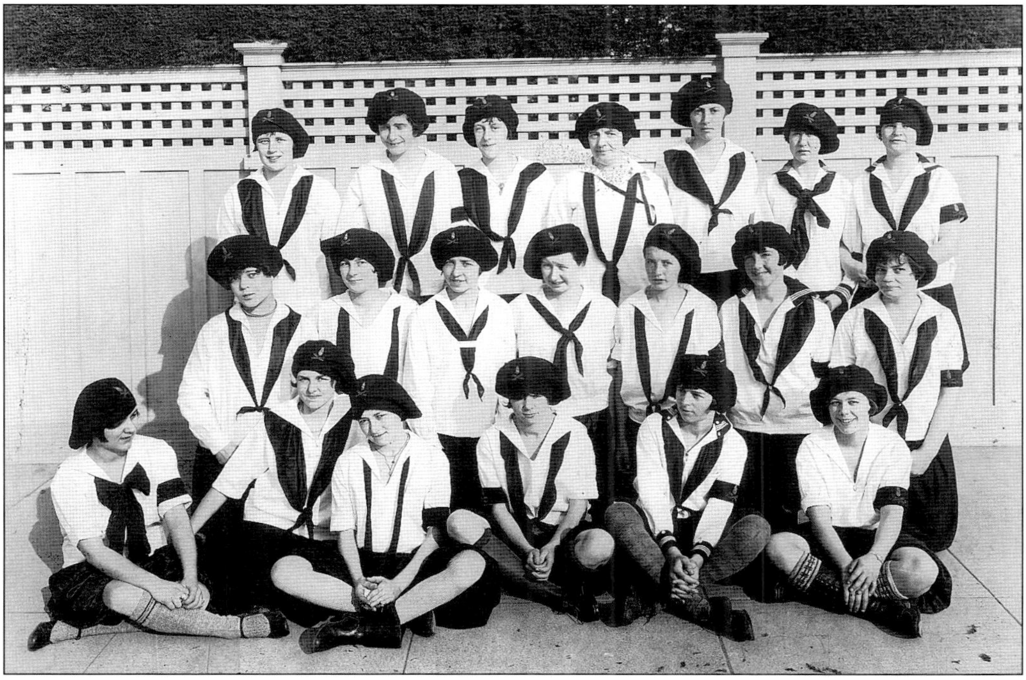

This 1924 photo shows Humboldt County's first troop of Campfire girls which was organized by Mrs. H.C. Brokaw. The Campfire girls became the dominant girls organization in the county.

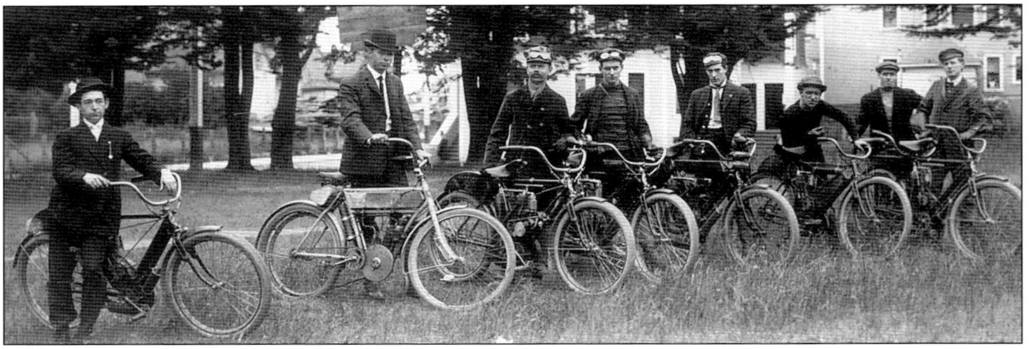

Bicycling was always taken seriously in Humboldt County. Here the Arcata Bicycle Club prepares for a ride.

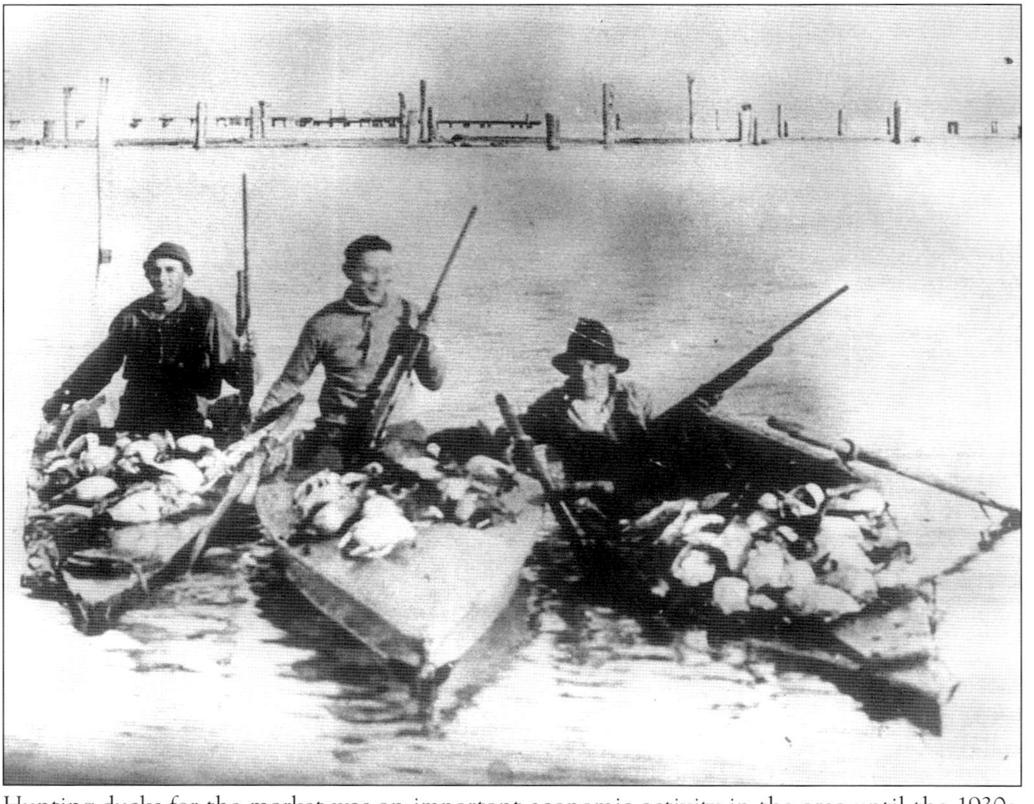

Hunting ducks for the market was an important economic activity in the area until the 1930s. The low riding "scull boat" was developed first on Humboldt Bay and was ideally suited for moving undetected towards waterfowl. These men are identified as George Dean, Harold Carson, and Henry Domeyer.

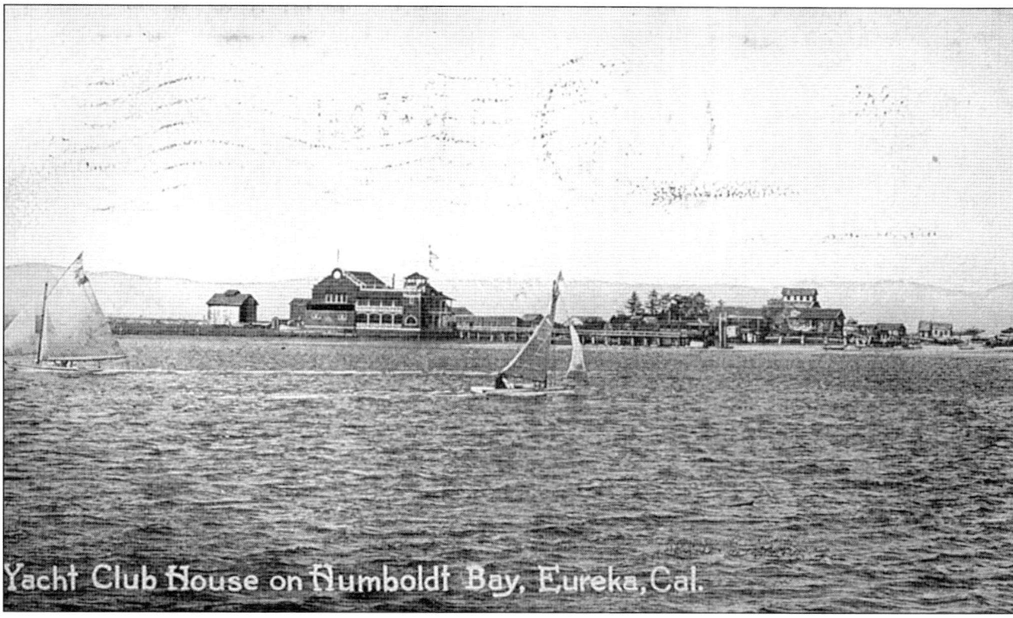

The Sequoia Yacht Club was a center for Humboldt County "society" in the early 20th century but declined in popularity after the First World War. The building, on Indian Island, boasted an indoor, heated swimming pool.

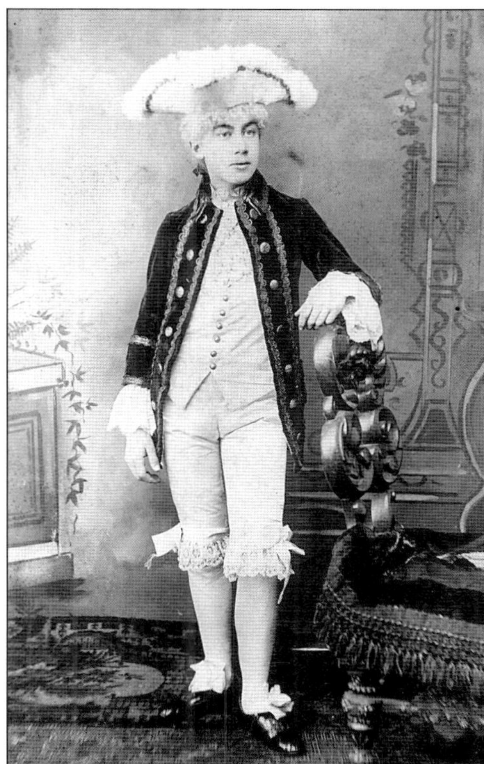

In 1880s Eureka, one of the highlights of the social year was the Mask Ball. Here Frank Sweasey, from a prominent Eureka business family, poses in his elegant costume.

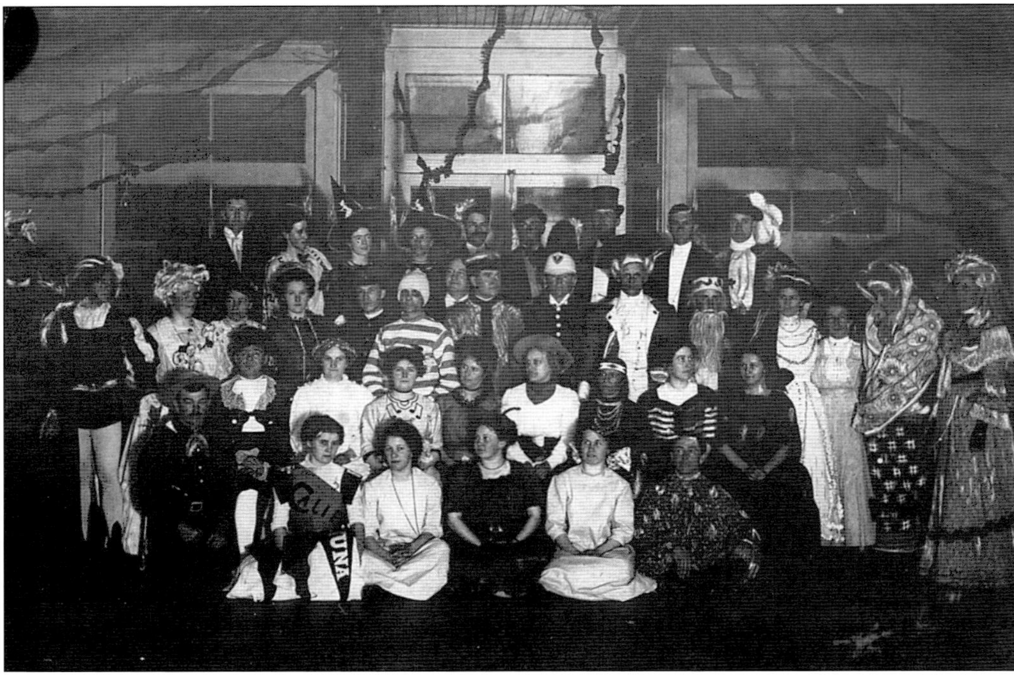

Halloween parties such as this high school event also called for elaborate costumes.

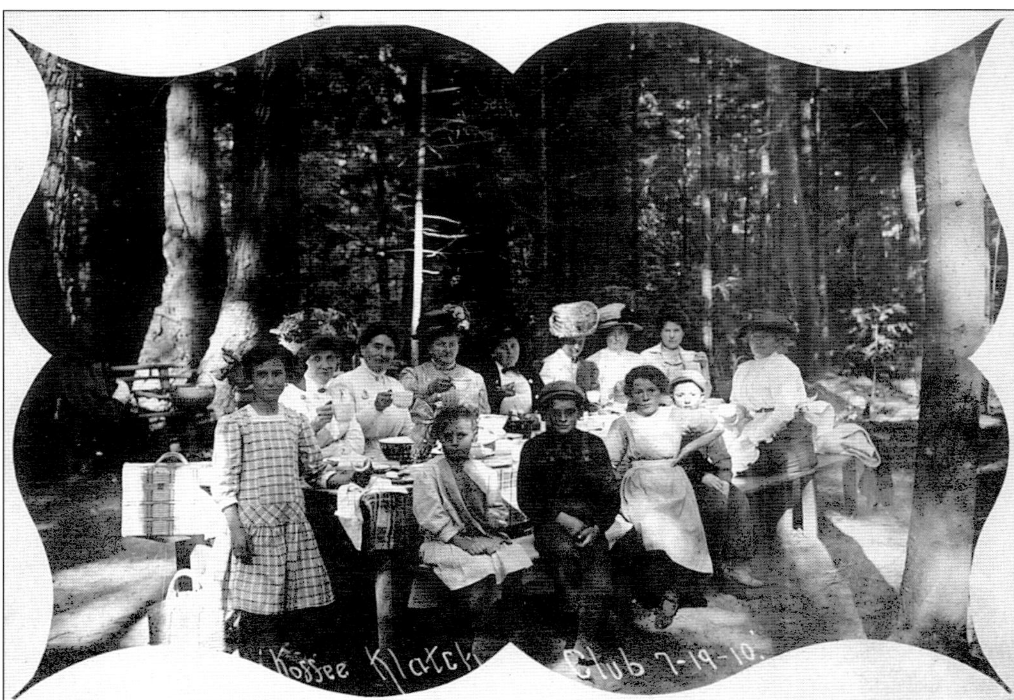

Coffee clubs were among the many women's organizations that thrived in the late 19th and early 20th century. Here Eureka's "Koffee Klatch" meets and socializes at Sequoia Park.

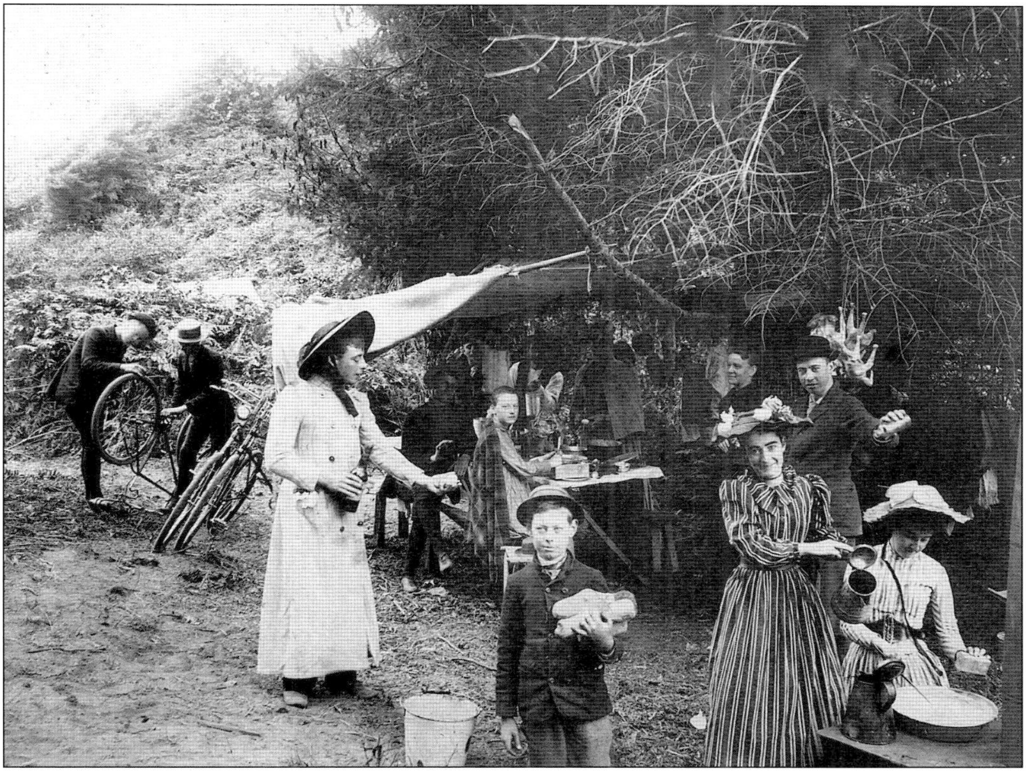

This gathering is identified as "Camp Jolly" at the mouth of the Little River. These campers seem to have brought to the rugged outdoors all the conveniences of a 1890s home.

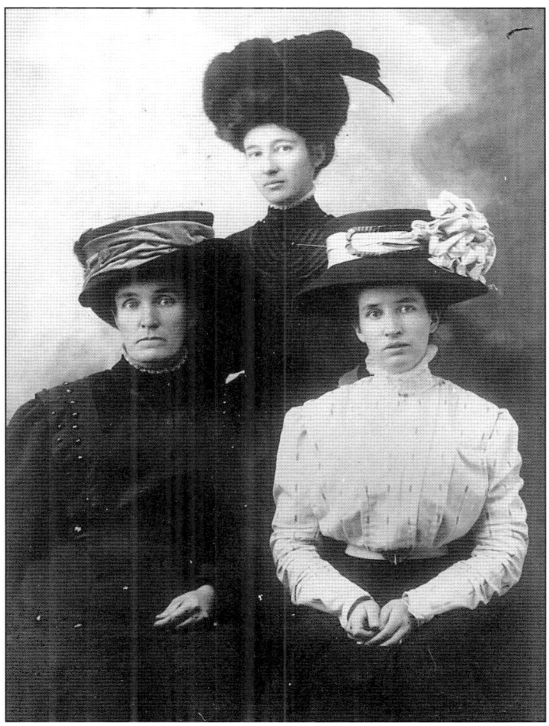

Although relatively isolated, Humboldt County women were attentive to fashion. Through newspapers, magazines, and catalogues, they made certain to keep up with the latest styles. Here three generations of Fisher women (Rhoda, Myrtle, and Ida) pose in an Arcata studio in the large hats fashionable around 1900.

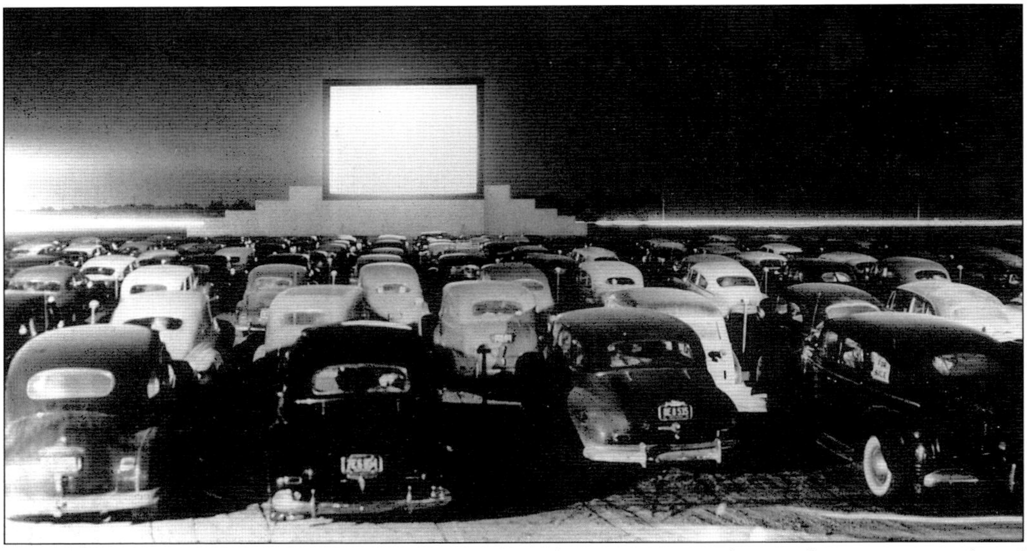

Like most of America, Humboldt County took to drive-in movies during the car-centered mid 20th century. Here the Midway Drive-In, midway between Eureka and Arcata, is packed for a show in the 1940s. The lights of Highway 101 can be seen beyond the screen.

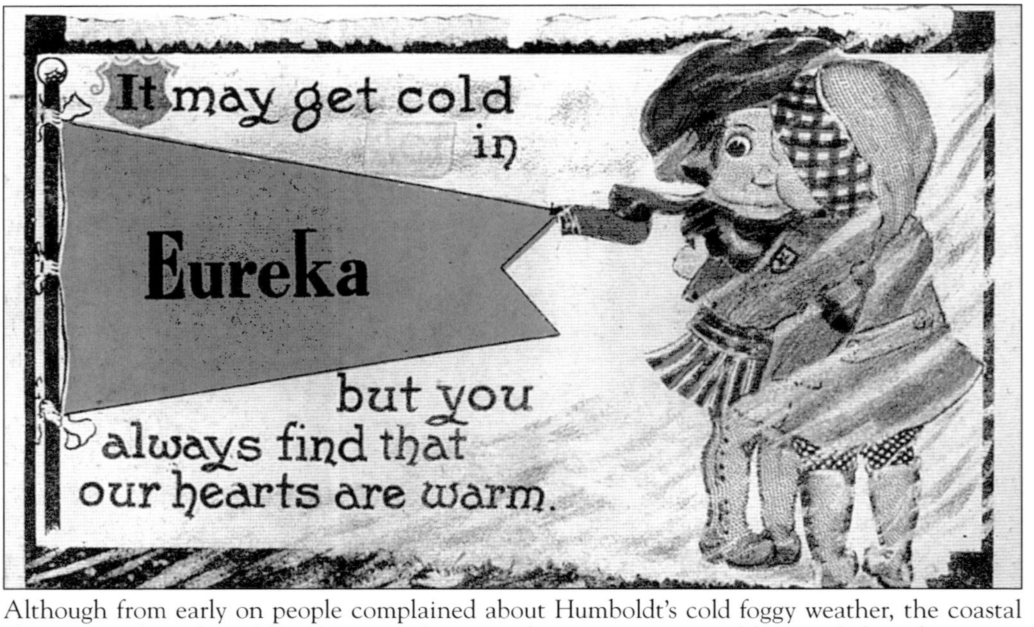

Although from early on people complained about Humboldt's cold foggy weather, the coastal climate is relatively mild and unvaried. In Eureka, temperatures seldom go below the 40s or above the 60s. The highest temperature ever recorded in Eureka was 87 degrees in 1993—the lowest recorded "high" in the lower 48 states. But whatever the weather, the saying on this 1913 postcard is still true—you can always find a warm welcome in Eureka.